THE ROGUE: A RIVER TO RUN

by
Florence Arman
with
Glen Wooldridge

(The story of pioneer whitewater river runner Glen Wooldridge
and his first eighty years on the Rogue River.)

Copyright ©1982 by Florence Arman

All rights reserved. No part of this book may be reproduced by any means
without written permission from the publisher except for the inclusion of brief
quotations in a review.

Published by  **Wildwood
Press**

209 SW Wildwood Avenue
Grants Pass, OR 97526

Library of Congress Number 81-52732
ISBN 0-9607260-0-4

Printed by THE BULLETIN PUBLISHING CO., INC.,
Grants Pass, Oregon, U.S.A.

9 10 11 12 13 14 15

This book is dedicated
to the memory of
Sadie Wooldridge
and
Glenn Ballou
who helped make it happen.

Ted Trueblood and Glen, 1972.   Glen Wooldridge collection

FOREWORD

This is the story of a unique man. One of the definitions of **unique** in my dictionary is "being without a like or equal." That fits Glen Wooldridge to a T. He is a river man. There are none like him and I contend he has no equal.

He first ran Oregon's Rogue River from Grants Pass, 120 miles inland, to Gold Beach, on the Pacific, in 1915. He is still running it as I write this in the spring of 1981. He built the boat for that first trip and he is still building them. His boats, or others patterned after them, are used on every wild, fast, dangerous river in the West.

He began guiding Rogue River float trips in 1917 and he was the first to run it upstream from Gold Beach to Grants Pass, in 1947. The next year he accepted the challenge of Idaho's River of No Return, the Salmon, so-called because early day boatmen could run it downstream, but not back up. Wooldridge ran it upstream from Riggins to Salmon City, virtually across the state. He was the first, as he was to run the Klamath upstream.

Other rivers he has mastered are the Yankee Jim Canyon of the Yellowstone, part of the Colorado, the Hells Canyon stretch of the Snake, the Yukon, and in British Columbia the Bella Coola, Atnarko, Dean and the North Fork of the Thompson.

But his first love remains the Rogue and if you move a rock anywhere along it I'm sure he would notice the change. He was the first Rogue River guide and the most famous. His clientele included Zane Grey, Victor Moore, Guy Kibee, Clark Gable, and Herbert Hoover, as well as many others who could afford to go anywhere they chose. One reason was that he is a superb boatman and splendid angler. Another is his personality. I've been on the river with him when the gray clouds hung in the tree tops, the cold rain would have chilled an otter, and fish were not to be found.

Yet he was never cross, never impatient, and if he was ever discouraged he concealed it well. His conversation is spiced with witticisms and he has a story for every bend in the river.

He is the best story teller I know. Most of this book is in Glen Wooldridge's own words — the same stories that charmed his guests for more than 60 years on the Rogue River. Florence Arman has had the good judgment to leave them the way he told them. They can't be improved upon.

Ted Trueblood
Associate Editor
FIELD AND STREAM magazine

ACKNOWLEDGMENT

There was room on the cover for only Glen's name and mine, but so many people shared in making this book it became a community effort.

Graphic artists Pam Daft and Mike Murphy did a lion's share of the work. Pam typed the manuscript, made the maps and logo. Mike did the cover painting, the back cover and helped select the photographs. They worked together on the layout. Martha Murphy proof-read and edited the manuscript. Walt and Jim Walstrom, at **The Bulletin,** did the excellent printing and answered a million questions for us.

Writers like Ted Trueblood, who wrote the foreword; Con Sellers, Gene Olson, Kay Atwood, Olga Johnson and others helped by example and encouragement. Other writers, some long gone, left their articles about Glen for me to glean. And I never would have made it without help and encouragement from the members of the Monday Writer's Workshops.

Photographers who saw the chance for a good picture and collectors with fore-sight in saving them provided the illustrations. Special thanks go to Glen and Bruce Wooldridge, The Josephine County Historical Society, Jerry Acklen and the Grants Pass Courier, The BLM, the Siskiyou Forest Service, and others for letting me choose from their collections, and to Frank Prosser for the copy work.

Corrine Hemphill passed along research information she gathered. Talks with river guides Bob Pritchett, Squeak Briggs, Taylor Cain and Bob Pruitt; with passengers on early drift trips; and with long-time friends of Glen's gave me a sense of time and place on the river.

My thanks go, too, to the people who support the Josephine County Library and the historical societies of Southern Oregon where I spent so many hours reading microfilm. The staffs of these places couldn't have been more helpful.

This could go on and on, but most of all to Bob, my patient and long-enduring husband, to others of my family who supported my efforts, and to Glen and Mary Wooldridge, who opened their home and their lives to me for so many, many hours that I felt I was one of the family, to all of you a big THANK YOU.

Florence

CONTENTS

MAPS

INTRODUCTION

It was Glen Wooldridge's rig. Any whitewater addict along the rivers of the Pacific Northwest in 1969 would recognize the distinctive lines of that shiny red Wooldridge sled boat. Or, missing that, couldn't help seeing his name emblazed on the door of the equally red, but battered, five-year-old pickup Glen parked in front of our house that morning. He'd asked my husband, Bob; our daughter, Mary; and me to go with him to Illahe on the lower section of Southern Oregon's Rogue River to do some boating. We were waiting in the yard for him.

When he hollered, "Who wants to ride with me?" I hurried to claim a seat beside him, leaving my place in our pickup to Glenn Ballou, Wooldridge's friend and fellow boatbuilder of some quarter century association.

Glen's gift of story telling is almost as well-known as his skill at whitewater running, and I didn't want to miss any of his stories on that long ride over Bear Mountain between Grants Pass and Illahe.

Since the early 1920s when he started the Rogue River Drift Trips and issued the invitation, "Ride the Rogue with Wooldridge," thousands of dudes have responded. The designation, "dudes" is a part of Glen's whimsical idea of being a country slicker taking the city dudes for a ride. He guided such people as then-president Herbert Hoover, Clark Gable, Zane Grey and Ginger Rogers. Others enjoyed the trips, too; working people like you and me; secretaries, nurses, loggers and doctors.

Writers, especially, were attracted. Their newspaper and magazine stories about Glen and his wild river trips circulated from New York to San Francisco. One article was published in Arabia.

They gave him titles such as; DEAN OF WHITEWATER BOATMEN, WHITE-WATER COWBOY and THE OLD MAN OF THE ROGUE.

Where else could you find such a combination of droll humor, common sense and daredevilry? Glen would give you a wild, tumultuous ride down the rapids, land you safely, then keep you laughing with tall tales around the campfire while peeling potatoes and frying fish for your dinner.

Glen had retired from guiding the drift trips when Bob and I met him, but not from river running. You might see him on the Snake, the Salmon, or along some Canadian waterway. If he couldn't get someone to go with him, he'd go alone, but he's rarely had occasion for a solo boat trip.

As we drove the road along the Rogue past Jump-Off-Joe Creek, we caught glimpses of rough whitewater, then dark Hellgate Canyon before taking the Galice Creek turnoff. The mountain road led us to higher evergreen-clad ridges where tatters of snow still clung to the forest floor in sheltered coves, although a riot of rhododendrons warmed the underbrush.

Bare rock cliffs and jagged burn-killed snags marked the dusty, graveled road snaking along the ridges. Blue-green carpets of fir undulated, hump after hump, to the canyon floor miles below.

Glen told me this was the road he and Sadie, his second wife, drove for many years, towing boats home from downriver trips. Glen would make a drift trip with a load of dudes every three to five days during the summer and fall seasons. Sadie would drive the 140 or so miles over the mountains to bring home the party and the boat.

"And," he said, "this was one of the better roads. You should have seen the ones we had to use in the early days."

He told me of the people living in these secluded canyons during the years he had been running the Rogue. As he talked they came alive; old hermits crazed by the solitude, packing rifles and hunting the ultimate game, each other. Grizzled miners, pockmarking the hills and riverbanks with shafts and potholes, meagerly existing in shacks along the river, with eyes for nothing but the bright, elusive gold. Tomorrow was always the day they would strike it rich. Early settlers made their way into the lower canyon, bringing Indian wives, either bought or taken in trade for a mule. They built homes and reared their families in this remote canyon enclave.

The old mule packer, Hathaway Jones, brought the necessities for existence across the mountains from West Fork, the railroad flagstop. But equally important to the secluded families, Hathaway brightened their lives with his Paul Bunyan style stories made-up on the lonely forest trail.

These tales, told and retold, spread across the nation when journalists boated the Rogue with Glen and heard them from Hathaway or from Glen, which was almost as good.

Glen is someone you can enjoy silence with, too, and his stories were interspersed with periods of quietness while he remembered.

At Foster Bar, near Illahe, we put the boat in and Glen ferried us upriver. A great blue heron flapped just ahead of the boat, stopping on a rock at the water's edge for us to catch up, then leading the way again. Vultures ganged a downed log and gulls circled, searching for a feast of spawned-out eels or salmon.

Sea lions, Glen told us, often came upriver the forty miles from Gold Beach, feeding and playing in the water. Bald eagles, golden eagles, osprey and many other birds patrol this wild section of the Rogue and beaver are returning to its banks.

We docked at Tom Staley's Wild River Lodge and, using that isolated cabin as base, we spent the next four days boating, fishing, hiking or just plain loafing. It would be hard to find more amiable companions than those two. Glen W., noted for his green suspenders and always wearing some odd sort of hat, usually had a mischievious grin that started in his eyes. He was always up to something, as active and full of surprises as the riffles on the Rogue. Glenn Ballou, tall and lanky, was like its peaceful stretches, always tidy and serene.

We came to know why they loved this secluded place. You could sit on a rock and watch an otter playing in the water, or dash for your camera when a bear galloped through the yard. But, like all Wooldridgeites, our number one priority was boating with Glen. This was my first thrill at real whitewater boating and I was glad it was with the old master boatman himself.

A run up a rapids where the water was, in Glen's words, wiggly, showed his mastery of whitewater running. He stood in the boat, hand to tiller, concentrating on the river's every movement, as though mesmerized by it. Then, with the agility and grace of a bull fighter who plays with the bull, allowing it to almost catch the cape with its horns before frisking away from it, Glen capered with the chuting water. He dipped the bow of the boat into its frothy edge, then, using the force of the water to turn the boat, he shot on up the stream.

You get a false sense of security boating with Glen. His lifetime intimacy with this wild river, knowing its every rock and riffle, reading the water to know what is below the surface by what's happening on top, makes it all seem too easy. As though the river isn't the deadly enemy it has been proved to be, taking its toll of two, three, six who knows how many lives this year.

Most memorable were the trips upriver through Solitude, just at sunset. We counted seven bears strolling along the high, rocky banks one evening. Unperturbed by the jet motor's shrill, they gave us scarcely a look, except one old fellow. He turned for a second look and I vowed he knew Glen from a long way back.

Glen's boat was the only one on the river those few days, except for one party of drifters who passed in front of the cabin.

Evenings were soul-filling, too. After crispy fried trout and potatoes, followed by canned peaches and Glenn Ballou's special brew of coffee, we sat on the porch and watched for a steelhead explosion in the wide mirror of water where twilight still lingered. A silver twist, a resounding plop, then ever-widening rings in the dark green water were our rewards.

Renewed by deep draughts of moist, alder-scented air, we partook of the canyon nightlife. A black-tailed deer materialized from the dark woods near the smokehouse and stood silently with her twin fawns before fading again into the darkness. Tiny owlets strenghtened their wings from the limb of a madrona tree above the porch roof. Their energies exhausted (Glen said, "I guess they ran out of gas.") they'd thud to the porch roof and screech their toenails down the metal roof before dropping to the soft, leaf-padded ground.

Glen would sit with his green-paint-bespattered brogans propped on the porch rail and, cued by Glenn Ballou, spin yarns about the people living in the area when he first started coming downriver.

"Right over there," he'd point out, "is where Payton earned his hunting badge. He had been wanting to kill a bear and one morning he saw something brown in the bushes. He ran for his gun and shot it. Turned out to be the neighbor's mule. He had to pay $60.00 for the mule and $10.00 to have the guy that owned it dig a hole and bury it."

Or again, about one character he guided deer hunting in the early days. "He couldn't hit a flock of school houses," he might say, then throw back his head and laugh his infectious haw-haw-haw, lifting his glasses to wipe his eyes weakened by years of wind on the river.

Glenn Ballou would give a dry, closed-mouth chuckle and prompt him to tell some other outrageous story, until the mosquitoes drove us indoors for the night.

Since that time I have taped many of Glen's stories and gathered other Wooldridge and Rogue River lore. To give a clear picture of Glen's life on the Rogue, without too much repetition, some editing and organization of materials was necessary. I have used Glen's words in bold face type when possible to retain that zesty Wooldridge flavor.

Glen's rig, 1969, with Glen in boat, taken at Robertson Bridge on the Rogue River.
Arman photo

Bob Arman pushes off, with Mary Arman, left; Florence Arman, right; and Glen at controls. 1969.
Glenn Ballou photo

Glen, at left, tells stories to Mary, Bob and Florence Arman on porch at Payton cabin, 1969.
Glenn Ballou photo

Glenn Ballou rides the famous dinosaur tree at Clay Hill Lodge.

Glenn Wooldridge collection

THE RIVER

And the Rogue? What makes it a river to run?

Early settlers called it Rogue's River, after the temperament of the natives living on its banks. The Rogue or Tututni Indians, provoked by the encoachment of miners and homesteaders, didn't give up this river paradise without a struggle. It took the U.S. Army to remove them to a remote coastal reserve.

Through usage, the name became Rogue River, and it fits. Spawned by melting snow in Oregon's High Cascades, this brawling whitewater stream performs some awesome antics in its obsessive journey to the sea.

At a mile-high level, under subalpine forests of mountain hemlock, lodgepole pine and fir, the melting snowwater seeps through porous volcanic waste left by Mount Mazama's upheavel some 6700 years ago.

The water travels underground until it reaches a barrier of glacial clay, then is pushed to the surface again as Boundry Springs just inside Crater Lake National Park. That's the beginning of the Rogue.

It flows southwesterly through forests of mixed conifers and evergreens, under climax species of Douglas fir, broadleaf madrona, tan oak, golden chinkapin and canyon live oak. Continually fed by creeks and rivulets, it is shadowed at times by ponderosa pine, sugar pine and incense cedar.

Strengthened by the waters of Union and Red Blanket Creeks, then its middle fork, it falls and chutes, even going underground when its volcanic bed allows. Below Prospect the South Fork rushes to join its downward plunge.

The U.S. Army tried to tame the Rogue's race, too, with a man-made barrier, the Lost Creek Dam, built by the Corps of Engineers in the 1970's. Boaters cruise the swelling bulge of the reservoir, trolling for trout stocked from the Cole Rivers Hatchery a short distance downstream.

Along these upper banks vacationers in campers and RVs crowd the many riverside parks, angling for rainbow trout or enjoying the natural beauty of the area. An osprey reconnoiters the water for miles, then loops through tall firs on rugged peaks to its dry-stick nest in the tallest tree.

Some 3700 feet lower than its source, the stream enters the Rogue Valley. Bypassing historic Table Rock Mountain of Indian legend, it is joined by Bear

Creek, which waters the famed Harry and David orchards. It flows by Gold Hill, whose top had a core of gold.

It rests and loafs along through scanty stands of black and white oak and madrona, with occasional evergreen forests reflected in its depths.

Dropping only 500 feet over the next forty miles, it gains such tributaries as Evans and Savage Creeks above Savage Rapids Dam, then Jones Creek, Applegate River, Jump-Off-Joe and Galice Creeks before entering the wild area.

The next thirty-four miles, from Grave Creek to Foster Bar, was designated the "wild" section of the Rogue when the U.S. Congress included it in the Wild and Scenic Rivers Act of 1968.

The Rogue Trail, hiked by thousands each year, follows the river along this stretch, angling up to the high ridges, then again dropping down to the river's edge.

Explorers, trappers, and miners, who packed along this old Indian trail in the early 1850s, looked down into it waters and returned with astounding tales. Their talk gave a picture of the river, with descriptive names such as Devil's Stairs, Wildcat Rapids and Deadman's Bar. They told of thunderous Whiskey Creek Falls, roiling over its craggy rim and dropping into a stony cauldron below; of the constricted waters raging through the narrows of Mule Creek Canyon; and the strange phenomenon of the Coffee Pot's swirl.

Below Foster Bar the Illinois River joins the Rogue River at Agness and the wide, but still strongly-currented stream descends gradually to Gold Beach, where it joins the Pacific, some 210 miles from its source.

Who would attempt to run such a river?

Thousands of eager kayakers, rafters and drift boaters answer that question each year when they apply to have their names in the lottery for permits. Permits have been required for private boaters since 1978 and for commercially-guided parties since 1975, from the Memorial Day weekend to Labor Day. In 1980, there were 9211 who claimed their permits and boated the Rogue during that period.

But in 1915, Glen Wooldridge was one of the few who would answer the call. He laid claim to the Rogue on his first trip downriver, and in the sixty-five years he has been running it, he has left his indelible mark on the stream.

And if a river can own a man, Glen belongs to the Rogue. It worked its magic on him the day he moved to its banks.

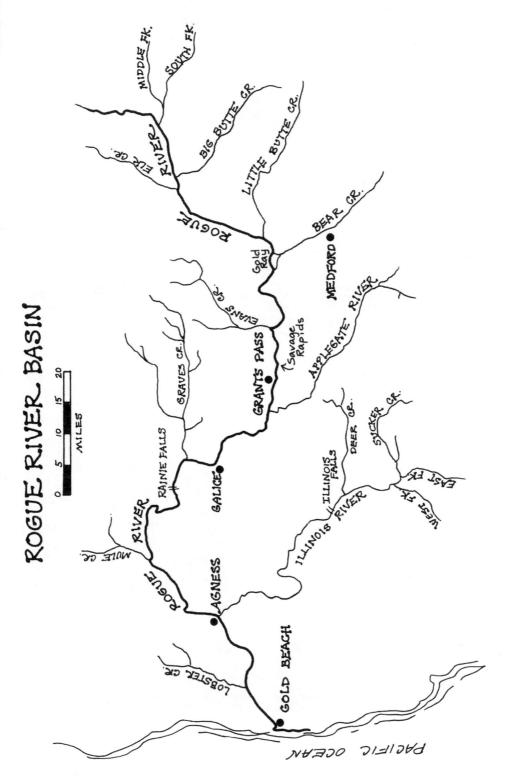

ROGUE RIVER BASIN

MIDDLE FK.
SOUTH FK.
BIG BUTTE CR.
LITTLE BUTTE CR.
ELK CR.
RIVER
ROGUE
BEAR CR.
Gold Ray
MEDFORD
APPLEGATE RIVER
EVANS CR.
GRAVES CR.
Savage Rapids
GRANTS PASS
SUCKER CR.
DEER CR.
ILLINOIS FALLS
ILLINOIS RIVER
EAST FK.
WEST FK.
RAINIE FALLS
GALICE
RIVER
MULE CR.
ROGUE
AGNESS
LOBSTER CR.
GOLD BEACH
PACIFIC OCEAN

MILES
0   5   10   15   20

Rainie Falls, a place to remember.   *Glen Wooldridge collection*

Chapter One

From Foots Creek Downstream to the Rogue

It was Granddad Cook who first told me about the salmon and steelheads, when I was just a little kid wading in the edge of Foots Creek. He said the old salmon came up the creek to spawn in the gravelly places, and when the little fish hatched out they stayed close to the bank where they would be protected. Nature provided them with food in the shallows while they were so small.

Then as they got bigger, they got more daring, swimming farther and farther out into the current, learning the dangers of the river, how to stay out of the way of bigger fish that would gobble them up.

They went down the creek, he told me, to the Rogue River and grew a little more and learned a little more until they moved on down the river to the sea. They spent some time in the sea and when they got ready to spawn they would always return to the place they hatched.

By some means, whether by smell, taste or the sense of direction, they would recognize the Rogue River when they came back to its mouth and make their way back up it. I thought that was a real good plan. I really liked that.

It was on his grandfather's Foots Creek mining claim that Glen Wooldridge was born, March 31, 1896, deep-rooted in family ties, with a toehold in the old ways, but with the exciting promises of the Twentieth Century ahead.

Granddad dug a mining ditch, when he first settled the claim in the late 1850s. He tapped the creek high above the place and brought water down the ditch. It went into rusty iron pipes, reduced smaller and smaller until it went into the hydraulic giant. He would turn the giant this way and that, using the force of the water to cut down the creek banks, then sluice the rocks and dirt away to get the gold.

Granddad called the mine the Cement Diggins, because it was so hard to get the gold out. I remember one time I found a little heart-shaped nugget down there along the creek. I gave it to the little girl who lived neighbors to us.

1

The melting snows high in the Southern Oregon hills added their flow to the creek, giving Robert Cook a good, long season working his placer claim. Then he would shut down the giant, clean up the sluices and start the dry season's work around the farmstead.

Gardens needed plowing; barnyard animals, dropping their young, needed tending. It was a good thing Henry Wooldridge, Glen's dad, had stayed on, after marrying the Cooks' daughter, Mary, some five years before. Henry was a good hand with the animals.

Spare time was spent blacksmithing; building wagons, hacks and buggies; or gunsmithing. Robert Cook had learned that a frontiersman needed to turn his hand to just about anything that came up, to earn a living. If he needed a tool, the quickest and cheapest way to get it was to make it. Neighbors knew where to come for advice, to use the forge, or have their rifles rebored.

Kinfolks came early in the morning, in wagons and buggies, or afoot, to spend Sundays and holidays visiting and enjoying the home-grown bounty spread on the tables under the plum trees on a hot summer day. Crusty loaves, made from grain stone-ground at local mills, came hot from the wood range oven. They tasted good with venison, or Chinook salmon from the streams. Grandmother Almira, adding garden vegetables and preserves to the board, was not above tweeking the back hair of a small boy or spatting a reaching, grubby hand.

Some things couldn't be home-grown, even in Jackson County's fertile soil. When the brown sugar in the barrel or coffee beans in the sack started getting low Mr. Cook would hitch-up the buggy for a trip to Gold Hill, eighteen miles to the northeast.

Glen; his brother Frank, who was three years older; and any cousins who were visiting, vied for the chance to go along. Wisely, Mr. Cook would only take one of them at a time.

One day when I was about five, I somehow drew the privilege of going to Gold Hill with Granddad. The only way he had of getting around was in a buggy hitched to his one-eyed bay mare, Old Nell.

We started off down the road, if you could call it a road. It was really just a trail down through the brush, but you could get through it all right.

I was sitting down behind the dashboard when the old mare got scared of something, like one-eyed horses sometimes do. She started running away, and here we went, downhill. I looked back at Granddad to see how he was making it. He was leaning back, hanging onto the reins, his long, white whiskers parted in the middle, just winging back over his shoulders on each side.

We were rounding a curve when the front wheel hooked onto a little pine tree. Away the old mare went, with Granddad hanging onto the reins. He went right out of the buggy, head first, landing on his belly on that hard ground. It knocked the wind out of him; he lost the reins and Old Nell went on down the trail.

I was still in the buggy, and I kept looking out over the side, watching him. Finally he got up. "You stay in the buggy," he told me, "I'll go catch the mare."

2

Well I knew I had to mind Granddad, so I sat there maybe a couple of hours. Then I saw him coming back with the old mare. Dick Swacker, who lived at the mouth of the creek, was with him. When Dick heard the mare coming down the trail he knew something was wrong, so he ran out and caught her. They brought back some wire and poles and fixed the broken shaft. We hooked up again and away we went, on to Gold Hill to do the trading.

Big, bushy-bearded Robert Cook had a free-flowing stream of stories for the boys to enjoy. Cold winter evenings were spent gathered around the fireplace or the kitchen range, listening to him tell of the rivers of his own life.

When he was 17, about 1850, he left the Tennessee hills and made his way to St. Louis, where the Missouri pours into the Mississippi. He hired on to raft logs down the mighty stream. When each long raft of logs was poled and guided to market he hiked back upstream to help take another one down.

While in St. Louis he watched the wagon trains making up for the long trip to Oregon Territory. In 1852, he approached one of them and asked its captain if he could join up. Captain Smith hired him to drive one of his teams of bull oxen on the trail. Soon he was the captain's most dependable helper.

He couldn't help noticing the young Kentucky girl, Almira Wooldridge, with her parents and four brothers, traveling with the train.

There were other Wooldridges, too, distant relatives of Almira's family, making the 1852 trek. It was from that family line that Henry Wooldridge, Glen's father, came.

Grandmother Almira, too, had an exciting story to tell the boys about the wagon trip. Several of the young men, including her brothers, teasing her, offered to trade her to some young Indian braves for good ponies.

The Indians rode away, promising to come back with the ponies to swap for the pretty white girl.

Captain Smith, hearing of the joke, knew he had to get her away. The Indians were going to be plenty mad when their trade fell through. He emptied a big, wooden box, put it in the fastest wagon and had Almira climb into it. He sent her on to the wagon train just ahead.

When the Indians came back with the ponies he had a hard time convincing them it was all a joke and the girl wasn't there anymore. They looked into every wagon for her, even followed the train for quite a ways.

Captain Smith got a little rough with the young men, but they, too, knew the joke had turned deadly serious.

It was late summer when the train reached Salt Lake. Captain Smith decided to winter-over, get an early start in the spring. Some of the travelers protested; they believed that by traveling fast they could reach Oregon before winter. A vote was taken, with lines formed by the opposing sides. The men were almost evenly divided. Those who wanted to go on picked another wagonmaster and headed out.

Bob Cook and the Wooldridge families chose to stay with Captain Smith at Salt Lake. They found work helping build the Mormon Temple and were given food and supplies for their winter's stay, and more to start out again in the spring. They were promised wages, too.

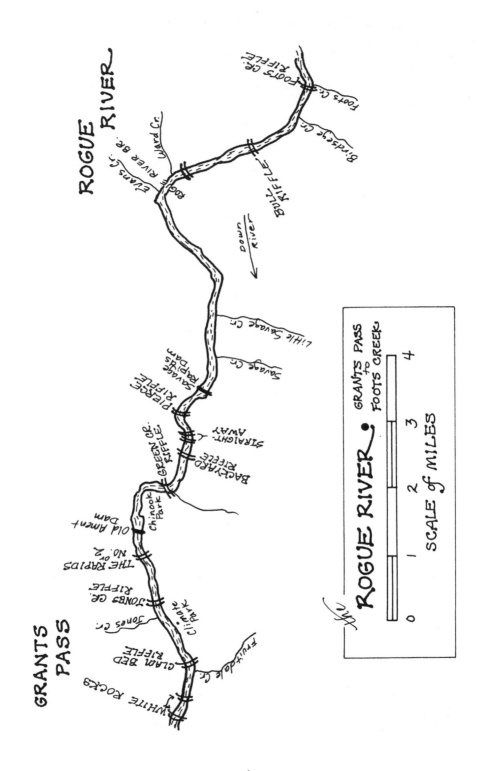

ROGUE RIVER

ROGUE RIVER • GRANTS PASS to FOOTS CREEK

SCALE of MILES

0   1   2   3   4

GRANTS PASS

Foots Cr. — FOOTS CR. RIFFLE

Birdseye Cr.

BULL RIFFLE

Ward Cr.

Rogue River Br.

Evans Cr.

Down River

Little Savage Cr.

Savage Cr.

SAVAGE RAPIDS Dam

PIERCE RIFFLE

STRAIGHT AWAY

GREEN CR. RIFFLE

BACKYARD RIFFLE

Chinook Park

Old Ament Dam

THE RAPIDS or NO. 2

JONES CR. RIFFLE

Jones Cr.

Clip Park

CLAM BED RIFFLE

Fruitdale Cr.

WHITE ROCKS

4

When Bob Cook approached Brigham Young, asking for his wages, the old patriarch told him, "The Lord will repay you."

And maybe He did; Almira Wooldridge became his wife, February 20, 1853, with Brigham Young performing the ceremony. The caravan started on toward the Columbia with the first signs of spring.

Making their way through the mountains they picked up three survivors, all who were left of the ill-fated group which split off from the train the year before.

On June 27, 1853, they reached Oregon City. Soon Bob and Almira headed south, taking up a donation claim on Long Tom River, north of Eugene. They lived there for several years before homesteading their claim on Foots Creek where Mr. Cook was postmaster of the Draper post office.

In the early days, Granddad was a Jackson County commissioner. He was in office when the big, brick courthouse was built at Jacksonville, the county seat, then. That's the building they use for the Jacksonville Museum, now. The area was bustling with miners when he first came here. He would hike over the trail, about six miles, to Jacksonville when they would have a commissioners' meeting, rather than go by wagon the twenty-two miles around the Old Stage Road.

At the beginning of the century, some forty years later, mining was still the big industry in Southern Oregon. Local miners thought the paydirt would last at least another hundred years. The gold shipment of 1900 was estimated at a half-million dollars for the area.

In 1902, the men stopping by the Cook place brought word of the new strike at the old Dry Diggins mine, located three miles up-river from Grants Pass. A couple of miners, Perkins and Pike, had hit it big there that year.

That was old mining ground, worked since the early 1850s, but water had always been a problem. A limited amount could be taken from Jones Creek and a small stream called Bloody Run, but after they were exhausted the giants had to be shut down.

Then word spread that the Aments, C.W. and M.C., were dealing for the Golden Drift Mining Company, buying up all the land in the area. Early in 1902, they bought eight acres from W.H. Hamlin for $250, which gave them access to the Rogue in just the right place, with frontage for a dam they proposed to build.

They planned to raise the water twenty feet above the river. Knowing it would take a lot of lumber for the construction work, they also planned to build their own mill to saw it.

Businessmen around Grants Pass were all in favor of the project. It would be a big boost to the economy of the area. The Aments promised that, at some future date, it would furnish irrigation for both sides of the river and more electric power. Grants Pass had a small water and power dam, but the businessmen welcomed additional power for homes and industries.

"Uncle" George Wooldridge, who was some sort of cousin of Dad's, came by and said he was going down to the damsite to work, taking his mule teams to help with the construction. Dad went down with him and got the job of tending to all the horses and mules they needed to do the work. He moved us down to a little frame house, just northwest of the damsite.

5

It was pretty exciting, living down there. All sorts of things were going on. Loggers would fall trees and drag them in with horses, to the sawmill. They were sawing the lumber they needed right on the site.

Of course Frank and I had to start to school when we got down there. That was my first time in school and I didn't think much of it. I liked the teacher, all right. We went to a one-room school on Jones Creek and my teacher was Miss Savage.

Extra shifts were run at the mill to saw the two and half-million board feet of lumber needed for the dam.

The huge steam shovel M.C. Ament designed and built tore at the riverbed, gouging to the bedrocks for a foundation for the dam. The steam shovel's whistle blasts punctuated the ringing sounds of pick and shovel crews and the scraping of mule-drawn fresnos moving the loose rocks away.

Stubborn boulders were blasted with giant powder, peppering the surrounding area with flying rocks and dirt. The noise and excitement drew the small boys, but it wasn't exactly a safe place to play.

Uncle George was there, one day when they were blasting, and even for him things got a little rough. A blast went off and a rock came flying toward him. It flattened a big silver pocket watch he always carried. It didn't hurt him, but sure flattened that watch.

He would let his mules run loose around the damsite, when he wasn't working them. The railroad went right through there and the mules liked to stand bunched on the tracks. A train came along and one of the mules wouldn't move; it just balked. There was mule meat scattered for a hundred yards along that track.

Glen's family didn't live there very long. His dad came in one day and told Glen's mother he had been offered a job as butcher at the slaughter house in Grants Pass. It would mean moving again, and the house that went with the job was right on the banks of the Rogue.

In spite of that, Glen's mother was happy. It would get the boys away from the construction site, and besides, the job paid a steady $40 a month cash money.

They loaded the wagon and headed west, entering town and turning south on Sixth Street, the wheels churning the deep dust of the small town.

The homes of its 3000 residents were scattered over a large area with open spaces for gardens, chickens and hogs. Milk cows grazed in vacant lots. Horses and buggies were still the only means of getting around and stables were common sights within the town. Large pine trees and black oaks shaded the unpaved streets.

The town boasted three banks; three newspapers; eight churches; a city hall; a volunteer fire department; an elaborate opera house; several fine hotels, including the Palace, the Western and the Josephine.

Front Street (now "G") was rising again from the ashes of the tremendous fire of July 17, 1902, that burned two blocks of wooden buildings and left the brick ones empty shells. It had caught in the wood piles in the Southern Pacific yards, leveling the roundhouse and machine shops.

I can remember that fire, and hurrying along into town with the other kids

6

and the women, following the men who rushed to fight the big blaze. I hid behind my mother's skirts to watch it.

Furniture and goods were piled into the streets and everywhere they thought they could get it out of the way of the fire. The militia boys were called out to guard against looters. The Ashland fire department came in on a special train, but by the time they got there the fire was under control.

That fire, the second one of the year, was a big set-back for the growing town. Earlier the box factory and sawmill had burned. But Front Street was being rebuilt; and the railroad yards. Soon the Rooster Club could perch on the railroad fence again, to whittle, spit tobacco juice and watch the trains come in.

The Wooldridge wagon, with its scanty load of furniture, followed Sixth Street south to the river, crossed the bridge and Henry whoaed the team in the yard of a large white frame house.

Before they started unloading Glen dropped from the wagon's tailgate and made a break for the willows lining the banks of the Rogue. From that moment, when he didn't show up for supper, or was gone when the folks got up mornings, they knew where to find him. They had moved him into a boyhood wonderland.

Glen, on right, and his brother Frank, taken about 1900.   Glen Wooldridge collection

Ament Dam while it was under construction.

Josephine County Historical Society

Grants Pass fire on Front Street (now "G") 1902.

Josephine County Historical Society

South end of Sixth Street Bridge and the Grants Pass Water and Power dam, about 1900. Wooldridge home is at center, with slaughter house on far right.

Josephine County Historical Society

*Glen's father, Henry Wooldridge, holding
Glen's son Bobby, about 1929.*
Bruce Wooldridge collection

*Glen's mother, Mary Wooldridge,
1929.* Bruce Wooldridge collection

Robert and Almira Cook, in early 1900s.
Glen Wooldridge collection

Chapter Two

Huckleberry Boyhood

I was drawn to that river. It was alive! Things were happening under its surface. There were fish — lots of different kinds — and they did strange things.

Salmon coming upriver to spawn were so thick in the water you could almost walk across the river on their backs. The female would build her redd, her nest, by digging the rocks out with her body, flopping and twisting until her tail and head were white. She would have patches of white on her body, too. The male is like a mad animal, protecting its young. He keeps guard on the redd and when a steelhead comes near he darts out at him, slashing with his jaws.

I'd get up mornings before the family was awake and fill my pockets with cold biscuits and meat, then sneak off down to the river. I'd bellyflop on a big, flat rock, studying the water. The current doesn't always run the same; rocks and logs are washed in and out, causing changes. Sometimes I'd make little boats out of pieces of bark and set them adrift, watching to see how they moved in the current or swirled in the eddies.

In January, following the Wooldridge family's move to their riverbank home, Glen had a chance to see the river in all its awesome power. The Rogue went on one of its winter rampages.

Heavy rains fell, saturating the ground, and it kept raining. The creeks, flowing into town from the north, rose and flooded the streets. Sixth Street was a river of brown, muddy water. The engorged Rogue kept rising toward the bottom of the bridge, known at that time to be the longest single span bridge in the United States.

Our house sat on a ridge of land with a low spot to the south of it. The river cut around the house, circling us, stranding us on that little ridge.

George Fowler came over in his boat to ask if we needed any help. Mother decided to take Frank and me over into Grants Pass, but Dad stayed there.

The swollen current cut around the south end of the bridge, undermining the approach, twisting and pounding at the wooden structure. It broke away a forty to fifty foot section, swept it downstream, lodging it against the power dam.

It flooded the powerplant, putting out the fires under the boiler and blacking out the lights of the town. It washed away timbers and small buildings from the Golden Drift Mining Company, but the dam itself held. There had been a lot of speculation as to whether it would.

Other bridges in the area, including the Grave Creek wagon bridge, were washed out or damaged too much for horse and buggy traffic.

The next day, Sunday, when the rains stopped, the town people turned out on the riverbanks, watching the deluge recede. They estimated the damage it had done and the costs of restoring the bridge.

It took a little doing. Politics got into the way when it came to restoring the bridge, but neighbors pitched in and put up a ladder to the remaining main span, to accommodate foot traffic into town. It made it pretty hard on the farmers, having to stop on the south bank, walk into town, then carry their supplies back across and down the ladder. Children from the south side had to climb the ladder and cross to school.

Frank had to go to school. The folks thought he was old enough to climb the ladder and cross the bridge, but they thought I was too little. I got to stay home; that was all right with me.

There was talk of building another ferry, like the one they had in 1890, after the bridge washed away, but eventually the approach was rebuilt and Glen had to continue his schooling.

That autumn, the Rogue through the valley almost went dry for a spell, but it wasn't caused by the weather. Another new dam was being built about three and a half miles above Gold Hill and it had to take the blame.

At that time, if a person decided to dam the river and owned the land adjacent to it, about all he had to do was post his intent to build a dam. There were some requirements; the fish warden had to approve the fishways, but that was about all.

Dr. D.R. Ray bought the Condor place and in August of 1902 started building a dam of logs cribbed and filled with rocks, declaring his intent to use it for mining, irrigation and power. When it was completed, in October of the next year, instead of closing the gates gradually and taking the water to fill his reservoir accordingly, he just shut the gates down tight.

The river dropped to a brook-sized trickle. Below the Grants Pass dam 20 to 25 pound salmon flopped around in the mud. The stream dropped too low to operate the power plant's wheel and Grants Pass spent the night in darkness again until the river rose.

Glen was always the first one to notice changes in the river and come bounding in with the news. He and Frank didn't have too many interests in common. Frank loved horses more than anything. All the Wooldridges were horse lovers, until Glen came along. Back in Kentucky, where their ancestors raised fine racehorses, even the family's cemetery plot had horses on the tombstones.

Grants Pass was a horse-racing town. In the early years, doctors, dentists and lawyers would whip up their famous imported racers, right down the main drag of Sixth Street, trying their best to win.

I remember the Baber brothers, Archy and Graphy. They used to be

jockeys in their early years. They had a big barn over on Foundry Street where they kept race horses. My dad used to go over there quite a bit and Frank and I would sometimes tag along.

The old man, Bob Baber, their dad, was always full of big stories. One time his wife left him and he said, "Women are just like bunch-grass horses, give them a few good meals and they want to have a runaway."

Back then they hauled stuff on drays with horses. I remember Henry Shade and his brother ran the drays, then after that the Babers had them.

They hauled barrels of beer from the brewery to the saloons. There was a lot of saloons in those days. Kids used to catch rides on the drays. One time a little boy, whose last name was Everely fell off and the horses backed the dray over him and killed him.

That brewery was started by a guy whose last name was Kinland, I think. He was a big, potbellied Dutchman who would weigh 300 pounds. Then someone else bought it and turned it into a saloon. They had artesian water there, a really fine well.

Dad managed to get Frank and me a little pony from somewhere along about then and Frank was really happy about it. We called it Goog Eye, because it had one bad eye.

The Holmes family, with three boys about our age, lived just over the ridge from us. They had a little white pony, maybe a little bit bigger than a sheep, but not much. Frank and Bill Holmes got up a bet — twenty-five cents — on which one of their ponies was the best.

We went over to the racetracks, or anyway where they were going to race. It was where Redwood Avenue is now. At that time loggers were hauling lumber in here, by horse team, and the dust was about a foot deep on the road.

Now Bill Holmes was a long, tall, skinny kid, and riding that little white "sheep" his feet almost dragged the ground. Frank was riding Goog Eye, of course.

They stationed me down at a certain spot to judge the outcome of the race. Then they got all set and I brought my arm down to start them and away they went. Things were going pretty good, until that little white pony fell. It looked like a bomb went off, dust flew so high.

I couldn't see anything for a while, but pretty soon I saw ol' Bill come crawling out, his eyes full of dust, spitting mud. He was a hell of a looking thing. Frank was pretty proud, though; Goog Eye won his first race.

The old dam, below Fifth Street, soon became Glen's favorite playground. It was built of cribbed fir poles, filled with rocks. The workers had barged the rocks down from the White Rocks area, east of town, using pike poles to move the barges up and down river. It was built about 1889, to furnish electricity and water to the town, making Grants Pass one of the earlier Oregon towns to have electric power.

It was the first dam built across the Rogue, although there were diversion dams and small ones on creeks and feeder streams used for mining.

A bunch of us little river-rats played on that old dam, scrambling around on those peeled poles. They were wet and mossy, slicker than fish slime. We'd fish for trout from the race, or gaff salmon in the fishways. It had two fishways so didn't hold back the fish from going upriver to spawn.

The law was pretty loose, back then, and nobody said anything if you helped yourself to all the salmon you wanted. We'd take a couple, all we could carry, up to Ahlf's meat market on Sixth Street and sell them to him. It was a good mile to the main part of town, from the dam, and carrying a wet, fifteen pound salmon isn't easy for a small boy. We'd cut a willow limb and run it through the gills then a couple of us would carry it between us.

If we were lucky we'd get ten cents a pound for them — three dollars — that was a lot of money, back then. We would divide it up, buy stick candy or ice cream at Rothmund's store, or maybe more fishing gear.

Sometimes we'd catch a farmer going home in his wagon after doing his trading in town. We could ride back to the bridge with him, or if we still had the fish, maybe sell them to him.

This Huck Finn sort of life was great for small boys, but hard on a mother's nerves. Glen's mother was always afraid he would drown. She had a good right to be, too. A couple of boys were trying to walk the slick poles of the raceway, hanging onto one another, when one slipped, dragging the other in with him. One swam out, but the other didn't make it. The river took its toll.

Another time two boys were playing around in a boat above the dam when the current caught it. They weren't strong enough to row back and went over the dam. Glen's mother was already busy, at that time, with a new baby, Glen's brother Russell. She heard them and went running down there, just knowing it was Glen and he was drowned. It didn't hurt the boys, just threw them into the water. But it was exciting for a while, Glen said.

The folks worried a lot about me being down there on the river. They tried just about everything to keep me away, except whipping me. They didn't go in for that much.

They'd send Frank down to watch out for me. But he couldn't have done anything, if I fell in, except maybe point out the spot. He didn't like the river much. He would sit on the bank and think about the race horses he would have someday.

The lake above the dam was the town's resort area. It made a good swimming place. All the kids in town learned to swim there, but the Rogue collected its toll there, too.

The riverbanks across from the Wooldridge home was the gathering place for the younger adults on Sunday afternoons. Young men would rent canoes or rowboats from Mr. Costain's little marina and take their girl friends for rides, or maybe pay a nickel each and get him to take them up to White Rocks and back. He would take them in his little motorboat with the fringed canopy over it.

White Rocks were just above the railroad bridge, straight across from the city's present water intake. Someone blasted them out, years ago. I never did know why.

I can still remember old Costain's boat, putt-putting along up there. He used to try to sail on the lake, in a little sailboat.

The park wasn't developed, back then. Mr. Boyington was the one who did

14

the work on the park, after the bank bought the property and deeded it to the city. He spent years there, as the landscape gardener. He took his horse in there and pulled out the manzanita brush and planted trees. He had just about every kind of tree in there you can imagine. And he dug a well, but I guess it has been filled in now.

There was a big field where the park is and travelers in wagons would camp there. That's where I first met the Bearss boys. Their family camped there when they first came to Grants Pass 75 or more years ago and we were friends all those years.

Below the old dam there was considerable activity, too. The commercial salmon fishermen (gillnetters) had their net-drying racks on the riverbank, just about at the end of Fifth Street, not far from the Wooldridge home. They fished at night, when the river was dark enough that the salmon couldn't see the gillnets. During the daytime there was always someone around the drying racks, getting ready for the night's fishing. They would be drying their nets, checking them for rips and mending them, or caulking their boats.

I was down there, late one afternoon, when I was still just a little bit of a kid, when they were getting ready for fishing. They had campfires going, coffee pots boiling, frying sidemeat and the like. Nobody paid any attention to my being there. Sometimes the fishermen would bring their families along, so extra kids weren't noticed.

When it got dark they loaded their nets into their boats and started fishing. At that time they just fished in that one area. They would take turns rowing their boats up toward the dam, casting their nets, then drifting back. They'd haul in their nets, take out their fish; they really didn't know how to fish at the time.

Commerical fishing was just getting started here, then. It was started on the Rogue, here at Grants Pass, by two brothers, Emil and Frank Oldenburg. They came here from the Clackamas River.

When I didn't show up for supper my folks started getting worried. As it got later and later they turned the whole neighborhood out, looking for me. Finally one of the neighbors, a fellow by the name of Robinson, found me. It was away along in the middle of the night, but I was so interested in what was going on I didn't think about it being so late.

I can tell you the names of some of the fellows who were fishing there that night: Mr. Bearss; Woody Raines; a fellow by the name of Sullivan; and Shorty Talmadge.

Grants Pass during flood thought to be around 1900, possibly the 1903 flood.

Josephine County Historical Society

Sixth Street Bridge during the flood of 1903. Note the south approach has been washed away. Wooldridge home at right.
Josephine County Historical Society

Babers' dray with Glen Wooldridge hitching a ride, about 1906.

Bruce Wooldridge collection

Boatman enjoying scenery at White Rocks area, now Baker Park, at the old railroad bridge, Grants Pass.

Grants Pass Courier collection

Chapter Three

"Company" for Aunt Laura

Glen's folks got used to his being on the river all the time. They finally accepted it. He didn't get far away from its banks very often.

But when he was about thirteen, "Aunt" Laura Wooldridge, George's wife, came into town on the horse stage and wanted Glen to go home with her. She and George had moved to Missouri Flats, away out in the brush of the Applegate Valley.

George was running his string of packmules, carrying supplies to the miners. The backroads of Southern Oregon were still just wagon tracks at the time, rough and muddy during the mining season. George was away from home a lot and Laura wanted Glen "for company," she said.

Now I didn't really care much for the idea of going home with Laura. I was about half afraid of her. She was a big, dark-complected, hard-boiled old girl. At least, that was what I thought at the time.

Dad heard her dinging at me to go home with her and called me aside. "I think you ought to go home with Aunt Laura, stay out there with her for a while," he told me. "You can take my new shotgun, do some hunting while you are out there."

Well, that changed the picture considerably when he said that. I never had any experience with guns up to that time. A young cousin, Tommy Cook, was accidently killed with a gun and they kept them away from us. So when he said I could take his new Winchester pump shotgun along, that made a big difference.

It was a late, dry spring when they jolted out through the deep dust of the Applegate Valley on the Williams Creek Horse Stage. The coach was built on a wagon running gear, but wasn't fastened directly to the frame like the chassis of a wagon. They swung it from leather straps so it would rock and teeter, to ease the passengers' ride over rough roads. It was built high and could get over rocks and deep ruts.

We had to leave the stage and walk quite a ways uphill, probably a quarter

mile, to Aunt Laura's house. I was itching to try out the new shotgun. When I saw some squirrels in an oak tree I wanted to shoot them, but Laura wouldn't let me.

"They've still got little ones now," she told me.

We went on to the house and the first thing I saw when we stepped in the door was a new rifle, a 25-20 Winchester.

Boy, I thought, what wouldn't I do with that if it was mine. But that was Uncle George's gun, I wouldn't dare touch it. I was pretty certain George didn't like kids.

After I had been there a few days I decided to go out hunting. There was a big field, fenced with rails, out from the house a ways. You had to take the gate down one pole at a time to get through.

I took my shotgun, went up to that field and saw a wildcat sitting there, looking for a squirrel, I guess.

Dad had told me how far the shotgun would shoot, and the wildcat was quite a ways from me, so I knew there wasn't any use shooting at it from that distance.

I thought of Uncle George's gun.

I started for the house, down the hill, across a little bit of a creek, then around a big mudhole the stock had trampled out while they drank, through the gate and to the house.

As I ran I built up my courage to ask Laura if I could use the gun. I told her I saw a wildcat and needed it to shoot him.

She did a lot of deliberating, but finally said, "Now that's George's new gun, but if you will be real careful I guess it might be all right."

She gave me some shells, but before I could get out of the house she called me back, telling me, "Take that old mule up to the field and stake him out where he can get some grass."

George had a sleepy old mule standing in the yard, too old and broken down to use in the pack train.

There she was, taking up my time when I should have been out killing wildcats. But we finally got everything rigged up, found a long rope, an iron peg and hammer; everything necessary to stake the old mule. She left to go to the neighbors, and I led the mule through the gate around the mudhole and up the hill.

At long last I got him anchored and went to look for the wildcat. I guess I thought he would be sitting there, waiting for me, but he was gone. I hunted around up there for a while then decided to go back to the house.

I collected the peg and hammer, rolled up the rope and led the mule to a stump and climbed aboard.

Now that mule wanted to get to the house in a hurry, so away he went, down the hill. I couldn't do anything but hang on; trouble was, there wasn't anything to hang onto. I was sliding around on his back, trying to stay on. When he came to the mudhole he jumped — when he jumped I went off — clutching all that gear. I landed right in the mudhole.

The mule went on to the house and I crawled out of the mud. The rope went with the mule and I found the peg and hammer, but the gun was gone.

My first thought was that it got tangled in the rope and the mule dragged it to the house. I trailed him all the way, looking for it, but no gun. Then I knew where it had to be — in the mudhole.

I found a long stick and waded back into the mud, poking around until I located the gun. When I brought it up it was covered with gook. And it was broken — all but just a rod that went in the center, and that was bent to just an L shape, and full of mud.

I could just hear Aunt Laura again, saying " . . . George's new gun . . . you must be real careful with it . . ."

I found a spot in the creek which was tolerably clear and washed the mud out, then took it across my knee and straightened it out the best I could. When I got to the house I set it back in the corner where it had been. I sure was glad Aunt Laura was visiting the neighbor that afternoon.

By the time I found some dry overalls and changed into them a neighbor boy came by. I hadn't seen him before, so of course, I wanted to show him my gun Dad let me use. I was really proud of it.

We went into the living room and I filled the gun with shells and started pumping them out. I guess I pulled the trigger, anyway the gun went off and blew a hole through the door to the kitchen.

I just stood there, staring at that hole in the door, wondering what to do. I can still see it, yet. I finally got up courage enough to open the door, to see what happened in the kitchen. Aunt Laura's pretty enameled wood range was splattered with a load of shot. Oh! Gosh!

I knew Laura would be mad when she got home, so to try to make amends I talked this boy into helping me cut some firewood for her.

An old fir tree had blown down, below the house a little ways, so we decided to cut the limbs off it and haul them up to the house with that mule. We rustled up enough harness to hook him up to a sled that was in the yard and I made some lines out of the rope.

The neighbor kid took the axe and went on down to the tree while I was getting the mule harnessed. I got him hitched to the sled and was standing up in it, headed down where the kid was. He was chopping away at one of the limbs, trying to show me how good an axeman he was.

I drove the mule up too close. The axe glanced off that hard limb and hit the mule right in the face, cutting a gash about three inches long, right under its eye.

That knocked the old mule crazy. He started running backwards — right over me and that sled. He wound me up in the harness — stepped on me, I guess. Anyway I was down and didn't have any breath left in me.

The boy came running over, asking me if I was hurt. I didn't say anything; I didn't have any air left to say anything with. But I finally got up, caught my breath and we got everything straightened out. We took the mule to the house and unharnessed him.

I went straight into the house, got my shotgun and went down the road on the run. I had to get out of there; I didn't want to be around when Aunt Laura got home.

I guess the boy told her I went home, when she got back. I walked down the Applegate River to the mouth of Board Shanty Creek, then over the hill. There was a wagon road through there.

It was a fourteen mile hike and I got home in the middle of the night. I took my shoes off when I got to the porch. Maybe no one would know just when I came in. But that didn't work; I had no more than got into the house until Mother was up, wanting to know what was the matter. I told her I didn't like it very much out at Aunt Laura's house and decided to come home.

I never did tell the folks what happened out there, and Laura and George never told them, either. But I sure was afraid they would. Once in a while they'd come to visit and when I saw them coming, out the back door I would go, on the run, and down to the willows by the river.

I was talking to Uncle George, many years later, and asked him if he remembered when I came out to visit Aunt Laura, chopped the mule in the head, shot a hole in the door, broke his new gun, and a few other things.

Well, he said, he knew all about everything but the gun.

"What gun?" he asked.

I described the gun to him.

"Oh, Laura traded that gun off before I got home. I didn't know it was broken," he told me.

Aunt Laura wasn't half as mean as I thought she was. She covered up for me. But I didn't get any more invitations to visit her after that. I got that all fixed up.

Stagecoach, 1910, at old Red Barn, Kerby, Oregon. This stage coach was similar to the one Glen and Laura rode to Williams in 1909.   Edith Keyte collection

River Scene, Grants Pass, Oregon, showing Steel Bridge over Rogue River.

Captain Costain sails the Rogue, about 1910, between the bridge and old dam. This was a post card picture, note postmark upper left.
Southern Oregon Historical Society.

Massie's stagecoach ran between Merlin and Galice, shown loading on Massie's ferry to cross the Rogue.   Edith Keyte collection

Massie's ferry with stagecoach aboard in middle of Rogue.   Edith Keyte collection

Josephine County Historical Society

The stagecoach arriving at Barlow's store, at Galice.

Williams postoffice, 1911, mail stage at right, with Ed Herriot, driver.   Arline Gray photo

"Uncle" George Wooldridge, driving the horse, with his brother, Logan, standing at right.
L. Z. Swinney photo

Chapter Four

George Fowler — A Friend in Time of Need

No doubt Glen was glad to get back to his so-called river-rat friends around the old dam. Even a week away from the river was a long, dry spell. Along with swimming, fishing, and catching a ride in a boat once in a while, you could hear lots of interesting things about the downriver area. There were miners coming around with their tall tales of the dangerous riffles and falls. Glen couldn't hear enough about this remote and unknown section of the river.

There was talk of building a wagonroad from Grants Pass by way of Galice Creek, all the way down to John Mule Creek, as it was then called. Mule Creek is in the remote section of the river and there was quite a bit of mining going on. Supplies and equipment had to be sent in by rail as far as West Fork, on Cow Creek, then by packtrain to the mines in the canyon.

The promoters of the road estimated it could be built for $10,000. Alex Watts, pioneer and old time Indian fighter from the Williams area, said he had made a survey of the area in 1890, and that the roadway could be built successfully by laying it out on the north side of the river, just above the high-water mark.

The Siskiyou Forest Service offered a $5,000 appropriation for the road and promised another $15,000. Not much came of the project, but it was talked of for many years.

The existing road ended just past the mining camp of Galice. To cross the river, to get to Galice, you had to catch Massie's ferry below Hellgate, about where the Indian ranch was.

That's the Josephine County owned, much-used, Indian Mary Park. Umpqua Joe, Indian Mary's father, was a friend of the whitemen during the Southern Oregon Indian War of the 1850s. After the war he came into possession of the place and started the ferry there. Mary married Albert Peco, a mule packer, in 1885. The next year after they married Umpqua Joe and Peco had a shoot-out over Peco's killing Joe's dog. They were both killed. In 1894, Mary received the deed to the land, signed by President Cleveland. It is called the smallest Indian reservation in the United States.

ALMEDA

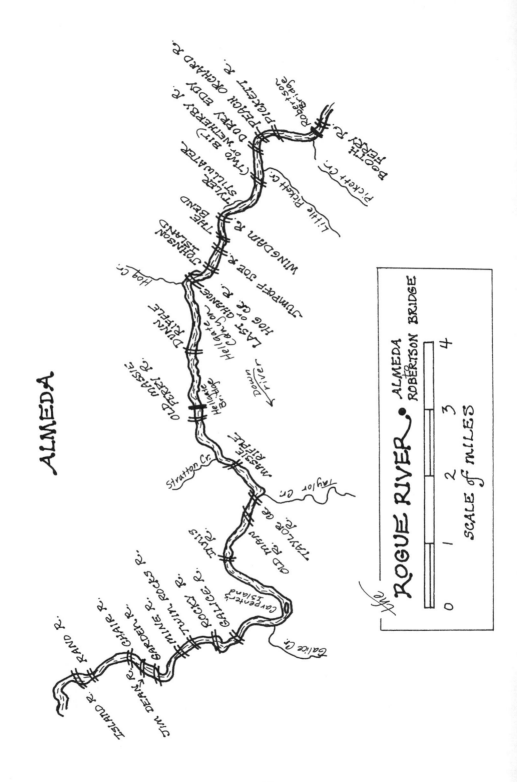

ROGUE RIVER
ALMEDA
ROBERTSON BRIDGE

SCALE of MILES

0   1   2   3   4

ISLAND R.
RAND R.
JIM DEAN'S R.
CHAIR R.
GARDEN R.
WINE ROCKS R.
GALICE R.
ROCKS R.
OLD MASSIE
Carpenter's Island
Galice Cr.
Taylor R. OR
OLD MAN
Stratton Cr.
MASSIE RIFFLE
Taylor Cr.
OLD FERRY R.
DUNN RIFFLE
Helle Briff
Hellgate Canyon
LAST CHANCE R.
HOG or R.
Hog Cr.
down river
JUMPER JOE R.
JOHNSON ISLAND
THE BEND
WINGDAM R.
TYLER STILLWATER
(TWO BIT) or WETHERBY R.
DORSY EDDY
PEACH ORCHARD R.
PICKETT R.
Little Pickett Cr.
Pickett Cr.
Robertson Bridge
BOOTH FERRY R.

The Almeda mine was working around 1910, and the Big Yank Ledge was being talked of as one of the heaviest producers of gold and copper in the nation. They built a log bridge across the river in front of the mine to transport ore and bring in supplies and machinery.

It was so low that boatmen going downriver had to stop and lift their boats over the bridge. This wasn't a big problem, as the traffic on the Rogue was pretty scarce at that time, but one riverboatman, Amaziah Aubery, found it very inconvenient. He made trips downriver to the Red River Mining Company, at Mule Creek, in 1910, 1913, 1915 and 1916, about one trip per year. When he would come to the bridge he would have to unload all the heavy machinery and supplies he was hauling, from the boat onto the bridge, lift the boat across, then reload.

The boats used in hauling the freight were built in Grants Pass especially for the trip. They were 27 feet long, with an 8 foot deck beam, a 4½ foot bottom and 37 inches depth of hold. They were built extra strong to withstand the strain of the trip and the boatmen took along a supply of oakum, pitch and planking in case they hit a big rock. These boats were dismantled at the Mule Creek mining area and the lumber used in construction, as there was no way of getting them back upriver.

One of the trips must have been extra scary, because four of the men with Aubery refused to go with the boats through some of the rougher places. Aubery had to hike downriver to the lower settlements and bring back some of the men who had freighted with him down there, to help take the boats through.

Another fascination for the young boys of Grants Pass was the "booze wagon", although at their age they couldn't hope to indulge.

That was the local name for the fancy railroad motor car the Southern Pacific had put on a daily roundtrip between Grants Pass and Ashland. This rain-proof, dust-proof passenger car was powered by six gasoline motors that could generate 250 horsepower. Sixty passengers could ride in comfort in its compartments and smoker, as it was well-ventilated in summer and heated by hot water pipes in winter. Glen remembers a ride on the car.

They called it the "booze wagon" because at that time Josephine County was dry and Jackson County wet. The bootleggers brought liquor across the county line on the train. There was a saloon out near Savage Rapids that did a big business.

I don't know how they got the booze across the river without the sheriff catching them when they crossed the bridge with it.

Around the Sixth Street bridge, in 1910, one of the distractions from fishing and boating was Spauldings' monstrous Best tractor, hauling lumber into town from Swede Basin. The old wooden bridge had been replaced with a steel one, and when the seventeen-ton traction steam engine, towing its four trailer loads of logs, crossed the bridge the noise was enough to scare the fish right out of the water. During one of its crossings a support under the bridge snapped, sounding like a rifle shot.

The bridge was then judged unsafe for the tractor and lumber loads. The gravel haulers, bringing gravel from the quarry near White Rocks to pave Front and Sixth Streets, were also banned from the bridge. A guard was posted to keep them from crossing and also, to warn other wagoneers to keep well to the left side while crossing. As soon as the guard was removed the lumber haulers started using the bridge again, even before it was mended.

But the main attraction, of course, was boating. It was as natural as going barefoot in summer for the boys who hung out with Glen along the river to learn to row and pole their families' boats.

In the Bearss and Briggs families, each with several sons, boating lore passed from father to older son to younger ones. But, in reality, even the older fishermen on the Rogue didn't have much knowledge of boating. They just had to learn by experience. They were always willing to give a boy a boatride, but teaching him to handle a boat required many hours at the oars or pike pole.

Glen's father and Frank weren't interesting in boating. His dad was busy making a living. He was butcher at the slaughter house, which was located a ways behind the Wooldridge home. Farmers sometimes called on him to doctor their sick animals, also. He wasn't trained in veterinary medicine, but knew a lot about it.

When he wasn't busy, he ran his race horse, the Grey Dude, at the local races. It usually came in well ahead of the rest. Frank always managed to have a horse or two around to occupy his time, so Glen had to look to someone else to teach him boating.

George Fowler was a familiar figure along the river. Glen would watch him rowing and poling his boat along. He remembered, too, that George had given him his first ride on the Rogue during the 1903 flood. George was an excellent boatman, able to maneuver his boat in tight places, and, too, he had the strength to haul it up and around the dam for an upriver trip.

He was a regular old mountain man, making his living trapping, hunting and fishing. He must have recognized a kindred soul in Glen; when Glen was big enough, George let him tag along.

George was stocky built, muscular and pretty good-sized. He was a kind of cranky old coot, but I could tolerate that, as long as he let me go along.

He would pole upstream as far as Ament Dam (Golden Drift Mining Company's dam) then drift back, fishing on the way. Sometimes he would take me to the woods with him, hunting and trapping.

He always carried his old shotgun, an unusual old Remington, single barrel, with the hammer on the side. You had to press down on it to cock it. There wasn't many of those around. He'd kill a duck for dinner, once in a while, with it.

He was a pretty good fisherman, too. The first salmon I ever saw caught on a fly, George caught it just below that old dam. Back then they didn't know a salmon would strike anything.

In the winter, George set his trapline down the Rogue from Grants Pass to the mouth of the Applegate River. He would run it about every second day, drifting and pulling his traps. He would check them, see if he caught anything, rebait and reset them, then maneuver his boat back to Grants Pass with a pike pole.

Pike poles, made of fir, were about as big around as an oar haft and about sixteen feet long. They were sharp with a steel point on the end to catch on the river bottom or between rocks so the boater could push the boat upstream. A

good pikesman could pole his boat about as fast as he could walk, but that's a lost art, now.

Boats weren't easily come by, back then. Each man usually had to build his own. They were narrow, like a canoe, sharp on both ends with hardly any rake so they could be poled up riffles with the pike, or easily rowed. Most of them were made of white cedar plank (Port Orford cedar) and had two sets of oarlocks so two people could row at the same time. Oars were made of ash and sold for $3.50 a pair.

When I first knew George, he lived in a tent where the Riverside Park is now. He came here from the logging camps at Yaquina Bay. His tent was pitched at the upper end of what is now the park. Mrs. Beverly's peach orchard was in there. Later he moved farther down into the park, into an old bachelor shack that stood just about where they start the Memorial Day boatraces now. Later on, the bandstand was built there, then they tore it down a few years back.

George would have hides and furs hanging from the ceiling of that little shack. It was just about fifteen feet square, and he would have skunk hides, coon, wildcat, otter, mink, just about anything he caught and skinned out. His traps, too, everything had to be inside the house, out of the rain. But he didn't have a dog; he didn't like dogs much.

He probably made a good living. A mink fur would bring $5.00 at that time and there was a lot of them around. A coon skin would sell for $2.00; an otter around $15.00

He was pretty much of a loner. I was around him about as much as anybody. He never married, but was a clean living old guy. He didn't smoke or drink, but did chase the women some. I guess people would have thought something was wrong with him if he hadn't.

I remember one time I was with George and we were walking across that campground up toward his house and we saw where something had been dragged along the ground and down to the river. I told George, "Looks like something was dragged along here." We went on and didn't think anything more about it. Later on, a kid swimming in the river found a guy's body hung up there below the bridge.

It was John York. He had been camping there, with his wagons and teams, and working around the country. There had been a young fellow with him, but there wasn't any sign of him or York's wagons and teams, after they found York's body.

This young fellow's name was Mike Morgan, and York had picked him up along the way and gave him a chance to work with him, earn a little something.

They caught the fellow up at Glendale. He had killed York and dragged his body down to the river, weighted it down with chains and threw it in. Then he took off with the teams and wagons. York was supposed to have had quite a bit of money on him, quite a bit for those times, anyway.

They were going to hang Morgan here, but they took him up to Salem and I never did know if they hung him or not.

31

I called George "old", that's how I thought of him, back then. He mightn't have been over 40 or 45 when I first started tagging after him.

He knew his business, though, and was a pretty good boatman. He taught me to row and use the pike pole. He really was the one who gave me my start on the river.

George K. Fowler, showing a sample of his catch. Raccoon and mink in his hands, otter skin on board. "There were lots of mink on the Rogue, back then."

Squeak Briggs photo

Spaulding's monstrous Best tractor, hauling lumber into Grants Pass from Selma. It could haul four loaded trailers behind it. This is the one that broke the bridge support.

Josephine County Historical Society

Bill Fergerson and Al Hall with their season's catch of pelts.   Hattie Hogue collection

Bearss family with a big catch of Chinook salmon. Note pike pole being held by woman at left.

Howard Bearss collection

34

Chapter Five

River Politics Spawns Poachers

As long as Glen could remember, he had meant to join the gillnetters when he was old enough to take a job, to spend his nights in summer pulling the oars of a boat on that downriver trip to Hog Creek he had so often heard the fishermen talk about.

But things didn't look too promising for him, or for any other fisherman intending to make a living by commercial fishing on the Rogue.

The fight for the river's bounty didn't end when the Rogue Indians were driven to the Siletz Reservation in the 1850s. Even before the turn of the century each of the three counties the river flows through had its own ideas about its uses.

At the river's mouth, at the twin towns of Wedderburn and Gold Beach, the Hume Company controlled the fisheries. Robert Hume started building them in 1876, and earned his title, the Salmon King of Oregon, by successfully maintaining claim to all the fish in the Rogue.

Hume bought land bordering the river on both sides from the mouth to twelve miles upstream. His fishing fleets, manned by coastal gillnetters, strung seines in the tide waters at the Rogue's mouth, hauling in the bright, saltwater-fresh Chinooks, silvers, (and, upriver fishermen swore, big steelheads.)

The gillnetters in Grants Pass had organized in 1906, calling themselves the Rogue River Fishermen's Union, with the avowed purpose of building a permanent fishing industry in the area. One of their proposed projects was to have a fish hatchery for the benefit of this middle section of the Rogue. To say they didn't like the way the Elk Creek Hatchery, on the upper Rogue, was being run would have been putting it gently. They were demon-tempered about it.

Salmon were being taken on the racks of the Rogue-Elk station. Some of the eggs were hatched, and as many fry as the tanks would hold were kept until they were five or six weeks old, then released in the upper Rogue.

Surplus eggs were packed in damp moss, 25 pounds to the tray, then crated and put in boxes, said to be about as big as a Saratoga trunk. The spaces in the boxes were filled with ice and sawdust to keep the hatching process from starting.

They were hauled to Medford by wagon, then shipped in a baggage car on a passenger train. The Southern Pacific allowed them free passage to Portland or San Francisco.

There they were transferred to a coastal steamer (the *Berwick* was sometimes used) to be transported back to the mouth of the Rogue to the Hume fish hatchery. They were hatched there and released.

This system of releasing fish in the upper Rogue and the mouth left Grants Pass area with only the native fish which escaped the seines at Gold Beach, since salmon return to their place of origin to spawn.

But credit should be given to Robert Hume for helping set up the Rogue-Elk hatchery when he found out that the eggs of the coastal-caught salmon were not mature enough for propagation.

Another barb in the gillnetters' flesh was that some of the eggs were shipped to the Clackamas hatchery and the fry released in the Columbia.

In Jackson County, on the upper reaches of the Rogue, as early as the turn of the century sportsmen started filling the lodges being opened there. The Rogue was gaining a name as a fisherman's paradise, and wealthy sportsmen came from afar to angle for trout and big steelheads.

They, too, were concerned about the diminishing migration of big steelheads. In 1910, they formed the Rogue River Fish Protection Association, to promote a bill in the Oregon legislature to close the Rogue to all fishing except with hook and line.

The Grants Pass gillnetters, caught in the middle of the three-sided battle that developed, agreed with the upper river sportsmen that the Hume people should be stopped from stretching their seines across the mouth of the Rogue. They offered to abandon commercial fishing during steelhead season, but strongly defended their own enterprise. They said it brought an annual $20,000 buying power to the Grants Pass area.

The editor of the *Rogue River Courier,* published at Grants Pass, supported the gillnetters. He called the upper river sportsmen "the silk-stocking fraternity," writing that they had no sympathy for the fishermen earning a living in an honorable industry.

The sportsmen's group circulated an initiative petition to close the river to all but hook and line fishing. They got eleven thousand signatures and put the measure on the ballot in the general election of 1910.

Around Grants Pass protesters claimed more than half the signers were from Portland and shouldn't have a say in a local matter. The measure passed, closing the Rogue to all but hook and line fishing.

It was along about then, when I was about fifteen, that I took my first dude on a guided fishing trip. There was this fellow who came around and wanted someone to take him upriver aways and let him fish back down.

I got a boat from old Costain who ran the little marina in the city park, and poled the fellow up to just below Ament Dam. As we were drifting back he was fishing and I was star-gazing when the boat hit a rock. It dumped me right out into the water. The boat didn't capsize, just threw me out. I had to swim to shore.

The boat drifted on down, with my dude still in it, and caught up on the

Clam Bed riffles. I walked on down there, feeling kind of sheepish, and waded out and worked it loose, then took him on down to the park.

I really learned something then. That was a good lesson for me. It taught me that you have to be awake every minute you are running a boat.

Around Grants Pass, the poachers kept busy supplying salmon for local needs. They couldn't see the need to stop fishing when the salmon were piling up below Ament Dam.

This time the battle that developed was among the home folks, one side saying the dam's fishways were adequate for upriver passage for the spawning fish, the other disagreeing.

But the answer to that was pretty obvious. Reports in the *Rogue River Courier* told of dead salmon hanging up along the riverbanks, in the bushes and on the old power dam just below Grants Pass where the city got its water.

Local doctors said the stinking mess had to be removed because it was a health hazard. Boatmen were hired and sent out with rakes to pull the dead fish back into the current and allow them to be washed downriver.

In 1912, an attempt was made to remove Ament Dam by blasting. This was thought to be the work of persons angry because it blocked the upriver journey of the salmon. The explosion shook the buildings on the property and a serious break was made in the dam, on the south shore, but the entire structure didn't go. There was never anyone prosecuted for the blasting.

Most of the time when poachers were brought to trial, they wouldn't be convicted. Most likely the jurymen would have been out, maybe the day before bringing home salmon for their own tables. But Glen remembers a couple of times two boys weren't so successful in getting away with it.

He and Harry Briggs, another young fisherman about his age, were caught below Ament Dam and charged with taking salmon illegally. They were brought to court and found guilty, but appealed the case. In the end they had to spend some time in jail, but it wasn't too bad. The jailer always went home at night and they found a loose bar at the window. They would wait until he was gone, remove the bar, and spend the evening on the town, or maybe the river, then slip back into jail before he returned in the morning. The bar was stuck back in place with chewing gum.

Another time he and Art King were arrested for fishing too near the Ament Dam. The fish warden said they were using triple hooks weighted with lead and dragging them along the bottom. They pleaded guilty and Judge Holman fined them $50. Not having the money to pay the fine, they had to lay it out in jail. This time it wasn't so pleasant; the bar had been reset in the window.

That old Ament Dam was really an abortion. The salmon piled up below it and wouldn't go through the dark tunnel of a fishway. It destroyed more salmon than the commercial fishermen ever caught. It just didn't seem wrong to go in there and help yourself to salmon that would eventually die and wash back down to Grants Pass, hang up and stink up the town.

The first game warden I can remember around here was R.E. Clanton. He'd hide his boat up by Ament Dam and when we'd go there to fish below the dam at night we'd drive plugs in his boat oarlock holes, pour some water on

them, then break them off. He was stymied, then, for the evening. I guess he could have killed us guys for that, if he could have caught up with us.

The Fishermen's Union did all it could to keep the river open for commercial fishing. The Hume forces, whether because they felt secure in their strength or from lack of leadership after Robert Hume's death, had been strangely quiet in the newspaper battle that preceeded the bill's passage.

But now they saw the need to take up the fight. Their huge buildings full of machinery were shut down, rusting and deteriorating. Local fishermen were out of work.

They enlisted the aid of the Salem *Daily Capital Journal* and Representative Pierce, from the Coos-Curry area, introduced a bill to reopen the Rogue to commercial fishing.

The bill passed through the legislature okay, but when it was sent to the Governor's desk it was vetoed. He had held hearings with the people from the Hume estate and the Sportsmen's organization, but hadn't asked the Grants Pass people to appear. He chose to favor the sportsmen, denouncing the Hume fisheries in rather harsh language.

The Hume People let the issue drop. Mrs. Hume sold the fisheries to the Macleay Estate Company of Portland in 1912, and retired to San Francisco.

But the Grants Pass gillnetters weren't ready to give in. Backed by the *Courier,* which declared there was room for both commercial and sports fishermen on the Rogue, they reopened the fight in 1913.

The Medford sportsmen had mellowed a little, by now, and were willing to compromise. They offered a thirty-day open river to the Grants Pass gillnetters, but the middle river fishermen wouldn't go along with that. They swore they would fight to have the river closed completely to all types of fishing unless they were given as much time as the coastal fishermen.

Medford's district attorney announced he was going to call for a grand jury investigation of charges that the poachers were dynamiting salmon below the dams in Grants Pass and selling them. That was a penitentiary offense, he warned them.

Countering that, Senator Smith from Grants Pass, threatened to kill the bill for Medford's new armory unless the fishing measure was amended for a full season's open fishing in the Grants Pass area.

The Gold Beach people swung around, joined the middle river fishermen and compromised, allowing a sixty-day season in the Grants Pass area. Both the sportsmen's association and the governor were upset, but the law passed over the governor's veto, reopening the Rogue for the 1913 season.

When Cal Allen and C. Weare were caught at the dam, wet to the waist and with the appearance of having been cleaning fish, the Medford sportsmen were given new ammunition.

There were no fish to use as evidence, but the prosecution claimed they had a partner, Wallace LeClair, who took the fish away in a boat. The boat was found downstream, but it only had fish slime, scales, and a fish knife in it, no fish or net.

Prosecuting Attorney Kelly strongly appealed to the Grants Pass jurymen for conviction on circumstantial evidence. He told them the people of the area agreed to enforce the laws if allowed to keep the river open for gillnetting. He threatened that if they were not convicted the river would be closed again.

He said just because the fishways of the dam were such that the fish couldn't get up them and congregated in great numbers in the pond below, the defendants thought they would slip in and make a haul. He insisted that if the people in the area would stand for that sort of thing they ought to have the river closed.

The defense attorney, Fred Williams, said it was the boys who were on trial, not whether Josephine County should have an open river. He didn't care about the attitude of Jackson County, or any other county; the state had not proved its case. The jury was dismissed because of a split decision and another trial was scheduled, but during the second trial the boys were found not guilty.

About that time, other damsites were being considered on the Rogue. One was at Hellgate. The Rogue River Public Service Corporation had plans to build a 200 foot high concrete dam there, to furnish electric power and irrigation for the valley. When they filed for water rights on the Rogue in the Hellgate area, they paid a $2286 fee to the State Department of Engineers, one of the largest ever collected at that time.

Everyone was worried about what such a dam would do to the fishing on the Rogue. The dam was talked of for many years but was never built, possibly because the cost would have been prohibitive to a private company.

Cal Allen, in dark shirt and his partner displaying their catch. Cal's mother is at left. Note small girl with small fish. Bruce Wooldridge photo

Ament Dam. The first salmon piers on this stretch of the Rogue were built on the point where the men are standing. Bardon and Croisant built them.

Josephine County Historical Society

Early day gillnetters with catch. Picture taken looking upriver to Sixth Street Bridge and old dam.
Josephine County Historical Society

Early day fisherman with catch. Josephine County Historical Society

Early day aerial passenger tram over Rogue at Hellgate. Grants Pass Courier photo

Chapter Six

Gillnetting: A Man-sized Job

Glen was seventeen when the river was reopened for gillnetting in 1913. Under George Fowler's training he had developed strong shoulder and arm muscles. He was able to pull a boat in the current and ready to take on a man-sized job.

The river was open from 400 feet below Ament Dam downriver to the mouth of Jump-Off-Joe Creek. The season started the first week in June and ended the last of July.

It took two people to handle a gillnetter's boat; one was net tender, the other, boat puller. George Fowler took me on as partner in his boat that year, and we just split the money even.

The principal meeting place for the fishermen was downriver from the old Grants Pass dam, where their drying racks were. I had always hung around there from the time I was a kid. They'd be running around, mending their nets, patching their boats and talking about the river. It was an exciting place, so it was just natural for me to join them when I got big enough to start fishing.

The nets we were to use were eight-and-a-half inch mesh. That was the smallest legal size, but most used the nine inch. They would allow a pretty good sized salmon and most any steelhead to go through. Larger salmon were caught by the gills in the meshes when they tried to go through and were drowned.

You measured the mesh by pulling opposite corners of a mesh square tight, then measuring from knot to knot.

Nets were hung with lead weights along the bottom and floats whittled out of soft wood along the top, so they would sort of tent-out in the water. You have two twines when you are knitting a net; the hanging twine and the webtwine. The little string, the lighter one made of linen, is actually the body of the net. But the heavier one, the hanging twine made of cotton, is the one you tie it to the line and cork line with. The web is twice as long as the lines. You hang it so it is real slack and loose. If it was tight it wouldn't hold the salmon; a big

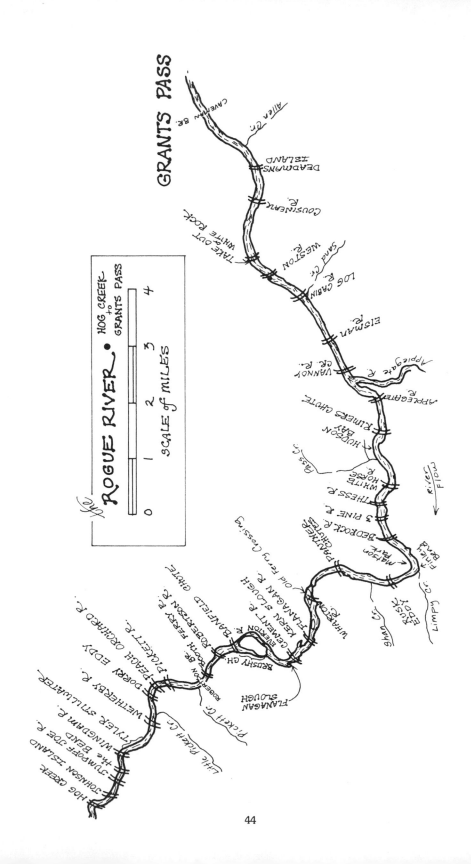

GRANTS PASS

ROGUE RIVER · HOG CREEK to GRANTS PASS

SCALE of MILES

0   1   2   3   4

CAVERON CR.

ALLEN CR.

DEADMANS ISLAND

COUSINEAU R.

TAKE OUT — WHITE ROCK

WESTON R.

Sand Cr.

LOG CABIN

EISMAN R.

VANNOY CR. R.

Applegate R.

APPLEGATE R.

RIMERS GULCH

HUDSON BAY

Bass Cr.

WHITE HORSE R.

THESS R.

3 PINE R.

BEDROCK R.

PRAIRIE CHUTES

MATSON PARK

Finley Bend

RUSK EDDY

LIMPY CR.

Shan Cr.

RIVER FLOW

WHARTON

FLANAGAN R.

KERN SLOUGH

CEMENT R.

GUERIN R.

BANFIELD CHUTE

Old Ferry Crossing

ROBERTSON R.

BOOTH FERRY

PICKETT R.

PEACH ORCHARD R.

ROBERTSON BR.

Pickett Cr.

Little Pickett Cr.

BRUSHY GH

FLANAGAN SLOUGH

DOREY EDDY

WETHERBY R.

TYLER STILLWATER

WINGDAM R.

the BEND

TUMOFF JOE R.

JOHNSON ISLAND

HOG CREEK

44

salmon would break it. If it hangs loose it goes with the salmon until it gets them caught in the gills. They can't break that.

The gill nets float with the water and the fish tangles with them. They would be from 200 to 300 feet long. Some people knitted their own, but most bought their nets. We bought our equipment at Rogue River Hardware. The nets sold for one dollar a pound and there were twenty-two feet to the pound.

You had to know how to knit or make the gillnet knot to mend your net when it would get hung up during a drift and get a hole in it. You knotted your twine around a mesh board, using that special gillnet knot, so the mesh would be uniform.

Net buoys were usually five-gallon coal oil cans.

The beginning of a drift or stretch of water that was free enough of rocks and submerged logs that you could let your net drift was called a towhead.

There were 32 towheads from Allen Creek to Hellgate and they were all named. There were: Allen Creek, Dean Man Island, Cousins, Weston, Sand Creek, Eisman Still Water, Eisman Riffle, Applegate, Whitehorse, Three Pines, Bedrock, Finley Bend, Shan Creek, Panther Chute, Ferry Hole, Stump, Cement, Dump, Bybee, Brushy Chute, Crescent Whirl, Pickett Creek, Peach Orchard, Dorry Eddie, Dorry Riffle, Tyler, Tyler Still Water, Wing Dam, The Bend, Jump-Off-Joe, Johnson's Island, and Hog Creek. Many of them were named after early fishermen and miners living along the river.

We fished at night, unless the river was muddy. You can't catch salmon in water clear enough for them to see the net. Mining, upriver, with hydraulic giants would muddy the water, but not enough. Once in a while we'd get a storm that would muddy it enough for daylight fishing.

We'd start fishing at dark and take out at daylight. Fishing was best just as it started getting light. The fish are moving more then than any other time.

We'd make a drift, pull in our nets, take the fish out, then go on to the next towhead and cast again. We didn't have any way to get back, unless we pulled our boat back by hand. We couldn't row back, because you can't fish in water dead enough for you to row in.

A few guys did become what we called "homesteaders." They would fish just one drift, then pull the boat back and drift it again. Just fish the one spot over and over. But if you were going on through to Hellgate, like most of us did, you didn't have time to do that. When we came to a place where someone was homesteading a drift we just fished on through. Nobody had a real claim to any one fishing spot.

You had to keep moving in order to cover the distance you figured on during the night. But we would stop along, pull up to the bank in a place that was easy in and out, and make coffee in the bailing cans.

When I first started fishing we were supposed to take our nets out at the mouth of Jump-Off-Joe Creek. If they caught you fishing farther down they would confiscate your net. They were supposed to destroy unlawful nets or seines, and there was a fine of $100 to $500 and from thirty days to six months in jail, but no one was ever convicted, or at least hardly ever.

The Burns boys were charged with fishing illegally with a net. The fish warden took their net and put it on display in the city hall, where the Golden Rule Store is now. They were going to auction it off. The other fishermen would go in and look it over, pretending they were going to bid on it. They would roll it around on the table where it was spread out. There was an open window right close to where the net was and someone rolled it up next to that open window, on purpose, I would imagine. The next morning the net was gone, and there went their evidence.

There hadn't been anyone fishing with nets for a few years and the river had lots of obstructions, tore the nets up pretty bad. We lost a lot of fish, too, that first year.

One fellow, John Hogue, who was about twenty-five years old was drowned. He was fishing with his partner, Pankey, and their net got hung up to something in the water and also got caught on an oarlock, tipping them over. That's the only commercial fisherman that I know of getting drowned. We had quite a lot of mixups, though.

The oldest Bearss boy was rowing the boat for his dad, drifting the Jump-Off-Joe drift. They ran into a rock, threw the old man Bearss overboard. Fortunately, they were close to shore and Mr. Bearss was able to get out. They had quite a load of fish in the boat and lost them all. We called that rock, Bearss Rock, after that.

We would fish through during the night, about fifteen miles of fishing water, then haul our boats back in the morning. We paid $4.00 for a man with a team to haul the boats back. The driver would be waiting with his wagon and team at Hog Creek Landing at daylight. Hog Creek was called Last Chance because that was the last chance you had to take your boat out, because of the lack of roads and places to get down to the river.

That road was made into Hog Creek to take the boats out. We'd load the boats on the wagons about daylight, by main strength and awkwardness, put the fish under the beds where they would be in the shade, then start back to town. We carried our beds right in the wagons, old mattresses and springs. We would throw them right in the boats, across the seats, and get in and sleep coming back to town. You wouldn't think you could sleep, jolting along over the chuckholes, but you would get to where you could, after a while.

It would take us three or four hours to get back to town. We would take the fish to the Fishermen's Union warehouse and dress them right on the river-bank. They had to have their heads cut off and be dressed before they were weighed.

After we delivered the fish it would be nine or ten o'clock before we got to bed. We'd sleep until about two o'clock then go down and see to our nets. We'd dry them every day and once in a while wash them with blue vitriol, to kill the fungus, to keep the nets from rotting.

The Fishermen's Union had built a little packing house, about twelve feet square, just down from the dam. They packed the salmon, 150 pounds to the box, iced them and shipped them by express. Most of them went south to the Bay area. H.E. Gething was president and manager of the union.

Rogue salmon were better flavored than Columbia River salmon, and these were Chinooks, fat and shiny, really the marketable fish.

The market varied from seven and a half cents to ten cents or more a pound. It sort of steadied after the Fishermen's Union was formed. We'd get paid once a week. We could figure six of those dressed salmon to average one hundred pounds.

There would be fifteen to twenty boats working and we would figure on catching up to fifteen fish per boat, but sometimes when a run was good we got lots more. The most I remember catching in one night was eighty-four for our one boat.

The *Courier* reported the 1913 season's catch as close to 200,000 pounds, but I think that was a gross over-estimation. That would be a lot of good eating. You can't catch good salmon like that anymore, and the best you can get sells for about five dollars a pound, nowadays.

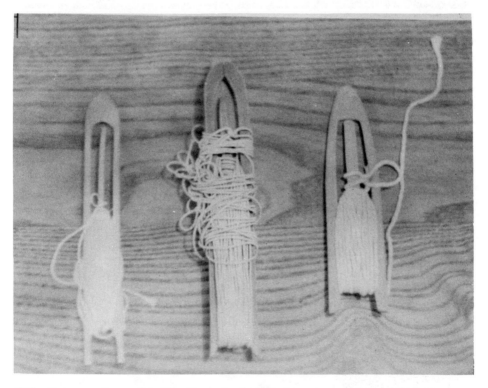

Gillnetters used needles like these to knit their nets and to mend them.

Arman photo

Gillnetters casting nets. Note coal oil can being used for buoy.
Josephine County Historical Society

Pulling in net with boat already heavily loaded. Note wooden floats near man's hands.
Pike pole under oar at right. Josephine County Historical Society

Boats were loaded on wagons at Hog Creek landing to be brought back to Grants Pass Fishermen's beds were brought along and they slept on way back to town.

Larry Sullivan collection

Fish were dressed out on river bank. Note fish-dressing stand at left. This picture was probably taken near fishermen's packing house at the end of Greenwood Avenue. Fishermen have been identified as Shorty Talmadge and George Ferry.

Glen Wooldridge collection

Chinook salmon in packing house, ready to be packed and iced for shipment to San Francisco market. Elizabeth Hiller collection

Gillnets were spread to dry on racks at foot of Fifth Street. Shorty Talmadge mending his net. What appears to be a tied package is a coal oil can used as buoy.

Josephine County Historical Society

Chapter Seven

Down to the Sea in a Home-made Boat

After we had been gillnetting for a couple of years, I was standing on the Sixth Street bridge one day, looking down into the water, when Cal Allen came along. He was another young gillnetter. We started talking about how we both wanted to go all the way downriver to the coast.

"Why don't we build a boat and go?" he asked me.

"Okay," I said.

So we pooled what little money we had, I think it was about six dollars between us, and went to Spaulding's Lumber Yard and bought enough lumber to build a boat. We got a wagon from somewhere, I guess we had to rent it from the livery barn, and hauled our lumber over to Ed Allen's planing mill on Ninth Street, by the railroad tracks.

We went in to talk to Ed, Cal's father, about planing the lumber for us and while we were in there the horses spooked. They ran around, got tangled in the harness, knocked over the railroad signs, broke the wagon tongue and dumped our lumber. They just made a circle then came around the second time and ran over the lumber, chopping it up pretty bad.

We finally got it all straightened out, sorted out what good lumber we had left and Ed Allen let us have enough to finish out what we needed to build the boat. He made a new tongue for the wagon, too and we paid him later.

We hauled it over to where my folks lived then. We had moved across the river to where the Bridge Motel is now. Really just from one end of the bridge to the other.

We built our boat there, and it was a hell of a looking thing. Heavy! It was made of cedar planks and 2×4s, and was about 20 feet long. We caulked up the cracks and dragged it down and heaved it over the bank just below the old dam. We rustled up some oars from someplace and got ready to start.

My folks thought we were crazy and tried to talk us out of going. Just the fall before Frank Marci had drowned at the Government Bridge and his body

51

was found at Illahe. He and A.R. Curtis had attempted to run the river and wrecked on the rocks. And a while before that a fellow by the name of Dunn had drowned at what became known as Dunn Riffle.

But I guess the folks could see it was no use trying to talk us out of going. Mother gave us three quilts to take along for a bedroll (that was before sleeping bag days) and we took a skillet and a gun and shoved off. That was September 5, 1915.

We hadn't got any farther than Eisman Riffle when we saw a really big run of salmon. The water was just thick with them. We talked about staying and fishing here but we had made a start so decided to keep going. We had taken so much ribbing about running the river we didn't want to back down.

We had been down as far as Whisky Creek Falls on a hunting trip, one time, but from there on down it was unknown country as far as we were concerned. And most everyone else for that matter. A man by the name of Amaziah Aubery had boated some mining equipment downriver. I think they broke the boats apart and used the lumber in them at the mines. And before that, back in 1896, or along that time, some men had gone downriver, but as far as we were concerned it was unexplored country. We never had talked to anyone who had taken a boat all the way down.

Dunn Riffle looked pretty bad to us. We looked it over pretty closely before we ran it, but we made it through okay. When we got to Almeda there was a low-water bridge across the river. It was used to go to and from The Almeda mine, called the Big Yank Ledge, back then.

We had to lift our boat over that bridge, which took a little maneuvering, and from there on down it was wilderness.

We would listen to changes in the sound of the water and when we heard something different we would tie the boat and hike down to see what was ahead.

We were just a couple of green kids, didn't know half as much about boating as we thought we did. But we sure learned.

At Grave Creek Falls we had to portage the boat, and at Whiskey Creek Falls we lined it down the fishway. That's a natural fishway, not man-made, and is still just about the same today as it was then.

To line a boat you have a long rope fastened to the bow. One fellow, standing on the riverbank, eases the boat down by letting out the rope, while the other fellow goes along the shore and uses a pike pole to keep the bow pushed away from the rocks and the banks. You can use an oar, but in those days we always had a pike pole in the boat.

In most cases it is more dangerous to line the boat than to run the rapids, but if it is a rapids you have never seen before it is a good idea to look it over and figure out which way you want to go before starting.

Old Man Ramey lived in a cabin on down from Whiskey Creek Falls, at that time. He gaffed salmon below the falls and packed them out to Glendale with two little buckskin ponies he used for pack horses.

Eventually the falls took his name, but it is a corruption of his name. They call it Rainie Falls, other versions of it you see now and again are Rainy, Rainey, and Reamy Falls.

There was a pipeline across the river, just above Horseshoe Bend. Amaziah Aubery hauled it in and put it there. It was the source of water for some mine, but I don't know which side of the river it served.

They were mining at the old Red River Mine on Mule Creek and the Forest Service was just finishing the trail around the face of the mountain that took the place of the one over Devil's Backbone across from Stair Creek. I remember as we were going along in the boat they shot off a blast and we were showered with broken rocks.

We would camp along the river banks at night, anywhere we could find a good camping spot. We fished and killed a deer so we would have something to eat. It was a pretty exciting time; hazardous, too, but we had a good experience.

We were awfully scared a few times, but that's good for you, as long as you don't get hurt. When you run one of the really bad rapids and get through it safely, then you have a great yen to do it again. Sort of like riding a roller-coaster, only much, much more exciting.

There was a flume hung on high rocks and cliffs that took water from Tom East Creek to Black Bear Mine on the south side of the river, really the east side there. Then on the opposite side, the Solitude Mine got its water at Tate Creek and the water in the flume flowed in the opposite direction than that one on the south side.

Looking down into Mule Creek Canyon for the first time is a frightening thing, but we knew we had to run it. So we did. That was really exciting. Then at Blossom Bar we had to rassle that heavy boat around and over those huge boulders; some of them nearly as big as a house. That sort of made us wish we never had started the trip.

We finally made it through and on down the river. It took us five days. We ran into a run of fish at Lobster Creek Hole and caught forty of them. We took them to the cannery at Gold Beach and sold them. We got a dollar apiece for Chinooks and thirty-five cents for silversides, so we had a little money to buy grub with.

The cannery had a campground where we pitched our tent, and we found some planks and boarded up around the bottom of the canvas about three feet to give us more head room. Then we gathered grass and weeds to make a bed. We had the three quilts we brought from home for cover.

There were other people around us, living in little cabins the cannery people had built. The men came down to gillnet and the women to work in Seburg cannery. Some made the trip over Hayes Hill and the Smith River Road, then down around the coast by Brookings, then over the Carpenterville Road. Others rode the train to West Fork, then hiked the trail to Agness and caught the mail boat.

We got all set up and started fishing. One morning after we had fished all night, we came back to the tent and found an old sow and a bunch of little pigs in our bed. They sure had fixed things up in good shape. Our beds were a mess, quilts dirtied, so I decided to wash them.

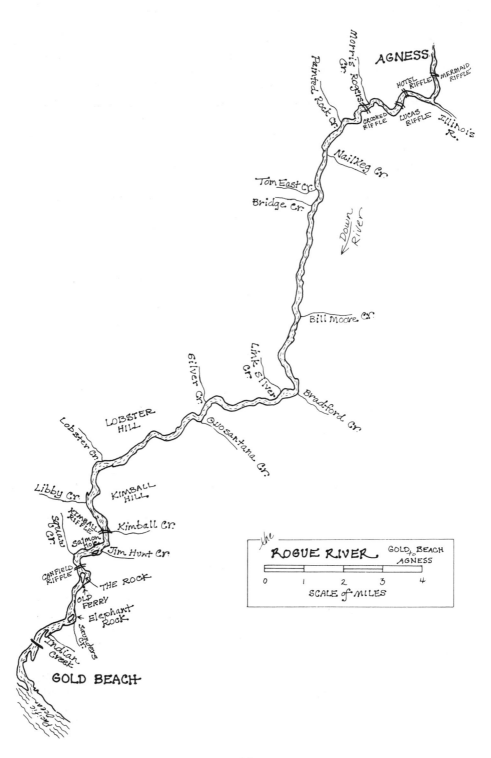

Morris Rogers Cr.

AGNESS

Painted Rock Cr.

HOTEL RIFFLE

MERMAID RIFFLE

CROOKED RIFFLE

LUCAS RIFFLE

Illinois R.

NailKeg Cr.

Tom East Cr.

Bridge Cr.

Down River

Bill Moore Cr.

Link Silver Cr.

Silver Cr.

Bradford Cr.

LOBSTER HILL

Quosantana Cr.

Lobster Cr.

Libby Cr.

KIMBALL HILL

KIMBALL RIFFLE

Squaw Cr.

Salmon Hole

Kimball Cr.

Jim Hunt Cr.

CANFIELD RIFFLE

THE ROCK

OLD FERRY

Elephant Rock

Saunders Cr.

Indian Creek

GOLD BEACH

Pacific Ocean

the ROGUE RIVER   GOLD BEACH to AGNESS

0   1   2   3   4

SCALE of MILES

I borrowed a washtub from a woman who lived in one of the cabins and washed the bedding. While I was at it, I washed my underclothing, too.

There was a wire fence on the east side of our tent I hung the quilts on and I spread my underwear on the bushes to dry.

The winds blow there all the time. I think that is the thing I didn't like the most about Gold Beach, the wind blowing constantly. In the summer it is wind, wind, wind! I really got tired of that.

When you are going downriver the wind would be blowing downriver with you, until you get to the mouth of the Illinois River, at Agness, then it's always blowing upriver.

We had to cook outside, as there wasn't room in the tent, so I built a fire to cook some supper. Then I decided to go down to the river to check on my partner. Cal was down there mending our net.

When I came back I found the wind had blown sparks from the fire into our bedding and it was burned up. Then when I went to the bushes to get my underwear the buttons were gone off them. What the hell has happened here? I thought.

When I took the tub back to the woman I complained about my buttons being gone. One of the women in camp came over and told me, "I cut them off. I thought you threw the underwear away, and I wanted the buttons, so I cut them off."

She took my underwear and sewed the buttons back and we were in business again. That was Ada Johnson who cut the buttons off. She and her sister, Hattie Hogue, both still live in Gold Beach. I go to see them when I go down there.

While we were there, Frank, my brother, showed up. I guess he was broke, like everybody else, and decided to try to make a little money, even though he hated that sort of job, fishing and boating.

One day we were tired of eating fish and decided we needed a deer. It was my job to do the hunting and while I was gone I came across a hog. It wasn't very big, about fifty pounds or so, but I killed it and skinned it. We were hungry for meat.

When I got back to camp I told Frank it was a bear and he didn't know the difference. He had fifty cents, all the money he had in the world, but he gave it to a woman to cook a ham off that hog for him. After he ate it I told him what it was. He wanted to fight me for letting him spend his last half-dollar to have that hog leg cooked. Oh, gosh, we didn't make any money but we did have lots of fun.

We took turns cooking and when Frank was there we made him take his turn, too. He didn't like it. One day when it was his turn to cook he got the food ready and stepped out the back, where we were called, "Come to dinner, you s.o.bs.

One evening there was a whole gang of us with our boats along there and someone said, "We ought to have a chicken roast."

One of the Indian boys, one of the Frys, said, "I'll get the chickens."

It was dark already, but away he went. After a while he came back, carrying a little fir tree about six feet tall with three or four old hens roosting in it. He had taken a saw and cut the tree off and here he came carrying chickens and all. He hadn't even disturbed them. We had our chicken roast.

An Irishman who was fishing with us decided it was time for a little relaxation one day. He took his boat and rowed down to Gold Beach and got drunk.

There was a little riffle, just in front of the cannery, not very rough, just a mild sort of riffle. And Frank and I were sitting on the bank, by that little riffle, when we saw him coming back, rowing upriver.

He would row up into that riffle then stop and rest. And, of course, his boat would drift back downriver when he stopped rowing. Then, when he rested, he would row back into the riffle and get tired, so he'd stop and rest again.

That riffle was where they threw the salmon waste when they dressed them at the cannery and hundreds of seagulls would be on the gravel bar, flying around, squalling and fighting over that garbage.

We watched this Irishman row up there a few times and drift back and after a while Frank waded out and caught up with him and helped him get his boat over to the bank.

When he got out of the boat he told us, "That's the biggest bunch of seagulls I ever saw in my life. I've been rowing for an hour and I haven't got through them yet."

Frank didn't stay down there very long; he came on home. I don't know how he got down there in the first place.

Cal and I stayed until the middle of November. Then we just abandoned our boat. Never saw it again. I sure wish I could see it now, or had a picture of it. I'll bet it would look awkward to me.

When we started home we rode the mail boat from Gold Beach to Agness. That was an early day version of the big mail boats that haul passengers along that stretch nowadays. Elihu Fry ran it. It had a motor, about a 5 to 8 horse, and he carried several pike poles in the boat. When he came to a riffle everyone had to use a pike pole to push us over the whitewater. Then we'd go bumping along to the next riffle with that little motor.

After that thirty miles by boat to Agness, we started hiking. There were 48 miles of trail to West Fork, on Cow Creek, the flag stop on the railroad. Boy, that was a long trail. It seemed like 148 miles over that mountain. They called it Ninemile Mountain. I think right then was when I decided to make a run upriver someday, by boat.

West Fork was just a store, a hotel and the train stop. There was a big warehouse to store things in until the packers could carry them down into the lower Rogue Canyon.

The provisions for the Marial Country came from there. You would see strings of pack stock in there, 15 to 20 head to a string, mostly mules. Mules didn't tire as easily as horses and could keep to the narrow trails better. They lived longer, too.

Hathaway Jones ran his pack outfit along that trail and carried the mail. He was there when we made that first trip downriver.

At that time quite a lot of mining was going on in those hills and canyons around the Mule Creek area. Before they built the trail around Mule Creek Canyon it went over the mountain next to the river. Straight up and down, over the top of the peak for four to five miles. They called that the Devil's Backbone. Everything had to go over it until they made the trail around the face of the mountain across from Stair Creek.

One guy told me a story, many years ago. He said he hiked down the Rogue Trail. Sometimes it was on the gravel bars, sometimes up the side of the mountain. He kept going and it turned into an Indian trace. He followed that and it turned into a game track. Later on it became a squirrel trail. He followed that and it went up an oak tree and into a hole.

That's sort of the way our trip to Gold Beach was. After all our efforts to build a boat and go down the river. After the troubles we had when we got there and all the energy we used fishing, we didn't bring home much money. I came home with eighty dollars.

Glen and gillnetter friends just before his first trip downriver in 1915. Left to right, unidentified man, Al Hall, Cal Allen and Glen.   Glen Wooldridge collection

Glen and unidentified man, 1915, taken the day he started his first trip downriver.
Bruce Wooldridge collection

Almeda Mine with low-water bridge, Galice about 1915. Boats had to be unloaded at bridge, lifted over, then reloaded. Amaziah Aubery's boat, hauling freight for miners downriver.
Bureau of Land Management collection

West Fork depot, about 1913.   Southern Pacific photo

West Fork Hotel, 1910, left to right, Jake Croy, Jake Fry, Charley Billings, Andy Huggins, unidentified man & Chauncy Fry.   Bureau of Land Management collection

Forestry crew building Rogue River Trail to bypass Devil's Backbone, 1915.
Bureau of Land Management collection

Blossom Bar before Glen opened it by blasting the boulders.   Glen Wooldridge collection

Chapter Eight

Fight, Fight, Fight, But the Rogue Always Wins

On the upper reaches of the Rogue, around Prospect and in the Rogue-Elk region, fly fishermen were discovering the wonders of the Rogue for rainbow trout fishing. The steelheaders, too, were making excellent catches, but they were concerned about the future of good fishing in the Rogue. Again, they laid the blame on the gillnetters in the Grants Pass to Hellgate stretch of the river.

The newspapers took up the fight and sometimes it took on a comicality. The Medford sportsmen were labeled "Bearcreekers," indicating they weren't really on the Rogue and should stick to their own waterways. And when the Portland Commercial Club members stopped in Grants Pass, while making a tour, the young boys of the city gave each of them a paper bag of Grants Pass air to be opened and breathed while they were in Medford.

The Medford newspapers countered by saying the dams in Josephine County needed signs on the fishways to show the fish how to get over them.

But this old problem of what to do about the Ament Dam was still a major one. A movement was started by the upriver fishermen to have it destroyed. They said it hindered the fish from reaching their spawning beds. There were still people around Grants Pass who swore this was not so. They put forth their case that the fish wardens had time and again had the fishways changed to their own specifications.

In June, 1915, game wardens Applegate, from Gold Hill, and Walker, from Medford, counted fifteen poachers taking salmon with unlawful tackle, and fishing too near the dam.

When they tried to arrest them five shots were fired by someone and all of the poachers disappeared into the brush. The fish wardens managed to catch five of them. The poachers demanded a jury trial, but this time were convicted.

In the meantime the Josephine County road department decided to do some work on the steel bridge across the river. The workmen needed a boat to get around in the water, but after they got it, they didn't know how to maneuver it.

Glen was around there quite a bit of the time so they got him to row the boat for them. They called him their boatologist. When the bridge was finished they presented the boat to Glen.

That was the year I got my first boat motor, but it wasn't any good. I bought it from someone, I don't remember who. It was an Evinrude outboard, and once in a while I could get it to run a while. It was made of brass and had a magneto and a hotshot battery. That's three big dry-cell batteries in a package. It had a flywheel with a knob sticking up and you had to stick the wires on the sparkplug to start it.

You'd turn the knob this way, and bang, it might go the other way, kick right out of your hand. Maybe it would run forward, or maybe backwards, you never could tell which.

If it went backwards you'd have to jerk the wires off the plug and start over again. Maybe this time you'd get it to running the right direction.

I had it around here a long time, then Charley Holland came along one day. He was an old friend of mine. He wanted to borrow it.

So I said, "All right, you take it."

Charley was one of those guys who would monkey with something like that half a day at a time to get it to run five minutes.

I had forgotten all about the thing, until one day he brought it back "I've had your motor fifteen years," he told me, "and decided it was almost time to bring it back."

I wish I still had it, but I let it get away from me. I don't know who I gave it to, but somebody. I bet it would look funny now.

Glen and Charley Holland after a fishing trip, note old motor in center.

Glen Wooldridge collection

Glen and Cal worked with the commercial fishermen again, in Grants Pass in the summer of 1916, then used the boat the bridge workers had given Glen to make another trip to Gold Beach.

They gillnetted again at the mouth of the river, camping out and selling their catch to the canneries. That year Macleay's cannery was paying $1.50 per fish.

Seeing the cannery's big seine strip the river of all the fish in its path raised the ire of Grants Pass fishermen. It didn't seem reasonable for the upper river people to think this was all right and to object to their gillnetting at Grants Pass.

Gillnetting and seining are two different methods, altogether. In using a seine they use one boat, anchoring one end of the seine to something on the shore then laying the seine out around the pool. Then they come back and the fish are in the puddle so they work it gradually to shore and take the fish out.

Salmon haven't got sense enough to jump over the cork line, but stupid carp will jump over it and go on out.

The seine would be about 250 to 300 fathoms long (six feet to the fathom) and they fished to a depth of forty feet. Macleay's crew would spread it just above the jaws of the river and, at times, even out into the breakers, then circle and pull in everything in its path.

There would be thousands of fish of all kinds; salmon, perch, steelheads, carp, suckers, flounders, shad and others. One sweep of the seine, in 1915, brought in 600 large Chinooks along with the other fish. There were twenty-five men working the seine. At times, in earlier years, the seines were drawn in with horses.

The men were supposed to throw the big steelheads back, and most of the time they did, but the smaller fish were nearly all dead from the pounding they took from the large salmon caught in the bunt of the seine.

Glen and Cal didn't get into a hassle with the Macleay outfit, but another young Grants Pass man did. It was Claud Bardon, who was well known locally for his quick temper. He had a battle with Mr. Macleay, himself, right in the river.

Bardon laid his drift net, then the Macleay crew spread their seine, trying to get around him and cork his net. He pulled for the opposite shore, blockading their seine.

After trying to get by, Macleay jumped into the river and pulled Bardon's net down, trying to let the seine boat and the seine cross over. Bardon warned Macleay off, but when he didn't go, Bardon jumped into the water and tussled with Macleay, forcing him to turn the net loose. The seiners avoided Bardon after that, but Macleay brought charges against him for assault and battery. Bardon had to pay a total fine and court costs of nine dollars, the price of six big salmon.

Old timers around Grants Pass say that Bardon's escapade was the basis for Zane Grey's novel, *Rogue River Feud.*

Glen and Cal had a tussle in the river, too, but it wasn't with the Macleay outfit.

One night Cal and I were fishing. It was a moonlit night and the river split into two channels just where we were fishing. We had to go down the left channel and there was quite a little riffle there. I was rowing the boat and I looked around and saw something in the water ahead of the boat. It was a bear, swimming the river.

Gee, there we were right out in the middle of the river. I took off after him.

Allen climbed up in the bow with the bowline, going to lasso him. So I rowed right up to him and Allen put the rope on him all right. He let him swim a little ways from us then gave the line a big pull. That just turned the bear upside down and the rope came off.

Before we could catch up to him again he got to shore. I often wondered what would have happened if he had got a leg into the rope so he couldn't get loose. We had the rope tied to the boat, of course. We could have had some fun with him. Then, again, he might have climbed right in the boat with us. Anyway, we didn't get him; he got away.

Another time we were fishing right down at the mouth of the river, right where it runs into the ocean. We got too close and were washed right out into the ocean. It swamped our boat, sunk it, but the waves beat it up against the bank and we got out.

We lost our net, temporarily, but it finally washed onto shore when the tide changed. It had a couple of salmon in it.

It can be dangerous fishing down there at the mouth of the river, especially if the fog rolls in. Some of those fogs are so thick you can't see two inches in front of you. Take a dark night, then fog, the only way you can tell the directions is by the sound of the surf rolling.

Ruell Hawkins and his brother, Harry, came downriver to Gold Beach, one night, in later years. It was so foggy they didn't know where they were. They discovered they were out in the ocean, after a while. Ruell shut his motor off and let the boat drift. He had to conserve what gas he had as he didn't know which way to go.

When the sun came up he could see the shore. They had drifted down close to Brookings, someplace. When they started into shore their boat capsized and they had to swim in. Ruell told me that the worst part was trying to keep their noses out of the foam.

When the 1916 fishing season was over, at Gold Beach, Glen abandoned his boat, again, and with Cal, caught the mail boat to Agness, then hiked the trail to West Fork to catch the train home. That was the last season Glen fished commercially at Gold Beach.

The winters 1915 through 1917, Glen worked his grandfather Cook's old Cement Diggins mine on Foots Creek. One season his dad and brother worked with him; the others, a friend of his, Sherman Estelle, was his partner. They stayed with Glen's grandfather at the farmstead. The old pioneer was in his eighties at that time; Glen's grandmother had died in 1912.

The old ditch was still usable and they operated the hydraulic giant to wash the creek banks down, sending the paydirt and gravel through the sluices. If a boulder was too big to move with the stream of water from the giant, sometimes they would build a fire around it, heat it as hot as possible to crack it. If the heat alone didn't do the job, a stream of water from the giant, on the hot rock, generally would. Otherwise they had to use a sledge to break it up.

Many of the mines in Josephine County, and even as far away as the Idaho mines, used a Ruble "grizzly" to move the rocks out of the way. This invention of the Ruble brothers on Coyote Creek at Golden, was a system of iron bars set at an incline so that boulders and coarse gravel could be forced up and over them by the powerful stream of water from the giant. The gold-bearing sands would go into the sluice boxes below.

The Cook-Wooldridge operation wasn't profitable enough at that time to warrant the cost of such an outfit. It took several tons of steel and iron to construct a grizzly.

The bedrock of one fork of Foots Creek had been stripped with a steam dredge, just after the turn of the century, but it hadn't worked the Cook claim.

When preparations for the 1917 fishing season rolled around, the Grants Pass gillnetters invested in a big truck to haul their boats back from the Hog Creek turnaround. That would save their having to sleep in the boats on the wagons, jolting back to town, as well as the cost of hiring several wagon drivers.

When the season was over upriver, they used it to haul their outfits to Gold Beach, going by way of Roseburg and Bandon. They started their own business of marketing fish, hauling them to Coquille and shipping them to Portland.

The next year, during the Grants Pass season, Lawrence Middleton, whom they hired to drive the truck to pick them up at Jump-Off-Joe, ran the truck into a train which was coming down the steep grade near Merlin. The young driver was killed and nine-year old Jack Bearss, who was riding with him, was badly injured.

In 1917, Glen took his first dudes on a guided trip downriver all the way to Gold Beach. They were Bruce Cornwall, a real estate broker from San Francisco, and his son.

I remember it very well. It rained like hell and we caught one fish. But this time we didn't leave the boat at Gold Beach. I had someone with a truck come over and pick us up and haul the boat back.

It took at least two days to come back over the hill from Gold Beach, in those days, and sometimes in the old Model Ts we were using then, you had to get out and push.

The road didn't follow the ocean then, and it does now. When you got out of Gold Beach a ways, you had to go up to Carpenterville, then down to Brookings. That was a long and crooked road. Some people named Carpenter ran a little store there. From Brookings the road took over the mountain again, then turned off at Patrick Creek, going up and around the hills by Monumental, then down to O'Brien. It was a miserable thing, getting over that mountain — much worse then Carpenterville. It was just a trail around through the boulders.

If you happened to meet a car, there weren't very many, one of you would have to back up until you found a wide spot in the road. There was always someone going off the road and down into the canyon. They reported six in one week's time, back then.

Squeak Briggs said when they went over to fish at Gold Beach one year, they had a 1923 Chevy with an open flywheel. The road was so full of mud holes that flywheel would get packed with dirt and they would have to get down and scratch it all out before they could go on.

Hattie Hogue, at Gold Beach, has a funny story about a trip over that road. She said one time when she and her husband came to Gold Beach, in the

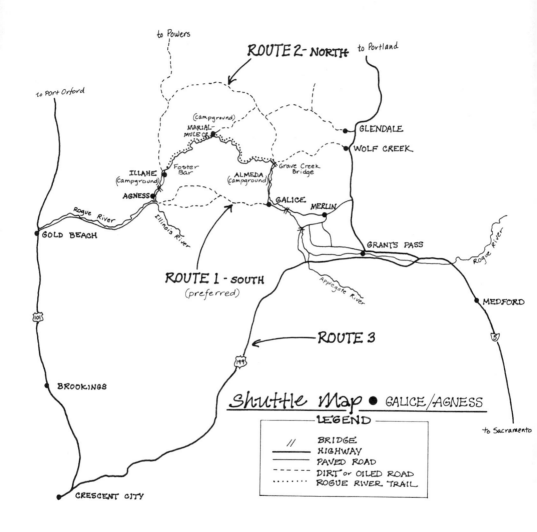

to Powers

to Portland

ROUTE 2 - NORTH

(Campground)

MARIAL-
MULE CR.

GLENDALE

WOLF CREEK

ILLAHE
(Campground)

Foster
Bar

ALMEDA
(Campground)

Grave Creek
Bridge

to Port Orford

AGNESS

GALICE

MERLIN

Rogue River

Illinois River

GOLD BEACH

GRANTS PASS

Rogue River

ROUTE 1 - SOUTH
(preferred)

Applegate River

MEDFORD

101

ROUTE 3

5

199

BROOKINGS

Shuttle Map ● GALICE/AGNESS

LEGEND

to Sacramento

//	BRIDGE
———	HIGHWAY
———	PAVED ROAD
- - - -	DIRT or OILED ROAD
·······	ROGUE RIVER TRAIL

CRESCENT CITY

1920s, it took them two days to make it over that Carpenterville Road. She and her husband didn't have car trouble, but there were some people traveling along with them in a Buick. It was built so low that when they'd hit one of those oversized mudholes they would have to push and pull the car out. Finally they hit an extra deep one and the old Buick plunged down into it and broke the gas line.

There wasn't any way they could fix it. The woman who was with them got out her hot water bottle and they filled it with gasoline. She kept her arm sticking out the window, holding that hot water bottle while the gasoline dribbled into the carburetor through the rubber hose. They would have to stop every time that quart or so of gasoline burned and refill the hot water bottle.

Mrs. Hogue said the same woman had carefully handled a couple of dozen fresh eggs she brought all the way from Grants Pass. She kept them in her lap, making sure they didn't get shook up. Finally, when all the excitement was going on about the gas line and having to hold the hot water bottle out the window, she got so aggravated she just threw the eggs, bucket and all, out the window and down into the canyon. "To hell with them," she said.

I'd always had Model Ts, but then I got ahold of a Dodge. That was better. It was one of those old slow-motion rigs, but it would pull on those bad roads, go shaking and chuckling along.

One of the first hunting parties I guided was an old man and a boy. I had my suspicions about the old man's being a hunter, right from the first. He told me he never used the sight, just shot from the hip, and he carried an old lever action 30-30.

Well, we got up there on Evans Creek and camped out. We got up early next morning and went out to hunt, just the old man and me. We hadn't got very far from camp when I pointed out a doe to him, saying, "There's a deer." Or at least I tried to point it out to him, but I didn't mean for him to shoot it.

He said, "Where? Where?" looking around and swinging that old rifle around. I wasn't too sure I was safe, even where I was standing next to him.

Finally he caught sight of the doe, standing on a hill of dirt about a hundred yards in front of him. But he didn't wait to check and see if it had horns, just started pouring the lead.

"Did I get him?" he hollered.

I said, "No, I don't think you did." The bullets had spattered the hillside all around the deer, and of course she was gone.

But he insisted I go down and look for her anyway. So I went down into the brush, looking for the old doe, but didn't see any sign of her, or any blood.

Well, we hunted around there for a while, and finally the old man said, "I've got to go back to camp. I'm out of shells."

So I took him back and that afternoon the boy and I went out, leaving the old man resting at camp. It wasn't too far from camp that we jumped a couple of nice three-points and killed them both.

We dressed them out and dragged them back to camp, but the old man wasn't there. When he didn't show up all that afternoon, we got worried, but finally, about sundown, he came splashing in, right down the middle of the creek, soaking wet from falling around in the creek and tired out.

I asked him why he was walking down the middle of the creek and he told me that's what he had always heard to do, if you got lost, to follow a creek downstream, and that was what he was doing.

He came on into camp, sat down on a log and told the boy to get him a drink of water, that he was dying of thirst.

"You were right in the creek," I told him. "Why didn't you get you a drink?"

"How could I?" he asked me. "I didn't have a cup."

The battle of the Rogue wasn't all the fighting that was going on, at that time. Overseas the first World War was raging. Young men aged 21 to 30 were required to register for the draft. Glen registered in Jackson County because he was working the Foots Creek mine on his twenty-first birthday.

By the time he was called up, the war was almost over, and he wasn't sent any farther than the Presidio at San Francisco. The men in his outfit, called up so late in the war, weren't given any military training, so to keep occupied they took up boxing.

Their trainer arranged exhibition matches for them in San Francisco, Oakland, Stockton, Berkeley, and other towns around the camp. Glen was pretty serious about boxing. When he was discharged from the army he came back to Grants Pass and trained with Joe Gorman, a professional fighter who ran a gymnasium on Sixth Street, between "G" and "H". Gorman was lightweight champion of the Pacific Northwest and had just missed taking the world title a few years before. Glen worked as his sparring partner for a while.

I got so I would do pretty good, although I never did consider myself a really good fighter, but among the amateurs I could handle myself pretty good.

I thought I was going great guns, whipping everyone who came along, until I was over-matched with a red-headed guy from Yakima, Washington. His name was Wildcat Kelly, and he licked the socks off me. After that I didn't think I was such a good fighter.

There was a time when I considered taking it up professionally, but I guess the lure of the river was too great.

One of Glen's friends from that time said Glen had the fastest hands on any man he ever knew. He said Joe Gorman may have been as fast as Glen but he didn't think so, and either one of them could hurt you.

During that period, just after the war, in addition to his gillnetting, Glen worked on a road-building crew and did some logging on the North Fork of the Coquille, above Myrtle Point. Both the logging camp and road building gangs gave him lots of opportunities for fisticuffs, but the Rogue always won in the end.

Glen in his World War I army uniform.   Bruce Wooldridge collection

Early day mail boat on lower Rogue.
Siskiyou National Forest collection

Modern mail boat.   Rogue Mail Boat Service photo

Josephine County Historical Society

Giant at work in the Josephine County area.

71

Glen Wooldridge and Robert Cook, his cousin in front of their grandparents Cook's house on Foots Creek about 1970.
Arman photo

Chapter Nine

Fishing and Hunting; A Way of Life

By now the Rogue's fame as a steelhead river had spread and people were coming from all over the country to fish it.

A high-ranking English official, Collie-MacNeill, who was consul to Mexico, came up with his wife and daughter in a chauffeured limousine. He was on his way to Canada, but stopped off long enough to fish the Rogue. He said it was the best fishing he had ever had in his life, and he had fished all over the world. He promised to come back the next year and build a lodge on the river.

He bought property near Savage Rapids and built his lodge and made it an annual pilgrimage to spend several months each summer and fall fishing the Rogue.

Zane Grey's party came in July, 1919, and spent some time fishing the Rogue and other rivers, and also Crater Lake. His wife; his brother, R.C.; and a Miss Ackerman, from New York City, made up the party. Other famous people who came in the early years were Jack London, Irvin Cobb, Boseman Bulgar, and Babe Ruth. Even Winston Churchill paid a visit!

Salmon fishing with hook and line was gaining in popularity, and to make it easier to fish for them, salmon boards or piers were built out into the river.

The first salmon boards on the Rogue, that I remember, were put in at Ament Dam on the little point of land just below the dam. That must have been about 1912 or 1913. They were built there by a couple of local fellows, Croisant and Bardon, to catch salmon, mostly for their own use. But Bardon did peddle fish around town. He had a little wagon with a bell on it and he would go along, ding-dinging that little bell so women would come out of the houses and buy fish from him.

The piers were built out into the water, set on legs, but the high water would come along and wash the legs from underneath them.

The fishermen used bamboo poles and big brass spinners. They'd set their poles where the spinners would work in the current, then go back and sit in the

shade, hoping they would get a strike. That was quite effective, back when we had lots of fish. And we really did have a lot, and all kinds.

The spring Chinook salmon was the kingpin of the whole caboodle. That's the best fish there is. When they come into fresh water they are prime, reaching their peak right in that period, and they hold up pretty well.

They start coming in here, well, the earliest I ever knew them coming was in February. Not many come in that early, though. Later on, in April and May, is really the best time, then another run comes in August.

They would hang around the salt water and the fishermen downriver would catch most of them. They had to get used to the warm water of the river and wouldn't come right on through in a hurry like the springtime run. When the water is cold they come right on through in a few days, but the summer run wouldn't do that. They would school down there.

I don't know if the spring and summer runs of Chinook are the same species, but you can't tell them apart by looking at them. They run at a different time, but a few would be coming up all summer long.

They spawn in two different periods. The very first spawning we would see would be right around the middle of August. That would be away on the upper part of the river. Then, as time went on, they would spawn on down river. By mid-September they would be spawning around Grants Pass, but October was the big month for salmon to spawn. That was what we called the fall Chinooks, but they weren't quite as good a fish as the spring salmon. They weren't so fat — not really as prime a fish. I don't know if it was the age of the fish, the hot water, or just what caused it.

The biggest fish I ever landed was a fall-run Chinook. That was in December, 1934. I caught a 54 pounder on a number three spinner, just below White Horse Riffle.

Steelheads spawn in a shallow, gravelly place, just the same as salmon. Steelheads will bite even when they are spawning. You can catch them on bait right in their spawning beds.

There are a few summer steelheads left, but very few. There never were lots of them, like the Chinooks. They came in the springtime and early summer and went on into the upper part of the Rogue and would stay up there. They were nice little fish and easy to catch. They'd bite anything, but they never were a strong run of fish.

They got to calling those things they are catching now, summer steelheads, but that's not a summer steelhead. He's a different fish than that.

He's a nice beautiful fish, starts biting here in July then goes to that upper country. They make a dandy fly fish. They are red-meated, like a Chinook, and don't get very big. Most of them would be about three or four pounds, but sometimes they get quite a bit bigger. The best thing to catch them with was crawfish.

The cutthroat is not a migratory fish in the Rogue River. He stays in there the year around and goes into the little streams in the mountains to spawn in the springtime. When the water was taken out of the creeks for irrigation, there he went. We hardly ever see a cutthroat anymore, and the silversides, or Coho salmon, went the same way.

They used to make a pretty good run here, and in the Applegate River, coming in in the late fall, along in October or November. They didn't last long, though. They were just about ready to spawn when they came in and they'd go right on up into the tributaries. As time went on water was taken out of the tributaries for irrigation and they used to spread the little fish out across their fields by the thousands. I think that's what destroyed the silversides, or Coho salmon runs. I haven't seen one in five or six years.

They have a very prominent nose, real hooked, the males especially. As they near the spawning season they turn red on their sides — a kind of orangey-red streak down the center. Some steelheads get that, too, in the fall, as they near their spawning season.

Silversides are good fish to smoke; they aren't too fat. Chinooks are pretty fat and juicy. There are still quite a number of silvers in the ocean, so they do spawn in some rivers, maybe the Klamath. They don't take the water out of the Klamath like they do the Rogue, for irrigation. They take some, but not as much. They don't drain the tributaries and the silvers have a place to spawn.

They used to spawn here in Gilbert Creek and Jones Creek and lots of them went up the Applegate. The big floods didn't do too much damage to the redds, just shifted the gravel around. They spawn on the riffles, so the shift of the gravel doesn't do much damage. It's a wonder any of them live to maturity, with everything that feeds on them.

They didn't seem to catch the silvers from the piers so much, maybe because there wasn't many people fishing from the piers when they made their runs.

I wish I had one of those old brass spinners; I'd like to show you what they looked like. Some fishermen said the silversides would strike a copper spinner better, but I don't know whether they did or not; anyway, it was easy fishing for them, back then.

The sturgeons, now, I never saw any over six feet long, but if you catch them three feet long they are a dandy fish. I really liked them. They are protected now. In the Snake River, they stopped sturgeon fishing completely. They are getting scarce. They grow very slowly. They say a sturgeon six feet long is sixty years old. It takes them a long time to mature, and they are the homeliest things I ever saw.

There was still concern about the fishways at Ament Dam. In 1919 Representative Sheldon, from Jackson County, introduced a bill in the House directly aimed at it. The measure required the fish warden to serve notice on owners when a dam was blocking the fish runs and to make repairs, himself, when needed.

Shortly before that, the fish warden had dynamited a wing dam on the Ament structure, and the company was upset about it. They claimed they were not warned that the fishladder was faulty. On more than one occasion the fishway had either been repaired or rebuilt.

That year, while the company was rebuilding the dam, a fire of unknown origin burned the entire wooden structure above the water. The company officials said it was more of a blessing than a deterrent to their work and continued to repair the dam. Glen said he believes it was never put into good condition again, though.

That year, again, there were bills in the Oregon legislature concerning fishing rights on the Rogue, and some unusual groupings and regroupings occurred. First of Medford people, joined by the Grants Pass fishermen, pushed for the banning of seining, but the measure failed to pass.

Then the next year the Jackson County sportsmen joined the Macleay officials to form a treaty. They proposed the banning of seines, limiting the size of drift net mesh to 8½ inches, and limiting commercial fishing to the twelve mile point above the mouth of the Rogue. This, of course, cut the Grants Pass gillnetters out completely. They called the treaty an unholy alliance.

The state attorney general judged the treaty to be illegal and there was a shifting of sides, with political strings being pulled to get the measure passed. Grants Pass fishermen came out of it better, in the end, with a five-day extension to their fishing season.

The gillnetters started the 1920 season with a fleet of only five boats. They sold their fish to Charlie Gray and Emil Harbeck at the City Meat Market on the corner of Fifth and "G". Walter Sweetland originally started that fish market.

Harbeck had an elevator built right up through the sidewalk, so it was handy for the gillnetters to drive up and toss their fish onto the elevator to be taken to the basement for processing.

There was a tremendous run of salmon that year, the biggest in the memory of the earliest fishermen. The fish schooled at the mouth of the Rogue and were hanging back from coming upriver. Downriver fishermen credited the huge run to be salmon liberated in other streams that were schooling in the river's mouth. They reported many fish marked with the Columbia River identifications, as well as fish from other streams.

The Savage Rapids dam was started in 1920, about seven miles upriver from Grants Pass. It was quite a big project, built of concrete, 480 feet wide and with a 400 foot spillway. Shattuck Company was the builder, with E.J. Carillo, the engineer.

They had the state fish warden down to okay their fishway built on the north side of the river and ten feet wide. They wanted to avoid the controversy that had plagued Ament Dam.

The project was started for irrigation, and almost immediately after it was put into use their first problem arose. The small fish were being pumped into the fields and pastures around the countryside. One man brought in a bucketful he had scooped up out of one small pool in his field. They counted one hundred fry in the bucket. The irrigation takeouts were eventually screened, and when the green moss from the river clogged them, special revolving screens were designed to take care of that problem.

Through the years the fishways were rebuilt several times. Later, on the south side of the river, the company was able to put in satisfactory fishladders. A wide parking area was cleared for tourists to stop and see the big salmon going up the ladders.

After that dam was built, someone installed salmon boards below it, putting in quite a lot of them and renting them commercially.

Alfred Smith, who owned the property just below the dam, cut some of the trees on the property and used them to build a lodge, the Weasku Inn. He built several small cottages, with rough bark exteriors, to rent to the out-of-town fishermen. There were wood stoves and beds, but the fishermen had to bring their own cooking outfits and bedrolls. The fishermen could fish from the salmon boards or hire guides to boat them up or down river. It was a good place for a guide to contact a fishing party to fill-in during off-season for gillnetting.

Hunting, too, took up a lot of Glen's time. He would hunt the triangle between Murphy, Williams and Grants Pass, and also the Evans Creek area.

Evans Creek was a good place to hunt. There were a couple of old log cabins up there, on West Evans Creek, which we used to camp in. They were still in good condition and we didn't have to use our tent. The old salt vats were still there, on Salt Creek, when I first started hunting that country. That was probably the major source of salt for the Southern Oregon area, in the early days, other than what they packed in by mules.

On the left fork we used to hunt Willow Flats. Just about the last time I ever went hunting with my dad we went up there. He was getting pretty old, by then, and he was the camp cook. He was a good one, too, because he liked to eat. He probably weighed around 250 pounds.

I remember one time, back when I was just a kid, Dad went hunting and he took along his black and tan hound, Bugler. They were hunting along when Bugler started a deer. He took off after it and Dad did too. He thought he had a good sight on the deer, but when he shot he hit Bugler.

He carried him all the way home, in his arms, but it was too late; Bugler died.

Back then about every second hound was named Bugler. There was this fellow, Smith, who lived on Evans Creek, had a hound named Bugler, too. He was almost as bad as Hathaway Jones for lying. Nothing would do but for me to take him hunting. He was going to show me where I could kill a panther. I had an old Model T Ford I had made into a pickup, so I stopped by and picked up him and his couple of hounds. So here we went, up Evans Creek.

In those days there wasn't hardly any road up there. You'd ford the creek, then go a little ways and have to cross back again. After we had crossed the creek half a dozen times, we were right out in the middle of a wide stretch of it when we got a sniffle of water in the carburetor and the old Model T died.

Well here it was, January and cold as the dickens, and us right out in the middle of this creek, and it's as wide again as a freeway. There was nothing to do but get out and try to crank the Model T. So we waded around and finally got the thing pumping again, jumped in and went on.

The dogs were tied in the back end of the pickup, so when we finally got to the place we were supposed to find the panther we stopped and got them out.

I didn't have much faith in the panther part, to start with, but I wanted to go anyway, just for the fun of it.

Those old hounds were so poor you could almost see through them. You

had to prop them up against a bush before they could stand up. This fellow said, "I will just turn Bugler loose; he won't run anything but a panther."

So I said, "Okay, turn him loose." I was hanging onto the rope on the other one.

Well, pretty soon Bugler found a track and away he went, tearing around through the brush. There was a series of little knolls up there and he went bawling off around the side of one of them. We took off after him.

Somewhere, during the chase, I lost Smith, but I followed Bugler, thinking maybe I could chase him through there.

Just about the time I got around the knoll up jumped a little deer, bug-eyed and just scared to death, with that old hound, Bugler, right after him.

That was Smith's wonderful panther dog — but that old hound was hungry — he was after meat.

I shot the deer, saying to myself, "Here's where I feed these hungry mongrels."

I skinned out a haunch and fed those old hungry hounds. I'd cut off a chunk and they would grab it and swallow it whole, pieces as big as my fist. To slow them down a little, I started cutting the pieces a little smaller. Finally the old hounds were so full of meat they were just standing there, stiff-legged.

I collected the dogs and started back and we ran into Smith. He was madder than the devil. He could see what happened — I'd fed his dogs. Well, he tied the dogs in the back of the pickup and we went chugging back through the rocks and chugholes, back and forth across the creek, bouncing around.

We had gotten quite a ways when we finally stopped and looked back at the hounds. Old Bugler had jumped out and we had dragged him until we were just dragging his hide along. Smith had tied the rope a little too long. I was glad I'd fed the old hounds — at least Bugler died with a full belly, but I wasn't very popular with Mr. Smith.

Another time, up on Evans Creek, I was hunting by myself, in barely open timber. It was raining a little and there was a thick fir tree that had fallen to where it was angling down the hill. I was going right up toward it and I saw this animal come out from behind it and go loping over the ridge and out of sight. I stood there dumbfounded, wondering what it was. I could have killed him easily enough; I was that close to him, but I waited too long. After he was gone I woke up to the fact that it was a timber wolf. He was dark grey, but he might not have been so dark if he hadn't been wet.

I had another experience up there, another time. I was going up a timbered draw and saw some wolf tracks in the dust. There were two or three tracks along there and I was watching real close, trailing them. The wind was blowing a little bit and I heard a growling noise. It would growl a little, then it would stop, then it would growl again. I finally pinned down the spot the sound was coming from, a little draw to the right of me.

I went sneaking up there, real easy, hearing this growling every once in a while. I visualized that they had killed a deer in there and were having a little argument about it. I kept sneaking up until I could get a good look. I discovered that it was two trees rubbing together in the wind, but it sure had me fooled for a while, scared a little, too.

Well, I never did get my panther, or cougar, but I guess you needed a good dog like Smith's old Bugler to get one of them.

"You slide through a little hole at Slim Pickins."   Glen Wooldridge collection

Woman angler landing big Chinook, is Mrs. Darling, Los Angeles. Note shallow depth of boat, old fishing pier on stilts, left.

Josephine County Historical Society

Savage Rapids before the dam was built.

Josephine County Historical Society

Glen in Hellgate Canyon, taken from the south side, looking downstream.

Glen Wooldridge collection

Chapter Ten
Rogue's Robin Hood

There was a big change in Glen's life, in 1924, when he married Eva Owens. The responsibilities of a married man sat a bit heavier on him than those of a foot-loose bachelor. He had to try for a more regular income.

Cal Allen and I went up to the Columbia, in the spring of 1925, and took my boat. We were going to gillnet up there, before the season opened on the Rogue. There were others who went up there to fish. Al Schmitz used to go just about every year, I think, and that year the Houcks went along; Lee and Henry and their dad, and Don Barnes went with them.

There was this tragedy happened while we were fishing up there. Lee Houck drowned. He was just a young man, about 21 years old, I guess, and he was a good boatman and swimmer. He had been working with his dad on the Rogue, here at Grants Pass, for several years.

He and Henry were in the boat, I think, with Don Barnes on the riverbanks, and their boat got caught in the whirlpool and swamped them. Don jumped in and tried to help them, but the boat broke up. Don and Henry caught onto the back part of it, and Lee tried to get ahold of the front part, but was caught in the current. The Houck boys' dad managed to get to Don and Henry in a motor boat, but Lee was carried on downstream. They didn't find his body for a long time.

That was the only time I ever went to the Columbia to fish.

Glen tried working at a few other jobs. He took Eva and his small son, Bobby, down to Dorris, California, and spent about sixteen months falling and bucking timber, but always returned to the river.

By now there were more out-of-towners coming to fish the Rogue, and he could occasionally find a party to guide at one of the resorts. On the upper part of the river several big resorts and hotels catered to the tourist trade, such as the Rogue-Elk and those around Prospect.

Some of these tourist-fishermen were writers, also. One, M.W. Mier, was the western editor of *Forest and Stream*. He found his hideaway at the Aberdeen Villa, near Kerby, where he stayed several months, gathering material and writing. He told a group of Grants Pass sportsmen in an address to their club, that they should be proud to have a stream with a world-wide reputation right on their doorstep.

Joe Wharton was another one who brought a lot of those people here. He wrote a lot about fishing on the Rogue. His stuff was published in some big magazines back east (*The Boston Transcript, Forest and Stream,* and others). They were read overseas and were influential in getting the English and Scottish fishermen coming over here.

Joe was a real good friend of mine, but then he was everybody's friend. He was in the sporting goods business for something like forty or forty-five years, starting in 1907. Before that he worked for the Hair-Riddle Hardware, that was the old name for Rogue River Hardware.

He had a little shop on the west side of Sixth Street between "G" and "H" Streets, at first. Then he moved down on "H" Street, close to where the Rogue Food Shop is now. His shop was the first tackle store in Grants Pass. Everyone told him he couldn't make a living just selling fishing tackle, but he was there for a great many years. They used to call him the Sage of the Rogue.

It was said that the English and Scottish fishermen introduced fly fishing and reel fishing to the area; that local people, before that, used cane and willow poles and just horsed the fish in.

Zane Grey, too, took credit for introducing the reel to the area. He was the one who urged Wharton to stock really fine fishing tackle in his store. Wharton designed his own flies; the Rogue and the Wharton Jungle-cock Specials. His store became the gathering place for fishermen for the Southern Oregon area.

There was a pine bench in his shop he made in the early 1920s that was called the Liar's Bench. It was worn smooth by the seats of fishermen who sat there telling of the big ones that got away. Over the bench was a poem which read:

> On this rude bench beside the wall
> Great men have rested, fishermen all,
> Each in his own way has told a great tale
> of marvelous fish caught from minnow to whale.
>
> Millionaire, pauper, bishop and bum,
> Pugilist, preacher — each has come
> with his tale of such a wonderful catch
> Even the story of Jonah never could match.

Wharton was the president of the first city planning commission and the city charter revision committee. He served on the water commission and, in the 1940s, he was mayor of Grants Pass.

Wharton was always telling people how grand the fishing was on the Rogue. He wrote a column in the Courier, and was on the radio, giving the fishing reports and telling about the good fishing on the river, but he never had made a trip all the way downriver.

Finally I got him to make a trip with me. Ted Morgan went along. After that he really knew what he was talking about.

Wharton, writing for *Oregon Outdoors* magazine, described the trip downriver. He wrote that the entrance to Mule Creek Canyon should have a huge sign erected reading: ALL YE WHO ENTER HERE, LEAVE HOPE BEHIND!

He said that a short distance above the gorge they pulled the boat into an eddy, tied up, then hiked down the trail to the Narrows to check the river. It was the first spring trip that year and Glen wanted to see if there was anything blocking the gorge. Seeing that everything was clear, they returned to the boat and prepared to shoot the gorge. His narration continued:

From the locker in the bow, Wooldridge brought out three life preservers and we each put one on. "No particular danger," said he, "but just in case something happens." Then he gave us our instructions, "Joe — you take the seat in the middle of the boat and help trim ship and keep her on an even keel!" "Ted — you get in the stern with this short pike pole and fend her off the wall if we get caught in a whirl — in the Narrows there will be no chance to use the oars and we may be thrown against the jagged rocks at the side. If we happen to get cross-ways in the Narrows the boat will be broken in two in a jiffy and the trip will end right there. Damn poor place to be put afoot in this gorge. So say your prayers and trust to Providence."

Then we shoved off and were immediately caught in the rushing current and headed for the Narrows. Looking back upstream just before going into the turn, I caught a magnificent panorama of wooded canyons and the sharp peak of Saddle Mountain silhouetted against the clear blue sky. At the Narrows the walls closed in, the whole volume of the river dashed through the narrow chute with tremendous velocity, the water at the edges dashed high on the rock walls making a "V" trough in the middle through which the boat rushed with ever increasing momentum. Under-currents hit the walls deep down and caused great boils and whirlpools, threatening to dash the boat against jagged jaws and reefs that seemed to reach out to tear the sides out of it. I gripped the seat and hung on for dear life while Wooldridge with eyes narrowed and face tense as he watched the shifting currents, ever alert to avert the disaster that lurked on every hand. Sometimes he stood erect dipping an oar here and there, again dropping to the seat and throwing his full power into the oars to hold the boat in the middle of the current and away from the rocks. At the Narrows a huge boil suddenly erupted under the boat and swung the stern toward the jagged walls. "Now! Fend her off!" yelled Wooldridge, above the roar of the water and Ted put his steelshod pike to the rock and straightened her out and we roared down the rushing chute. Below the Narrows the Coffee Pot boils and boils and there are more whirlpools that catch a light boat or canoe and turn it end for end in the twinkle of an eye.

An oar dropped overboard here may rear up vertically and disappear, not to be seen again for a quarter of a mile. At last the gorge widened a little and we drifted into quieter water where Stair Creek tumbles in and relaxed a spell. Wooldridge looked us over with an amused grin. "Cripes!" said Ted. "I didn't know that water had so much power. When I put that pike against the wall I was almost lifted off my feet."

"You did a good job — and just in the nick of time. Another fraction of a second and the boat would have crashed and they would have been looking for three derelicks somewhere down the river," said Wooldridge.

Wharton wrote that it took them less than ten minutes to make the two miles through the gorge. He continues his story with a very graphic description of Blossom Bar and other infamous falls and rapids downstream.

In 1925, Zane Grey started making trips down the Rogue. He made several; then, later, he bought a camp site at Winkle Bar and built his cabin there. I took him on several of the trips. Mrs. Grey didn't go downriver in the boats, but stayed in the hotel in Grants Pass. Then he got to riding the train in to West Fork and packing in over the trail. It wasn't far to Winkle Bar from West Fork. After that she would go down to Winkle Bar with him.

Grey was a dentist before he started to write. He always had a passel of people with him. His brother, R.G.; his sons, Loren and Romer; and lots of people he'd bring along. He always traveled with a full crew; his secretaries, a cook, a cameraman, and there would be tents and lots of equipment to haul in. But I never did think much of him as a fisherman. He just couldn't seem to get the hang of catching a steelhead.

One of the boats he had made for the 1925 trip is still down at Winkle Bar. He had the boats built here in Grants Pass. Claud Bardon built some of them, but Grey had someone else build some, too. He had a whole procession of them, seven or eight, but they lost one or two on the downriver trip.

Zane Grey wrote an article about that first trip downriver. It was published in the *Country Gentlemen* magazine and attracted a lot of attention to the Rogue. A book he wrote, called TALES OF FRESHWATER FISHING, came out about the same time and there was a story of the Rogue trip in it.

There were lots of other noted people who came up and fished the river. Jack London was here, in the early years, and Jim Jeffries, the fighter. I took him fishing several times. He was really a good sportsman. After he caught one or two fish to eat he would say, "Well, that's enough. I came here to catch a fish and I caught one, so that's it." And he would quit fishing. He came back a couple of times, after that.

Glen and Eva had two sons, Bob and Bruce. They bought a house on "H" Street, in Grants Pass, and Glen spent his winters building boats in the garage. The materials would cost him about $25 per boat, and he would sell one for about $75. Each one was a little better than the last one.

Glen didn't use plans, and didn't even make a drawing of the boat before starting to build it. He just seemed to see the boat as it would be and crafted the wood accordingly. He was still building them of Port Orford cedar planking, but they were taking on a more flared, dory style, with one end blunted for motor mounting.

Hugh Brown, from Brown Brothers Lumber Company, had a sawmill on Williams Creek. I bought lumber from him. He used to deliver it by the truck load, made lots of trips.

I was paying about $60 a thousand for Port Orford cedar, back then; now it is $1300 a thousand. Port Orford, or white cedar, is real good boat lumber. Spruce is a little lighter, a little tougher, but harder to get.

There was some real nice sugar pine out here in this country, between Grants Pass and the Applegate, in early years. It wasn't worth much, and was awfully heavy when it was green. I used to build boats out of that, some, too. When it is dry it's pretty light, but there's lots of sap in it.

You'd featheredge the boards and lap them over the edges and the bottom. That was the best way to do it. You'd get your boat so that it didn't leak, that way. But if it did leak, you'd put it in the river and soak it up. Then, when you took it out, it would dry and shrink again. The boards would get smaller than ever, and you'd have more cracks.

That old boat the BLM is saving at Rand is a real old one. We made two of them, years ago. I sold one of them to Anderson, who bought George Billings place. We must have made them out of yellow pine. Boy, did they get heavy. We made them out of little pieces of board, nailed them together. Must have used a hundred pounds of nails. Water would get in each one of those little cracks, then when you set it on the bank to dry it the cracks got bigger and you had to caulk it again and paint it.

I got so used to the boats being so heavy, I didn't pay any attention. I didn't know there was any other kind.

We bought the house on "H" Street from Dr. Elsworth's wife. He was the veterinarian my dad started out working with. The old man Elsworth died and my dad just kept being the veterinarian. They called him Dr. Wooldridge. Then Mrs. Elsworth started to move to Crescent City. She sold us the house for $400. That must have been fifty years ago. I have lived here ever since.

One time when the boys were little, my brother Frank came by. He had a little goat in his car. He was quite a trader. I imagine he traded three chickens and a tabby cat for the goat.

It was cold and rainy and I was keeping the boys indoors. When they found out Frank had the goat in the car they started clamoring to see it, so he went out and brought it in. It wasn't very big, and the boys played with it for a while, there in the house. Finally I asked Bruce what he thought of the little goat.

"It smells like Uncle Frank," he said.

Frank didn't like that much. My other brother, Russell, died when he was about eighteen. Frank never did have any kids.

Everybody was poor, back then. Nobody seemed to have any money. They were all just like we were. We got so used to it that we didn't pay any attention, as long as we could get a box of shells for hunting. Deer was a big part of our living. We had to eat, so we did lots of hunting. There was still plenty of deer around this country, then. I don't know what we would have done without them and salmon. That was just about all that kept us alive, until I got the guiding business going.

We had an old Model T Ford and we would take a fish or two out to the farmers and trade it for a sack of spuds, or anything else we could use. One thing about those times, if you did get ahold of a few dollars they were worth something. You could buy a lot of groceries for $10, back then.

I got arrested for salmon poaching, one time, just below Whiskey Creek Falls. That's the original name for Rainie Falls. There were three of us working at that. We had a net set in there, just below the falls. My car was at the Benton Mine, up the hill a little ways, and we would pack the fish up to the car. We had been doing that for quite a while and we were getting a good price for the fish. I think it was about twenty cents a pound.

One day we caught fourteen salmon and put them in four sacks to carry them up to the car. We each took a sack up to the little bench of land above the river, what we called Fir Flat. Then the other two guys started to take their sacks up to the car and I left my sack there and started back after the one we left on the riverbank.

"If you see anything suspicious, give a holler," I told them.

"Okay," they said, and started on. I went back down to the river to get the other sack. Just as I came up to Fir Flat with it I bumped right into the fish warden, Blodgett. He was there watching that sack of salmon we'd left.

Well there we were, Blodgett and me, and two sacks of salmon.

"Where are those other fellows?" he asked me; then I knew he had seen us all.

"I don't know," I told him, "I'll call them." Of course when I hollered they knew something was up, so they ducked out of sight.

Blodgett told me to help him carry those fish up the hill.

"Hell, no," I told him. "They are yours now, you carry them."

So we argued and argued. The first thing he did was point his gun at me. I told him I thought he had more guts than to stand there and point that damm thing at me. He put it away. I was trying to figure out how I was going to get away from him, because I knew I wasn't going in with him, and he ought to have known it, too.

"Where's your boat?" he asked.

"It is right down there," I told him, taking the lead down to the river, but of course I didn't take him to my boat.

"I guess it's gone," I said.

"I heard those fellows take it a while ago," he said. But they hadn't been near it. They went upriver and crossed in another boat and went up the other side. My boat was under the bank, just a little ways from us.

Well, I went along with him, back up to the fish. One of the sacks had four salmon in it and the other one had three. I made sure I picked up the one with three in it, and he shouldered the one with four. He was a big, heavy-set guy and it wasn't long until he ran out of gas, going up that hill with that load of salmon.

I kept getting ahead of him and he would holler, "Whoa, don't get so far ahead." Then I would wait for him. Well, I did that for a few times, then we went around a turn in the trail. I dropped my sack, ran down to the river, jumped in my boat and went across the other side.

The next morning when I came up on the other side I could see him still monkeying around down there.

The sheriff came out to the house and arrested me and we had a trial in justice court. I lost, but appealed the case to the circuit court. The circuit court met in January, and that was in the summer time. I was free on bail.

That summer I was guiding a fellow from down south and when deer season opened down there, in August, he took off for a while and went down there to hunt. He killed a deer, or someone killed it for him, so he brought it back here and put it in the cold storage locker, intending to fish some more.

When he got ready to go home he told me, "Part of that deer is in cold storage. You had just as well go and get it, if you want it."

So I went up to the lockers, on "F" and 7th Streets, to get the deer. You could see right into the locker boxes, as they were just made of slats. So when I went in to get the deer meat, I saw the sack the game warden had packed in, with a tag sticking through the slats. It had my name on it.

I knew the fellow who lived across the street from the cold storage. It was Robins on, who ran the feed store. I went over to his house and borrowed a screwdriver and a gunny sack. When I went back I went in to the back of the cold storage building and took the hinges off that box. They were on the outside of the box. I opened the door backwards and took the fish out, then put them in the gunny sack and put the screws back in the hinges.

I took the fish out the back way and over to Robinson's and told him, "Do something with these. I don't care what, but just get rid of them."

When it came time for court, I pleaded my own case. I objected to as many of the jurymen as I could, but finally the jury was picked and it came time to start the trial.

The game warden came in and went up to the judge and whispered something to him. Then the judge rapped on the desk and said, "Case dismissed for lack of evidence."

We had a real hard winter, following that, with lots of snow. I was down at the river, dinking around, and I noticed the little birds along the edge of the water where the snow was washed back, pecking around, trying to find something to eat. There were lots of them.

I reported it to the game wardens and told them if they would furnish the grain I would take it down and distribute it to the birds along the river.

They agreed and this man, Blodgett, was the one who was to go with me. The snow was so deep we couldn't get down to the riverbank without carrying the boat through the snow. We didn't ever actually get down to the river: in fact, we had to give it up, but we went through the snow a good long ways. As we were carrying the boat along Blodgett told me, "I don't know how I am for carrying a boat, but I'm Hell for carrying fish."

We had a good laugh about that. He turned out to be a pretty good guy, after all, didn't hold a grudge.

Then not long after that, the prosecuting attorney on the case, Sherman Smith, and I went fishing together. He was born and raised here and I had known him ever since he was just a kid. I had on one of those red felt hunting hats and he told me, "I had one of those, one time, but it shrunk so I couldn't get it on."

I told him, "I'll bet that was about the time you were elected prosecuting attorney, wasn't it?"

He didn't have any comment about that, but he asked me, "What did become of those fish? I have no interest in it, anymore, but I just would like to know what happened to them."

I kidded him around, telling him, "I heard you and that game warden ate them."

There was another time, though, that they got my car with a load of salmon in it. There must have been forty salmon, loaded so high their tails were sticking out the window. They got my car, but I got away. When I got home, I called up the sheriff and told him my car was missing and someone must have stole it. They never did do anything about that.

The sentiment of the working people, at that time, was with men like Glen who defied authorities and kept their families fed with fish and game. Most of them were descended from the early-day pioneers who got along the best way they knew how. They believed the game was put there for their use and they didn't like the idea of rich people coming in and killing the game for pleasure.

Glen was a sort of Robin Hood figure to them. One of Glen's neighbors from that time said that many a widow or man out of work with a house full of kids, had fish or venison on their tables with the compliments of Glen.

Then Eva became ill with an incurable kidney disease. As was common in those days, the family, friends, and neighbors rallied around and helped Glen take care of her and the boys.

Eva died in 1933. She was such a little bit of a thing. One of her sisters took Bruce to live with her in San Francisco, for, maybe, two years. He wasn't much more than a baby when his mother died. Bobby wouldn't stay with anyone but me, if he could help it. He would raise cane if I left him with anyone else. I used to take him out in the boat with me, when I'd be fishing close in.

He was just a little fellow and he would curl up in the boat, big-eyed and shivering, and sit there for hours, but he was happy as long as he was with me.

Glen shows off a big catch of steelheads.   Glen Wooldridge collection

Josephine County Historical Society

Zane Grey's cabin at Winkle Bar.

Glen and Mr. Degner, a Grants Pass Courier employee, lifting the boat over boulders at Blossom Bar.

Glen Wooldridge collection

Glen, Eva 2nd from right in the old pickup he made from a Model T car, 1927.
←
Bruce Wooldridge photo

Joe Wharton, who owned the first tackle shop in the Rogue Valley. He was also on the first city planning committee and was the mayor of Grants Pass.
✓ Glen Wooldridge collection

Glen and Mrs. Degner admiring large buck deer shot on the trip.

Glen Wooldridge collection

Frank Wooldridge.

Bruce Wooldridge collection

Glen and Charley Foster taking a boat through Slim Pickins.

Bruce Wooldridge collection

Glen, taking boat through Coffee Pot in early 1920s. Louise Stokes, a Grants Pass Courier employee, was the photographer.

Glen Wooldridge collection

Chapter Eleven

Guiding Dudes Downriver

The guiding business sort of grew up with Glen. In the earlier years he guided fishermen from the resorts on the upper Rogue, in the Shady Cove, Trail and Prospect areas. As the out-of-town fishermen poured into the area, more and more resorts and lodges were built for them. Many of the lodges, such as General Electric's Genelec Lodge near Shady Cove, were built by big corporations as vacation places for their executives who made yearly treks to fish the Rogue.

Downstream, the Chambers of Commerce took up where the old Commercial Clubs left off, publicizing the wonders of the Rogue. The river was closed to commercial fishermen in 1935, this time without a battle. The Grants Pass and Gold Beach residents could see that the tourists and sports fishermen were doing more for the economy of the areas and tried to encourage the trade as much as possible.

Rainbow and Peggie Gibson bought the Weasku Inn, in 1927, and were making a tremendous success of it. They had come up from Big Bear, in California, and brought an established clientele with them. Rainbow was a noted fly fisherman, earning his title, Rainbow, by his skill. His sister was married to the English lord, Sir Morton Smart, who was orthopedic surgeon to the king of England, at that time.

Clark Gable discovered the lodge and made it his hideaway for many years. Carole Lombard, Ann Southern, Robert Sterling, Guy Kibee, Gabby Hayes, Jackie Cooper, David Niven, and many directors and producers from the movie industry made the Inn their headquarters. Mrs. Gibson said she couldn't remember all of the movie people who came to stay at the Inn, where they were treated as friends who came to visit.

Many guests had standing reservations year after year to spend a week to a month at the lodge. One couple in their eighties came back recently for a stay at the lodge, saying it was their thirty-ninth summer there.

Gable was around there so much he became almost a part of the Gibson family. He bought property adjacent to the Inn to build his own lodge, but never built it.

Clark Gable at WEASKU INN.
Weasku Inn collection

Rainbow Gibson built piers and salmon boards on barrels so that the rising water would float them higher rather than sweep them downstream as had happened in earlier years.

The fishing was tremendous in the river below the Inn. They would have five fishing piers and eighteen boats in operation, averaging 90 salmon a day. They would tow the boats down to the head of Pierce Riffle and anchor them so close together you could walk from boat to boat almost across the river.

It was a good place for a guide to book fishing parties for the downriver trip. President Herbert Hoover stayed there sometimes when he came to fish the Rogue. The Hoovers were familiar to the area, before Hoover became president. Mrs. Hoover was a mining engineer and she contracted to take over and develop a quartz mine south of Waldo, just over the state line in California, before he ran for the office.

President Hoover fished the upper Rogue several times and that is where Glen guided him, at first.

Glen would trailer his boat up to the Shady Cove area and set up camp at Casey's Camp or California-On-The-Rogue Resort. He would contact fishermen needing a guide if he didn't already have a commitment with someone. He and the fishermen would drift the river, fishing for rainbows or cutthroats, or the best fishing of all, summer steelheads.

If the going got too rough the dudes would get out and walk the banks while Glen took the boat through the worst places.

He would get someone to tow his trailer down to the designated take-out point to pick up them and the boat. It was usually at Dodge Bridge, or even as far down as Bybee Bridge, if the water was just right.

Rainbow Gibson, noted trout fisherman.   Josephine County Historical Society

Josephine County Historical Society

Rainbow Gibson at his lodge.

President Hoover was a quiet man. He didn't talk much except maybe to ask a question about fishing. I guess he thought I didn't speak his language. He was a good fisherman. I took him fishing several times on the upper Rogue, then he made one trip with me downriver to Gold Beach. After that I never did see him again.

The downriver fishing trips were made in the fall, when the steelheads were running. They started coming in in August and ran through to Thanksgiving. That would be our big season. People came from all over the world to fish the Rogue. It had a great reputation and certainly was a wonderful fishing stream.

In the early years we would put the boats in at Fifth Street, right below the bridge. The dudes always furnished their own fishing equipment. Most of them were pretty particular about it, anyway. But I would always carry a rifle along. There were always lots of deer in those canyons, and we would kill one along the first of the trip so we would have fresh meat.

We fished with lures, mostly. The flat-fish was very popular at one time, and the hot-shot, too, but before all that a small brass spinner was very good. It would be good yet, if we had any fish. Those were the best things to fish with.

And flies, of course: some people were fly fishermen, wouldn't fish with anything but a fly. Joe Wharton made some special flies to fish the Rogue, and of course, there was the Royal Coachman which was just about the best all-round fly. Then there was the Professor and another called the Cow Dung.

The steelhead is a wonderful fly fish. He will strike a fly, all right, if it is properly presented. They are a migratory fish. They come in from the ocean and stop along, here and there, maybe spend several days in one place. You would find, after fishing the river again and again, the spots where the fish would stay. You can't catch them just any place: you have to find the places where they stop. Then in comes a rain and they may move or not be in any of the places you have been catching them. You can usually see them jumping and get a pretty good idea where they are, but sometimes there will be lots of them jumping and they won't bite at all.

The fishermen would go to the grocery store and pick out what they wanted to eat, otherwise you'd have some unhappy people along. And they would bring their sleeping rolls; back then, not many people had sleeping bags.

We'd camp on sand bars or the river banks, anywhere we came out and it turned out all right, and there would be wood and water. We would usually camp by the creek as you shouldn't drink the river water. We pretty well had our pick of campgrounds. There wasn't anyone else on the river but us, so we'd always have a nice place to camp.

At first we took ten days to the trip. We would put in a lot of time fishing and hunting, if it was a hunting trip. Back then, before we blasted the channel, it took longer to get down the river. We had to line the boats around the bad places, and the dudes would pitch in and help if we had to lift the boats over the boulders.

In the springtime there was quite a bit of activity around Grants Pass, fishing for Chinooks. I had some salmon boards on the river at different times, back then. I had one at the mouth of the Applegate and another down by Robertson Bridge. Different location at different times.

I built some big barges, too, that I could move around with the motor boat. I would tow them down and put them out, anchor them here and there, then take the fishermen out to them. I put canvas covers, or flies, on them for shelter, and sometimes a little stove on them, and the fishermen would sit in them, out of the weather, keep warm and play cards while they waited for a salmon to strike.

I remember the first one I took down there. I built it here and just tied onto it with my boat and towed it down. Everyone said, "You won't be able to stop when you get where you want it." But I didn't have any trouble.

Back then I had a motor boat I had built, about twenty-six feet long, and I put a motor in it out of an old Star automobile. An inboard, of course, and it had a universal joint that came off the motor, with a shaft to the back of the boat to the propeller. It had a rudder and I could turn it this way and that to turn the boat, and raise the propeller out of the water.

It had a twelve-inch bronze prop, and a bearing made out of rubber. The steering apparatus, the rudder and drive shaft were all fastened together so they all raised. It would pull pretty good.

It wasn't the best thing in the world but it was better than nothing. I finally sold it.

One time a guy came in with a little boat and asked me if I minded if he put it in where we were fishing. I told him, "No, I don't mind, if you will stay out away from the fishermen."

He had a bottle with him and was kind of tippling a little bit. He fished awhile and when he came back he landed his boat and started walking up the bank. His legs got tangled up, he ran backwards and fell right in the river. He crawled out and down he went again. He had to crawl out a second time before he could get going.

One drunk, fishing on the barge down there, got sick and threw up and lost his false teeth in the river.

Then another time a couple of guys were on the barge, fishing and drinking. They didn't like the location, so they decided they'd just move the barge. They pulled up the anchor and took off, right down the river. I had another pier downstream, with an anchor line on it. They ran right under that line and it swept them off into the river. They were so loaded they didn't have sense enough to duck when they went under it. My motor boat was broken down, then, and I couldn't go out to get them. They had to swim out. I bet that sobered them up. The barge caught up downriver and I went after it when I got my motor going again.

Bobby was just a little guy, about ten years old, I guess, and he was down there with me one day. I had a pier up the river a ways and I took him up there and put him on it. He had his pole and I got him all set up, then went on to tend to my other piers and barges. When I came back, a couple of hours later, he had caught a big salmon. Up until that time I hadn't been able to get him too excited about fishing. He didn't seem to have much interest in it, but a guy came along and gave him $6.00 for the fish. That put a different flavor to this fishing business.

Another day Bob and I were anchored out in the river, fishing, and he was just sitting there, half asleep, gazing out across the river with his pole across his knees. I told him, "You'd better hang onto that pole: if a salmon hits it he will jerk it away from you." Sure enough, that's what happened. He lost his outfit, fish and all, and to make matters worse, we had borrowed the fishing gear.

The same thing happened to Bruce, later. A big salmon hit his pole and jerked it right out of his hand.

Sadie used to like to fish for salmon. That was lots of fun to get a big salmon on. I remember one time she fell in the river, down there. It was cold and she had on lots of clothes and big gum boots, Boy, was she mad!

Sadie Black was a young woman who had helped Glen nurse his wife, Eva, during her illness. Sadie was bringing up her own boys, Robert and Sam, alone. She often kept Bob and Bruce for Glen.

Another time we were fishing down at Robertson Bridge, when we had a pier with barges and boats there. Sadie and Art King were in a boat, fishing for salmon. A fellow came along, wanting to fish, and the boats were all filled up. There wasn't any boat to put him in, so I took him out and put him in the boat with Sadie and Art. He squeezed in between them and sat there and caught five big salmon and they never got a damned bite.

Boy, were they mad at me! He gave them one of his salmon when he left, but they were both still mad at me. I had a big laugh out of it. I told them that was the only chance they had of getting a salmon, for him to give them one.

Glen and Sadie Black were married in 1938, and she turned out to be the partner Glen needed to help him build up his guiding and boat-building business. They had the four boys together, but found there wasn't any more squabbling going on than in the usual family.

Sadie would take the boys and go with Glen to the upper river, in early summer, camping out and spending the days fishing or just riding herd on the boys. She would drive the car, with the trailer, down to pick up Glen and his dudes and haul the boat upriver.

On the upper river, that was day fishing. The trips weren't very long. We would fish up there during the spring season, until August 6, then start our scheduled runs from Grants Pass to the coast.

We did that, oh, probably ten years. That was wonderful fishing up there. The spring salmon went in there and the steelheads and cutthroats. That was really nice country, and it wasn't fished much, back then. Once in a great while you'd see someone, but not often. If I had wanted to I could have made a lot of money off that. I was charging twenty dollars a day, guiding, but I could just as well have got fifty.

The depression didn't affect the people who had money, and they were the ones who made the trips; it wasn't the poor guys.

The dudes wanting to make trips downriver contacted us by mail or telephone and scheduled a trip. Then they would come in by car or train. We would have them get here the day before so they could get things they needed and get organized for the trip.

We always carried the big skillet, kettle and coffeepot, and took the tarps or flies. We never used tents. By using a fly we could put up a lean-to sloping one way and build a fire out front. Then if we had any wet clothes, bedding, or anything we could easily dry them out. If we got caught in a rainstorm we might stop and put up the fly, build up a big fire, warm up and stay dry while the storm lasted. It didn't interfere with our schedule too much. We used a big fly so there would be plenty of room for everybody.

These trips, when we first started out, took ten days, but later we shortened them to five days which did about as well. We finally got around to using four boats. Two would start out, like today, then tomorrow two more would go. We broke up the schedule that way.

In those early days Glen had a lot of different men working with him, rowing the other boats, after he started using two, then later on, four. Cal Allen, of course, went down river with him the first two trips he made; then, for a while, he was guiding alone. Claud Bardon, Fred Popkins, Squeak Briggs, Prince Helfrich, and Sid Pyle each made one or more trips with him. Gail Huggins and Ruell Hawkins worked with him later, and Carl Ingraham was a regular for a number of years.

One day, in about 1935, I was in Joe Wharton's tackle shop and I met a man by the name of Charley Foster. We struck up a conversation and he told me, "I have been trying to catch one of these steelheads, but I never have learned how to catch them."

I told him, "Well, tomorrow, if you have nothing to do, we will go down to the mouth of the Applegate. I have a boat down in the river, and I will show you how to catch them."

We went down there and I showed him how to catch a steelhead. I think he caught six that day. That just spoiled him; from that time he spent more time at our place than he did at home. He had heart trouble when he first started working for me, but being active and on the river, out in the fresh air, must have cured him.

At that time I was building boats in the winter, when I wasn't guiding, and when I wasn't busy I would go boating. Charley worked for me quite a while, starting in on the boating. He was pretty awkward for a time, but he caught on, after awhile. He worked with me for fifteen or twenty years; became part of the family, actually, since Bruce married his daughter, Mary. He died in the 1970s.

After we made a trip we would usually stay over one day at home and prepare for the following day's trip; but later on, we didn't lay over. We would get in in the evening and leave again the following forenoon.

During the fishing season we carried only two passengers to the boat, but in the springtime we would take three to the boat. Those were sight-seeing trips and we just bounced right on through them.

When we started the three-day trips we couldn't get the local men interested in going with us. Then I had an idea: I started a campaign to get the women to going downriver. After that the men couldn't hardly refuse. I'd just

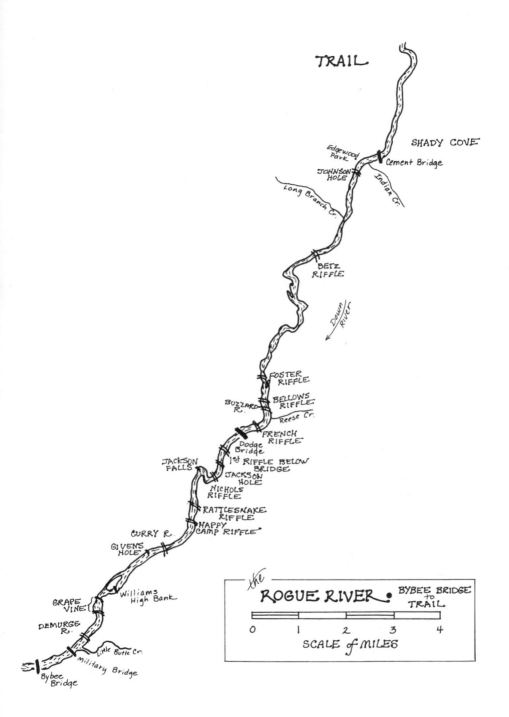

TRAIL

SHADY COVE

Edgewood Park

Cement Bridge

JOHNSON HOLE

Long Branch Cr.

Indian Cr.

BETZ RIFFLE

Down River

FOSTER RIFFLE

BELLOWS RIFFLE

BUZZARD R.

Reese Cr.

FRENCH RIFFLE

Dodge Bridge

JACKSON FALLS

1ˢᵗ RIFFLE BELOW BRIDGE

JACKSON HOLE

NICHOLS RIFFLE

RATTLESNAKE RIFFLE

HAPPY CAMP RIFFLE

CURRY R.

GIVENS HOLE

Williams High Bank

GRAPE VINE

DEMURGE R.

Little Butte Cr.

Military Bridge

Bybee Bridge

the ROGUE RIVER

BYBEE BRIDGE to TRAIL

0   1   2   3   4

SCALE of MILES

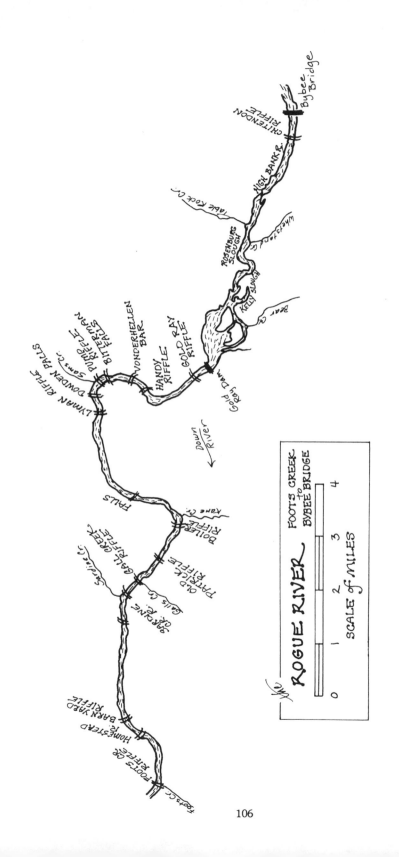

ROGUE RIVER
FOOTS CREEK
to
BYBEE BRIDGE

SCALE of MILES

0   1   2   3   4

Bybee Bridge

CRITTENDON RIFFLE

HIGH BANK R.

Table Rock Cr.

Wheelstone Sl.

ROSENBURG SLOUGH

KELLY SLOUGH

Bear Cr.

Gold Ray Dam

GOLD RAY RIFFLE

HANDY RIFFLE

VONDERHELLEN BAR

PURPLE RIFFLE

BITTERIS FALLS

Sams Cr.

DOWDEN FALLS

LYMAN RIFFLE

Down River

FALLS

Kane Cr.

BOILER RIFFLE

OLD PATRICK RIFFLE

Foots Cr.

GARL CREEK RIFFLE

Sardine Cr.

SARDINE Galls Cr.

BARN YARD RIFFLE

HOMESTEAD

FOOTS CR. RIFFLE

Foots Cr.

tell them the girls were making the trip. That boosted them up — got them started going.

We had lots of fun on the trips with the girls. They were really good sports. There were nurses from the hospital: Celia Barton Massie, Velda McFarland Jensen, Lucille Anderson Waterman, and secretaries. Evelyn Steele made a trip with us and wrote the story up in a magazine. Others were Martha White, Irene Hoyt, and Grace Woodrow, and lots of others made the trips with us.

We would put the boats in right under Robertson Bridge and drift down about twenty-five miles below Galice, to Black Bar Lodge. That was a really nice place to stay. Hal and Bea Witherwox built it there about 1935, and Red Keller helped.

We would stop there for the night. It was fixed up pretty good. They had good beds and hot water for showers, and of course the women liked that after a long day on the river. It had a big fireplace, and they fed us good, too. They had a garden, orchard, and raised a whole bunch of chickens to fry. Everybody always talked about the sourdough hotcakes Bea served for breakfast.

Then the second night out we would stop at Lucas Lodge, at Agness. Larry Lucas ran that. He was a guide on the lower Rogue for many years. He built up a pretty good business at the lodge. When the mail boats came up the river and more and more people started riding them for the sight-seeing trips, Larry started feeding them at the lodge.

They would cook a lot of food, real good food, like fried chicken, beef, corn-on-the-cob, garden vegetables and the like. Blackberry cobbler and beans, there always had to be beans on Larry's table. They would put the food on the table, in big bowls and platters like a farm dinner, and the people would help themselves. The Lucas family raised their own vegetables, fruit and beef; chickens, too, I guess. I say it was a good business, it is still a good business; Willard, Larry's son, and his wife run it now. They have some of the local people come in and help them cook and serve. Always have a full dining area when the mail boats come in.

Then the third day about noon we would land at Gold Beach and be on our way home a little while afterwards.

Sadie would drive the car over and meet us on the given day and we would load the boats on the trailer, piggy-back or double-deck them. Those early day trailers we used were home-made, of course. They were made on old Model T axles, with a 4' X 4' wooden frame and they just bounced the hell out of a boat, getting them home.

That was a long old drag back from Gold Beach to Grants Pass — about 150 miles and lots of it bad roads. Some of the time we went around by Powers, other times by Brookings, then Carpenterville.

One time we had a wreck coming home. The car went in the ditch and broke my leg. That was just at the start of the fishing season. I had to hobble around and row the boat and everything with a cast on.

If the dudes wanted to have their cars waiting for them at Gold Beach, Sadie would rustle up a crew here in Grants Pass to drive them down. She had a group of women she called on to drive with her. But she did practically all the driving, pulling the trailer to haul the boats back. It was a tough job, but she considered that her part of the job and she wouldn't let anyone else do it. She made a trip to Gold Beach and back about every other day for years and years.

That was a good business. I was charging about $75 a passenger for the three-day trips and I figure I cleared just about a hundred dollars a day.

Glen and Carl Ingraham at Argo Falls. These falls were completely filled in by the 1955 flood.   Glen Wooldridge collection

Sadie Wooldridge and Julia Young.

Glen Wooldridge collection

This wreck happened coming back from Gold Beach, about 1933. Mr. Christenson drove his Packard off the road and was seriously injured. Glen, riding in the back seat, received a broken knee-cap.

Bruce Wooldridge collection

Glen and Charley Foster at China Bar. This picture was used on post card. Note the right edge was painted on by an artist to extend the picture to fit the card.

Grants Pass Courier collection

This old mail boat at Gold Beach was like the one Glen built and equipped with an inboard Star automobile motor.
Bureau of Land Management collection

Hogline below WEASKU INN, at Pierce Riffle, Chinook fishing. Note salmon piers below building on left, they were the first ones built on oil drums to raise and lower with the water. "There was a lot of excitement when anyone yelled, 'Fish on!'"

Weasku Inn collection

Chapter Twelve

The Hermits of the Lower Rogue

The depression years brought gold prospectors back to the Rogue. Every little branch running into it had its sniper, panning for the bright flakes. One woman from that era said there wasn't any other way to earn money and even if you only panned a dime's worth of gold, that would buy a loaf of bread.

There were still hangers-on from the old goldmining days, so every cabin had an occupant. A man would get killed or die, leaving a cabin empty, and shortly afterwards someone else would be living there.

They didn't always give their real names and, in time, each of them acquired an identity on the river. There were many good men living along the Rogue, but there were some real characters, too.

Si Whiteneck lived in the Whiskey Creek Cabin when Glen and Cal made their first trip downriver in 1915. He was a good sort, a professional cook. He cooked for the forest service and the CCCs when they were working in the area. He was pretty well known for his sourdough pancakes, which he always shared with his horse, Nellie.

Then there was old Ramey, down at the falls. He lived at China Gulch, but used to gaff salmon at the falls. He was off his beam quite a ways. I never heard him talk about killing anyone, like some of the others did; but he thought everything belonged to him; the river, the fish, the deer, everything was his, according to his notion.

Back before Cal and I made our first trip downriver, we went into that country — had to hike in as the road stopped at Galice. We killed some deer, caught some fish and hired old Ramey to pack them out for us. He had two little buckskin ponies he used for pack animals, carrying the fish he gaffed out to Glendale to sell.

Well, he took our money. He wasn't at all backwards about that, but he growled and meowled about it. He said, "You fellows come in here, you kill my deer and catch my fish then get me to pack them out for you." He took them to the end of the road, to Galice.

He was there for a good many years. He used to have a partner. One day I was by there and Ramey told me his partner went down the river fishing and never came back.

They found Ramey dead, too, in his cabin. He had his rifle in his hand and a shell about halfway in the chamber.

There was another old guy, had one ear off, that lived just above the falls, on the mountain to the left. He told me about going down the river in a boat. He said when he got to Mule Creek he tipped over, fell out of the boat.

"Gee," he said, "there were some big boulders in the bottom of the river." If he had tipped over down there he wouldn't have been around to be telling me about it.

There were quite a number of cabins along the river, left by old miners and prospectors. There was one on the north side, below Almeda a little ways, then, just below the falls, there were four more.

In another cabin, up there on the hill, is where the old hermit, Colvin, lived. They found him dead in his cabin, too.

Joe Utassey lived in Ramey's cabin for a long time. They used to call him Gigolo Joe. Somebody found him on the trail and brought him down to the river. We went down in the boat to get him. When they put him in the boat I thought he was dead.

"Gee, he's dead, isn't he?" I asked them.

And a little, squeeky voice said, "No, Glen, I'm not dead." When the old miners or hermits died along the river, most of the time whoever found them just dug a grave and buried them close to their cabins.

Another fellow, Bill Graft, lived on the old Dutch Henry place on Meadow Creek, up near Horseshoe Bend. He was an Austrian. He told Hal Witherwox, at Black Bar Lodge, that he was going to kill me if I ever came around him anymore or around his place, but he never did get around to it. He fell out of an apple tree and broke his back. It killed him.

Black, the fellow that Black Bar was named for — somebody killed him and put him in his boat and pushed it off into the river. His body was still in it when it got to Gold Beach.

Then there was Bedrock Nell, who lived on Rum Creek. She was a gold miner. Some say she sold property up north to come down and mine gold. She was a wild sort of woman and when we'd go by in the boat we'd see her, out in the water about half-way up to the top of her gum boots, operating her sluice box.

One day we went by with a load of dudes and when we got on past her one of the fellows hollered back at her, "Why don't you get a man?"

"Man, Hell," she hollered back at him, "I can't hardly make a living for myself, let alone support a man."

Old Dutch Henry had killed a couple of people when he lived on Meadow Creek, but the law turned him loose. That was away years earlier than when Bill Graft lived there.

Hugo Meyer was the one they called the Hermit of the Craggies. He lived on the Illinois River, above Agness, about four or five miles up in the

114

mountains. He had some cables fixed across the Illinois and would slide across them on a Y-shaped tree limb. There were some pretty big yarns told about him being so wild.

His neighbors, Mr. and Mrs. Fauntz, ran a few head of cattle up the river several miles from his place. Fauntz had to go to look after his cattle and he always rode a mule.

On one of the trips his mule came home without him. Mrs. Fauntz got the people together, around there, and they tracked the mule back down the trail. They found his body where he had tumbled off down the hill. Larry Lucas came in with his boat and took the body down to Gold Beach, to the mortuary.

It wasn't until they got it down there that they found out he had been shot.

They suspicioned Hugo Meyer — I guess he and Fauntz might have been having a little trouble along. It must have happened in Josephine County; anyway, the sheriff brought him here to Grants Pass for the trial.

Tom Miller was the prosecuting attorney and he was pleading both sides of the case. I never had seen that done before. He instructed the jury, beforehand, "If you see that I am favoring the state the least bit, you acquit him"; and that is the grounds he was tried on.

Miller asked Meyer a lot of questions, of course, either on direct or cross examination. He asked him how he made a living and Meyer told him, "I trap."

Miller asked him if he ever ate any of the animals he caught in the traps and he said he did.

"Did you ever eat a coyote?" "Yeah." "A skunk?" "Yeah." "A coon?" "Yeah." "Well did you ever eat a rattlesnake?"

"Aw, you can't eat them," Meyer told him. "When you put them in the frying pan they curl up. If you straighten them out they just curl up again. They are tough."

Miller asked Meyer about an old injury he had and Meyer told him he was helping build a bridge and a wrench fell and struck him on the head.

Finally Miller got around to asking, "Did you shoot Mr. Fauntz?"

"Yeah." Meyer admitted.

"And did he fall off his mule when you shot him?"

"When I shoot them they always fall."

"Why did you shoot him?"

"Well," Meyer said, "my father died in Germany after the first World War, from starvation, and I didn't think I was going to live through the coming winter. I wanted to kill Fauntz before I died."

No more excuse than that.

When Miller asked him, "Do you feel you were justified in killing Mr. Fauntz?" Meyer said, "Sure."

The evidence showed that Mr. Fauntz had really been Meyer's friend, had on various occasions given him vegetables and other things he needed.

They sent Meyer to the penitentiary. I think they really thought he was crazy, but figured he might get out, if they sent him to the insane asylum, and kill someone else.

Clarence Burke was another hermit in that lower country. He lived on Wildcat Creek, not far from Rainie Falls. At that time there was a trail on the south side of the river. His cabin was built on the hillside, right on the trail. His porch stuck out toward the river, and it was off the ground a ways because of the way the house was built onto the hillside. The trail went right under the porch.

There were two guys living at Howard Creek, about four or five miles below there, and the young fellows came back and forth on the trail.

Burke had to carry his provisions on his back from Galice and down to his place, about six or seven miles. He suspected these guys were stealing his groceries, so he warned them about traveling the trail under his porch. He even built another trail around it so they wouldn't have to go under his porch.

One day he came home and found them up on the porch. When they jumped off and started to run, he opened fire and killed one of them. He shot the other one through the arm.

The one who got away came to town and reported to the authorities. They went in there, but Burke was gone. They found blood on the rocks where he dragged the guy to the river and dumped him in. But where he dumped the body it couldn't wash on down the river, so they were able to fish it out.

They caught Burke in Sacramento and brought him back for trial. I went to the trial because I knew the man and I was very interested. That happened in Josephine County. The county line crosses the river right at the mouth of Kelsey Creek.

The evidence brought out that they had robbed him on more than one occasion, and he had warned them to stay away.

Burke never did admit the shooting. He would have been foolish to do that. They acquitted him, and when the jury brought in the verdict, Judge Norton, who was judge here at that time, said, "You know, it is too bad there aren't more men in the country like Burke."

Then there was Mahoney, who killed Fox, but I guess I will save that one and tell you about it when I tell you about my first trip up the river. It fits better there than it does here.

It's the solitude, I think, that makes the hermits that way. Solitude. I don't think the human mind can stand solitude over a long period of years. Of course, when a person makes up his mind to live entirely alone, he's a little off to start with, seems to me. Then the solitude finishes the job. They would get the idea they owned the whole country, and when we would go through, they thought we were trespassing on their property. And, of course, they would see me more than anyone else.

Jimmy Coe, or at least that was the name he went by here, lived at Missouri Bar, back up on the hill about two miles in a cabin that originally belonged to Rupert Jones, Hathaway's brother.

Later he moved down to the mouth of the creek, and there he lived very much like a coyote. His house consisted of a few old boards he had found, and he leaned them up together. He had to get down on his hands and knees to crawl into it.

His stove was just the top of an old stove with a rock or two under it here and there, right on the ground. And his bed was a jumble of old rags and gunny sacks, just things he had picked up.

Altogether he lived around there for twenty eight years, he told me. I remember the first time I ever saw him. He was a little bit of a guy, and he had on some boots that were about nine sizes too big for him. One was white and the other black, and he cut the tops off them. He had found them some place. I bet his legs weren't any bigger around than my thumb, he was so awfully skinny and poor, but you could understand why.

He came to my house, here in Grants Pass, one day, and wanted to know where he could buy a pig. Well, I didn't know anybody who had a pig for sale, but we got to telephoning around for him and found somebody on Grave Creek who had a pig or two.

The next thing I heard about him, Mrs. Billings told me he was carrying this pig down the trail in an orange crate. She said, "I think he needed the pig for company."

Boy, that must have been a job, carrying that pig from Grave Creek to his place in a box. He kept one chicken for a while, staked out with a string. An old Plymouth Rock hen tied to a bush.

Others told stories about Jimmy Coe, too, how he would wander over the countryside, in the middle of the night, and sleep wherever night overtook him. He tried to make it to the neighbors, on occasion, to eat with them. He had bear traps set around his cabin, and people were warned about going up to it without him to guide them. You were supposed to stop at a certain big fir and give a holler before going farther.

Jimmy lived up there alone and was pretty friendly for quite a few years. When we would go by, if we saw him, we would give him a sandwich or maybe a fish. Then he went wild and, if we saw him at all, he would just be peeking through the bushes at us like a wild animal.

Eventually the solitude, or something, got to Jimmy Coe, too. Jimmy appeared at Marial in the middle of the night, and pulled a .32 Colt on a man who was there.

When this was reported to the state police, they went down and picked up Jimmy and took him to jail. The fellow was reluctant to press charges, but while they had Jimmy in jail the police processed him, sending copies of his fingerprints out to see if he was wanted anywhere. When the man didn't come in to press charges Jimmy was released to return downriver. After his release the police received information from their inquiries saying Jimmy was wanted in one of the southern states. He had escaped from the state's penitentiary many years before and they had assumed he was dead.

The state police went down and picked up Jimmy again and shipped him back down south.

John Billings, Abe Fry and Jim Fry were miners on the Klamath River in California during gold mining days. They purchased brides from the Karok Indian

117

tribe on the Klamath and, after living there several years, made the journey with pack mules to the lower Rogue country in 1868.

John Billings and his wife, Adeline, and their children settled near what is now Marial; the Frys at Oak Flats. They made their homes in the canyon for the rest of their lives, and each fathered ten children. Glen made friends with the children and grandchildren of these old settlers on his trips downriver.

Ruell Hawkins was a descendent of the Billings family. The Hawkinses lived up the river about fourteen miles from Gold Beach. I never did know Hawkins, Ruell's dad, but I got acquainted with Ruell boating on the lower Rogue. I don't remember that he did any commercial fishing, but he may have. He was just a kid when I first started going downriver. His brother, Harry, was murdered down there, I think.

Angie Hawkins, Ruell's mother, was quite a prominent person in that country. I think she did cooking at different places; the lodges, maybe. When she got old they took her down to Gold Beach to live, but she didn't like it. She started hiking home, but she never got there. She died along the way.

Gail Huggins was John Billings' grandson, too. He worked with me for a while, guiding. He and Marial and Ruell were cousins. Marial was Tom Billings' daughter. She is the one they named the post office after.

And Agness was named after Amaziah Aubery's daughter. He married one of Jim Fry's daughters and from what I hear, he was running the Rogue River before I was born.

Illahe got its name from an Indian word; it means home or valley, anyway some special place for the Indian people.

Grandma Billings, her name was Adeline, had tatoos on her chin. They called that the one-eleven mark. I don't know if they did that for any special reason; whether it was supposed to be pretty, or for identification, or just what, but she was a full-blood Indian. They were all related down there, eventually.

Clay Hill was where the Thomas family lived. Their daughter Flora married Hathaway Jones. That little creek, Flora Dell, is named after her. Her sister died when she was young and they buried her on the Clay Hill place.

Hathaway Jones had a cousin, Baldy Criteser, a person could have written a book about. He was just full of big stories. He was a good guy, though, and in some ways he had a heart like an ox, you know; he would do anything in the world for you. Boy, he sure could tell you some monstrous stories, though.

He lived on Bald Ridge. He and his wife, May, were both terrific drinkers, and they made their own liquor.

One time I met Baldy coming along the trail, leading his mule with a jug tied to the saddle horn. We stopped to talk awhile, you always stopped to talk to anyone you met on the trial, and he took the jug off the mule and offered me a drink, "It's three-star Criteser," he told me.

Another time, I was up to their place and Baldy had been sampling some of his product kind of heavily. He wanted to show me how good he was with a pistol. We were in the kitchen and he brought out this gun, and old .45 Colt.

He stuck his finger in the triggerguard and was whirling it around. It went off and shot a hole in his dishpan hanging on the wall. I tried to think up excuses for getting away from there fast, before he killed me.

Baldy was absolutely the worst-talking man I ever talked to. He could get more profanity into a sentence than anyone I ever met.

At one time, at the three post offices down in that country, each one of them had a postmaster whose name was George Washington. At Agness there was George Washington Rilea; at Illahe, George Washington Meservey; and at Marial, there was George Washington Billings.

Later on, when they got air mail service across the country, mail was still coming into that area by mule train. They used to have some airmail envelopes they sold at Marial that said:

This letter will go 16 miles by pack train to Illahe, 9 miles by auto to Agness, 32 miles down the Rogue River by mail boat to Gold Beach, then by auto stage, 152 miles to Grants Pass by way of Crescent City. Then it will be put on a railroad train and taken 32 miles to Medford and put on a plane and sped to its destination.

George Washington Billings.   Bureau of Land Management collection

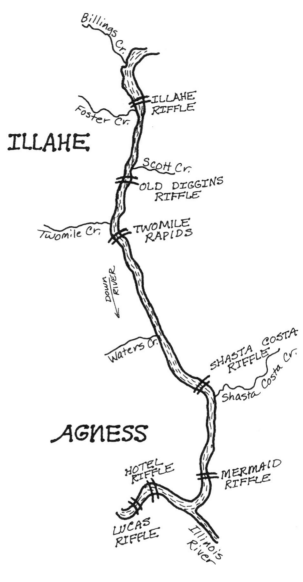

Billings Cr.

ILLAHE RIFFLE

Foster Cr.

ILLAHE

Scott Cr.

OLD DIGGINS RIFFLE

Twomile Cr.

TWOMILE RAPIDS

DOWN RIVER

Waters Cr.

SHASTA COSTA RIFFLE

Shasta Costa Cr.

Shasta

AGNESS

HOTEL RIFFLE

MERMAID RIFFLE

LUCAS RIFFLE

Illinois River

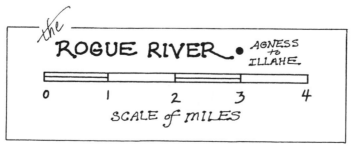

the ROGUE RIVER • AGNESS to ILLAHE

0   1   2   3   4

SCALE of MILES

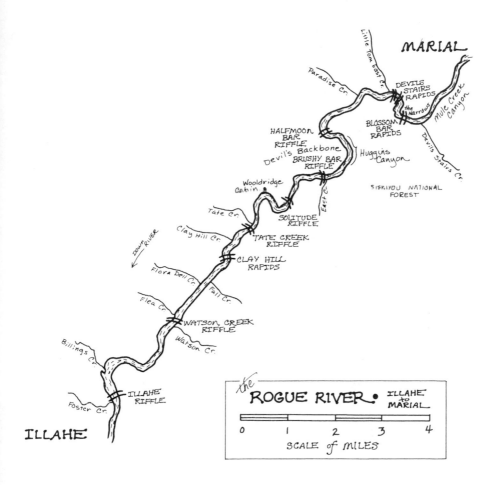

MARIAL

Little Tom Esst Cr.

Paradise Cr.

DEVILS
STAIRS
RAPIDS

Mule Creek Canyon

the Narrows

BLOSSOM
BAR
RAPIDS

Devils Stairs Cr.

HALFMOON
BAR
RIFFLE

Devil's Backbone

BRUSHY BAR
RIFFLE

Huggins Canyon

Wooldridge Cabin

SISKIYOU NATIONAL
FOREST

Tate Cr.

East Cr.

SOLITUDE
RIFFLE

Clay Hill Cr.

TATE CREEK
RIFFLE

Down River

CLAY HILL
RAPIDS

Flora Dell Cr.

Fall Cr.

Flea Cr.

WATSON CREEK
RIFFLE

Watson Cr.

Billings Cr.

ILLAHE
RIFFLE

Foster Cr.

ILLAHE

the
ROGUE RIVER • ILLAHE to MARIAL

0   1   2   3   4

SCALE of MILES

121

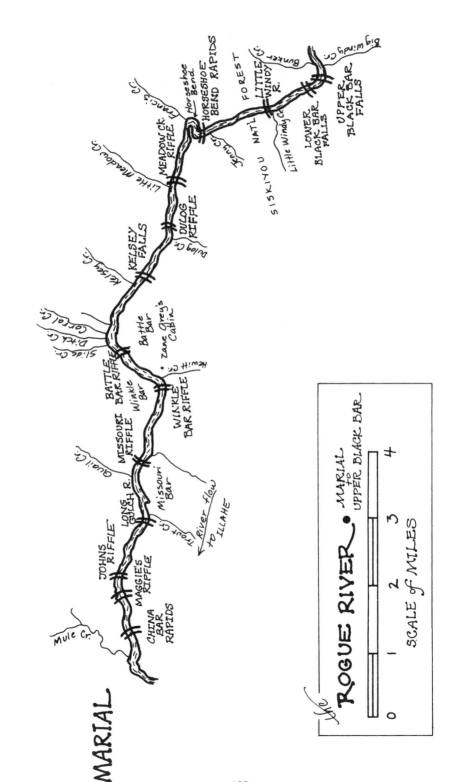

MARIAL

Mule Cr.

CHINA BAR RAPIDS

MAGGIE'S RIFFLE

JOHNS RIFFLE

Trout Cr.

Missouri Bar

River flow to ILLAHE

Quail Cr.

LONG GULCH R.

MISSOURI RIFFLE

Winkle Bar

Slide Cr.

Ditch Cr.

BATTLE BAR RIFFLE

WINKLE BAR RIFFLE

Hewitt Cr.

Zane Grey's Cabin

Battle Bar

Corral Cr.

Kelsey Cr.

KELSEY FALLS

Dulog Cr.

DULOG RIFFLE

Little Meadow Cr.

MEADOW CK. RIFFLE

Francis Cr.

Kenney Cr.

Horseshoe Bend

HORSESHOE BEND RAPIDS

FOREST

SISKIYOU NATL

Little Windy Cr.

LITTLE WINDY R.

Bunker Cr.

LOWER BLACK BAR FALLS

UPPER BLACK BAR FALLS

Big Windy Cr.

ROGUE RIVER

MARIAL to UPPER BLACK BAR

SCALE of MILES

0   1   2   3   4

122

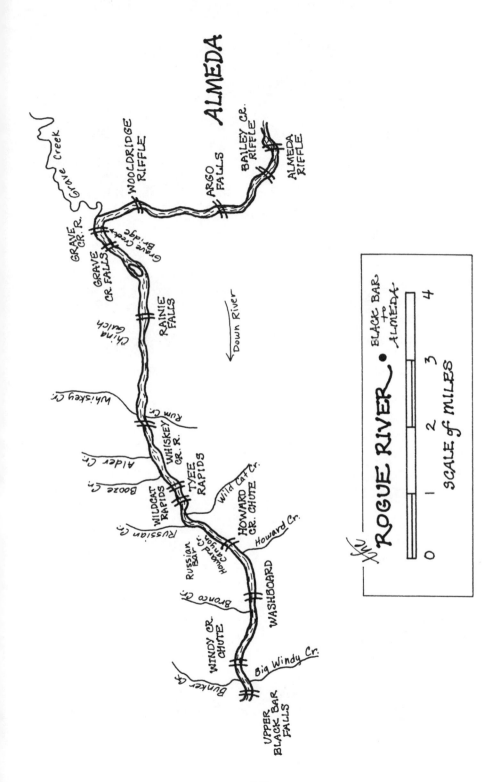

ALMEDA

Grave Creek

WOOLDRIDGE RIFFLE

ARGO FALLS

BAILEY Cr.

ALMEDA RIFFLE

GRAVE CR. R.

GRAVE CR. FALLS

Grave Creek Bridge

Down River

RAINIE FALLS

China Gulch

Whiskey Cr.

WHISKEY CR. R.

Rum Cr.

TYEE RAPIDS

Alder Cr.

Booze Cr.

WILDCAT RAPIDS

Wild Cat Cr.

HOWARD CR. CHUTE

Howard Chute Cr.

Russian Gulch

Russian Bar Cr.

Howard Canyon

Howard Cr.

Bronco Cr.

WASHBOARD

WINDY CR. CHUTE

Bunker Cr.

Big Windy Cr.

UPPER BLACK BAR FALLS

ROGUE RIVER

BLACK BAR
to
ALMEDA

SCALE of MILES

0   1   2   3   4

123

Forest bridge just above the mouth of Mule Creek. This is probably the one mailed by parcel post. Bureau of Land Management collection

May and Baldy Criteser at Bald Ridge. Bureau of Land Management collection

"Grandma" Adeline Billings.
Bureau of
Land Management collection

Billings Ranch at Marial. George Billings sold it to Andersons in 1931. The BLM purchased the property in 1970 for $251,700. It is now a walk-through museum with antiques from the Billings era on display. Glen hauled many of the furnishings downriver, including two cast iron bathtubs weighing about 250 pounds each.

Grants Pass Courier photo

Mr. Ramey and George Strong at Whiskey Creek Falls (now Rainie Falls) gaffing salmon.
Glen Wooldridge collection

Glen and Gail Huggins at Blossom Bar.   Glen Wooldridge collection

Chapter Thirteen

Hathaway Jones: Teller of TALL Tales

One of the people Glen and his dudes always liked to meet along the Mule Creek stretch of the trail was Hathaway Jones. Hathaway Jones was a mule packer who won a wide-spread reputation for his tall tales. He often defended his self-proclaimed title, The Damnedest Liar in the State of Oregon.

Hathaway was an old timer on the trail, having started carrying the mail between West Fork and Agness in 1889, as a hired packer for the mail contractor. Carrying mail in that country was no easy chore. Everything in the way of provisions for the 166 homesteaders and miners living in the canyon had to come by packsaddle. Flour, grain and feed, wire fencing, fruit trees, all had to come over the trail. Mail came this way for the 500 families in Gold Beach and Wedderburn, as well.

The Forest Service mailed a 2,000-pound bridge by parcel post, in 1914. It had to be packaged in 50 pound parcels to go by mail. It wasn't unusual for Rogue River Hardware to send sacks of cement, mining equipment, and farming tools by parcel post.

This was sent to West Fork, by railroad, then stacked up to await the mule packer. West Fork was just a little burg on the rail line; a hotel, a store, the depot, and a warehouse and barn, and houses.

The mail contract called for payment of $7,448 a year, in 1914, to the contractor, for a load limit of 600 pounds and 3½ cents a pound for excess of that weight. The trip had to be made in 23 hours, and to do that, the pack horses or mules must be made to trot part of the way.

A relay of men and horses waited at Marial, and it took twenty-five horses and four men to run the route. Sometimes the packs were raised from the horses or mules backs with a block and tackle in a tree, to give the animals a little rest.

In the winter the snow got pretty deep at the highest point of the trail, which was 4790 feet, and the mail was carried by men on snow shoes or skis.

The long hours on the trail gave Hathaway time to think up his tall stories, and he was ready to tell them on meeting anyone who would listen. Glen and other

127

people he met along the way soon spread the word and his cleaner stories frequently made the big national magazines such as the *Saturday Evening Post*. The *Oregonian*, too, often had stories Hathaway told in it.

Hathaway wasn't a very big man and he walked kind of leaning forward. He had an impediment in his speech, what we called a hare-lip, back then. And he also had a twang. But he had a way of telling his yarns that was really comical. He never laughed about them himself but was just as sober as if he was telling the truth. Everybody tried to tell his stories just like he did.

Of course, most of this stories had to do with things that happened to him every day. And he really had some funny yarns about his grandfather, Ike Jones, and his dad, Samps. There was no doubt about his being able to think up a yarn on the spur of the moment.

One trip I took along a friend, Sherman Estelle, who was quite a storyteller himself. And I had been telling Estelle about Hathaway and his tall tales.

We were taking our provisions out of the boat at the mouth of Missouri Creek planning on camping across the river from Long Gulch, just below the trail. I saw Hathaway coming down the trail and I said to Sherman, "Here comes the guy who tells us the big stories."

So we watched Hathaway come on down the trail and we all sat down on some rocks and Estelle started in on Hathaway. He told him about two fellows, the Oden brothers, Moze and Boze, who lived on Evans Creek, near Rogue River. Estelle told him people rumored it around that they hunted at night because they could see in the dark, just as good as they could in daylight.

I knew these guys; they called them albinos. Their skin was as white as chalk and they couldn't stand the light in their eyes, so the stories went around that they could see at night.

Hathaway sat and listened to Sherman for a while, then he said, "Yeah, I was up there one night. I was coming down Evans Creek on a horse, on the trail. It was raining and under the timber it was pitch dark. My horse got scared of something and wouldn't go any farther. So I got off the horse and struck a match to see what was the matter.

Well, there was one of the Oden fellows, sitting on a log. He was reading the *Oregonian*."

I thought that was pretty good. It just proved to me that Hathaway didn't have to stop and make up those stories. They just came to him naturally. We laughed all night about that one.

Hathaway rode a saddle mule, Monte, and she was a wonderful swimmer. He said, "One time I went down the river to the mouth of Missouri Creek and I wanted to cross to the other side and do some hunting. I rode Monte across. She always swam high, so I wouldn't get my feet wet."

"Well, on this trip I killed a big bear. I guess it would weight about 500 pounds. I put it on Monte and came back down to the river. Monte refused to swim across with the bear on her back. So I took the bear off her back and put it on my own and went swimming across the river, holding on to the reins.

"When I got to the middle, I noticed I was swimming a little deeper in the water than usual. I looked back and there was Monte sitting on top of that bear."

Most of Hathaway's stories were about hunting and fishing because those were things that were important in his life. They were all highly exaggerated, of course. One of the stories you'd hear around was about his goose hunt.

"One time a bunch of geese landed out in my field," Hathaway would say, "and there was a ditch running across there where they all went to drink. They were lined up at the ditch with their heads down, drinking, when I sneaked out with my rifle."

"I thought I would shoot right down the row of necks, get them all at once. So I gave a loud whistle and all their heads came up. I must have pulled a little too much to the left, though, because instead of their necks, all I got was a basketful of bills."

A lot of Hathaway's stories were about his family, his grandpa, Ike Jones; his father, Samps; and his brothers, Rupert and Todd. He told this one about when his brother Rupert had gone into the fox-raising business. There was quite a few people involved in raising foxes for furs around this country at one time.

"One time Brother Rupert lived up on Missouri Creek, and he was raising foxes and selling their furs. I went up to see him, and while I was there I went hunting up on the mountain. Rupert didn't go along, he had something else to do.

"Well, I hunted around a while and I slipped over a bluff and fell down in the canyon and broke my leg pretty bad. While I was laying there I noticed all these snakeskins around me. After a while a snake would come up to a certain little bush, nibble at it and then start to crawl away. As it crawled along its skin would just slip right off. Then there would come another snake and do the same thing."

"Well, Brother Rupert finally came and found me and while we were getting ready to go home I told him about the little bush and the snakes. So Rupert pulled the little bush up and we carried it home with us. When we got back to Ruperts he just tossed the bush up on the chicken wire on top of the foxes pen.

The leaves dropped off the bush, down into the pen and the foxes started eating them, but we didn't pay any mind to that, just went on in the house. But in three days you could just take them foxes by the heels and shake them right out of their skins.

Rupert sent the furs to St. Louis, to a big fur company. It wasn't long until that fur company sent a representative out and offered us $50,000 for the formula for tanning them hides. He said they were the best furs he'd ever seen. But we never could find that kind of bush again."

One time, Hathaway said, he was going over the mountain and the snow was pretty deep. In fact, he thought it was too deep for horses and mules in the packtrain, so Hathaway was just carrying the first class mail on snowshoes. It was about sixteen feet deep, he said.

When he got to the top of Nine Mile Mountain he saw a hat, just sliding along on top of the snow. He thought that was sort of a strange thing, so he went closer to get a better look. He reached down and picked up the hat and there was a fellow underneath it.

"Hey, down there, Mister," Hathaway said, "are you in any trouble?"

"No, I'm all right," the fellow said, "but my horse is having a hell of a time."

Hathaway's neighbor, John Hall, who lived somewhere back in there, about three miles above Marial's place, had a hound bitch that was a real good varmint dog. She could tree a bear, a coon or a wildcat, it was said.

She was about to throw a litter of pups and Hathaway wanted one of them pretty bad, so he asked John Hall for one.

John Hall said, "Yeah, I'll let you know when the pups are old enough to ween." So in due time, John notified Hathaway that the pup was ready.

Hathaway went over and got it, he said, and was carrying it home under his arm, on the trail, when a yearling deer crossed the trail. Hathaway put the puppy down to see if it would pay any attention to the deer track.

"He got interested all right, right away," Hathaway said, "but he went the wrong way. He tracked that deer right back to where it had been born the year before."

Hathaway liked to tell stories about the old black powder ammunition he used in early days. He always used it until John Hall gave him some smokeless shells for his rifle. They were supposed to have greater velocity and be more effective than the old black powder ones he'd been using.

Hathaway said he took his new shells and went off hunting, and as he went around a hill he saw a deer feeding on a bush. It was such an easy shot, he thought he would shoot him with a blackpowder shell and save the new smokeless ones for more difficult shots.

Hathaway took a shot at the deer, but it just went on eating, never looked up. He loaded his rifle with a smokeless load and shot at it again. It knocked the deer down this time, all right. Hathaway walked over to the deer and had just stooped over to cut its throat when something hit him, right in the seat of the pants. It was that black powder shot, just then getting there.

"One time," Hathaway said, "I had this big field of clover. I had fenced my field with logs, just cut them and let them fall around the field. Something got to eating the clover, and I couldn't figure out what it was. One day me and my little girl went out and sat down on an oak log, to wait and see what came out into the field."

"Daddy," my little girl said, "I hear something. I think it is in this log." We listened, then I pounded on the log and sure enough out of a hollow where a limb was broken off out came this bear and it ran out into the clover.

"I killed the bear," Hathaway ended the story, "But it was only a little one, weighed about sixty pounds or so, but it was the fattest thing I ever saw. Why, we got twenty-one gallons of bear grease out of it."

Another of Hathaway's subjects for stories was gold mining. It seems he went out prospecting and drilled several holes in the face of a ledge, back in that country. The next day he went out, going to put dynamite in them and shoot it off to look for gold. But he couldn't get the dynamite sticks in the hole. Gold was just oozing out of them.

He went running home to tell his Pap Samps, and Grandpa Ike, but they didn't get excited.

"Aw, Hathaway," they told him. "We know about the gold in that ledge, but you can't make any money off n it."

Hathaway asked them why not and they told him. "It is too far to the railroad. It would cost too much to ship all that gold. You'd better look for a strike that's not so rich."

He liked to tell yarns about rattlesnakes, too. One time Gail Huggins and I were going along down there, and when we got to Horseshoe Bend, Huggins killed a big rattler. Down the river a ways we met Hathaway. Huggins told him about the big rattler he had killed. We thought it was an extra big one, and he told Hathaway it had eight or nine rattles. Hathaway studied about it for a minute then said, "I never kill them with under 13 rattles."

He used to tell about how hot it got down in that country. He would tell about the lizards that went across a certain stretch of sand. It seems that just before starting across that particular stretch, they would pick up a stick, put it under their front leg and run as fast as they could until they got about half way across, then they would stop, put the stick down on the sand and stand on it panting and catching their breath, then they would pick up the stick and run on across. There never were any signs of the sticks because when they got across they would leave the stick on the other side and a lizard going the other way would take the stick back across.

Hathaway had a story about poachers that I liked. He told about the time they arrested his dad, Samps, for killing deer out of season and took him down to Gold Beach for trial. They took along a lot of his jerky to use as evidence. When it came time to present the evidence they passed out this jerky for everybody to sample, to see if it was venison.

When the first person got up to give testimony, they asked if it was deer meat, and he said, "No, tasted like dried salmon to me."

The next one they asked said, "No, must be mule meat."

Then all the jury had to sample it and the bailiff, everybody was chewing away on that jerky.

When it came time to bring in the verdict, the jury found him not guilty, but they recommended that he bring in a bigger load of jerky the next time he came to town.

Hathaway had another dog he was pretty proud of. When the dog would start getting particularly bothered by fleas, he would go down to the river, carry a stick in his mouth and swim out into the river until he was completely under, all but the tip of his nose. But he would hold the stick out of the water. The fleas would all go off him onto the stick, then he would drop the stick in the water and swim back to shore.

Everybody who told Hathaway's stories tried to tell them just like he did. There was another fellow, Will something or other, that lived down close to

Hathaway, and he wanted a bull Hathaway had. It was supposed to be an exceptionally fine animal.

He tried to buy it off of Hathaway, but Hathaway wouldn't sell it. One night he and Hathaway were sitting out beside Jones' house, probably doing a little drinking, and this fellow told Hathaway he could talk just like Hathaway. Well, Hathaway didn't like that at all, so they went around and around about it for a while.

Finally the fellow said, "I'll prove it to you, and if I do will you sell me the bull?"

So Hathaway agreed to the deal. Will went into the house where Flora, Hathaway's wife, had gone in to bed. Hathaway was supposed to stay outside and listen at the window.

Hathaway heard the fellow's shoes hit the floor, one after the other. He listened and heard the bedsprings rattle, then he heard Will's voice, sounding just like Hathaway's twang, saying, "Move over, old woman."

About that time Will heard Hathaway at the window, "Hold it right there, Will, you've gone far enough. The bull is yours."

Hathaway could tell some big stories all right. He was pretty proud of his title, the Biggest Liar in Oregon. When the *Oregonian* ran a contest and gave the title to someone else, he threatened to sue them for giving his title away.

He liked to ride his little black mule with white feet, Monte he called her. I don't know if he was riding her when he died. Some say the saddle turned on the mule, causing him to fall down into the canyon, hitting his head on a rock and killing him.

Hathaway was still carrying mail when that happened, in the late thirties. He was known far and wide for his tall tales, and people still talk about him and tell his stories over again. His obituary came out in the *Oregonian*.

Hathaway Jones, center, and his pack train.
Glen Wooldridge collection

Hathaway Jones.

Glen Wooldridge collection

Bureau of Land Management collection

Settlers along the lower Rogue swimming stock across the river.

Mule Creek Trail.   Bureau of Land Management collection

Hathaway's father, Samps Jones, and Hathaway's brothers, Dick and Todd.

Bureau of Land Management collection

Chapter Fourteen

Some Dudes Who Made the Downriver Trip

As more and more people came to run the Rogue, or to fish for steelheads in the fall, Glen's schedules filled months in advance, even with four boats making the trips.

Building his own boats gave him the opportunity to change the designs when he thought of something to make the trip safer or easier on the passengers. Splash boards were mounted along the bow portions of the boats. That gave them a deeper, heavier look but it kept his dudes from taking on too much water when he would hit the rapids.

Other changes in the boats were not so noticeable, as they were made so gradually. He held to the flared, dory style, built of cedar or pine shiplapped planking. These boats had two sets of oarlocks so that two men could row at the same time. The rockered bottoms made them easier to spin in the rapids with a quick twist of the oars, and to handle with a fishing party aboard.

Whitewater running called for boats with smooth bottoms, rather than V-bottomed ones. They would slide over the rocks in the water, or across them when the boats were being lined or portaged.

Learning to "read the water" was the best education a whitewater man could have. For Glen this came only by constant observation of the river.

There are several things about the water that tells you what is going on underneath, where the danger is. The color of the water, its motion, density, and sounds all tell you part of the story. You have to pay close attention to them, because your life and the others in the boat all depend on it.

There will be black, slick places; frothy whitewater; more dense whitewater; rapids; riffles; currents; falls; swirls and eddies; chutes and bends.

Slick, glassy water is sometimes dead water, but at other times it is swift rapids. It takes an experienced riverman to tell the difference before he gets into it. Frothy whitewater is full of air caused by the pounding of the water over a riverbed full of boulders. It is thin water and can't be run. White water that is more dense is over deeper boulders and you can run it. Fast, smooth water is deep and navigable.

You can tell the depth of a boulder under fast-moving water by the motion of the water over it. The wake of the water, over the boulder, tells its position underneath the surface.

A wave doesn't necessarily mean rocks; it can be just the speed of the river's current. Decisions must be made fast and constantly as to which whitewater is runable. There isn't always a clear, open channel to follow. In fact, in most whitewater rivers, there seldom is an open channel.

The riverbed changes constantly in high floods. Boulders move into what was open water. You have to know this and watch out for it. The sound of the water and how it is moving over the newly placed boulders just doesn't fit the picture the mind has memorized for that one place.

Always, after a flood, if we were the first ones going down the river, and we were for many years, I would tie up my boat and hike down around a bend to see just what was around there before taking my boat on down.

Sometimes a log would be jammed across the channel. I had to shoot logs out several times. Or a slide would change the channel and I'd have to find another way down instead of the one I'd been using.

I was doing nearly all the drift trips to the coast for many years, with the fellows working for me, of course. And I was doing most all the boat building in the area. Prince Helfrich was the first one that competed with me, but he didn't make too many trips, just occasionally.

Charley Foster was working with me, then Bob Pritchett. It took quite a while to get some of those fellows going, teaching them the river. Bob was a good boatman, but he hadn't had much experience with boating when he first started with me. He worked with me for something like ten to twelve years.

As word of the Rogue's excitement and beauty spread, film companies came in to make short movies of the river and of the fishing. In early years Fox Studios sent a crew in to film the steelheaders on the Rogue. *Pathe News* sent in two boatloads of writers and cameramen, and Glen took them downriver to make a newsreel that was shown nationwide. *Look Magazine* sent writers and photographers to make a trip with Glen.

The movie people; producers, actors, and so on, started using the Rogue as a vacation spot, but later bought land for lodges and cabins or farms and ranches in the area. George Murphy bought a ranch. Ginger Rogers bought an 1100-acre ranch that she called the 4R, for Rogers Rogue River Ranch. It is on the Rogue about sixteen miles from Medford.

I think one of the best guests we ever had on a trip was Ginger Rogers. She was really a good guy. She didn't hesitate to wash dishes or do any other thing that needed to be done around camp. She and her husband, Jack Briggs, came up and made the trip with us. Scotty Williamson and Jack Cooper were with them. We took some local people along, too. I remember Charles Cooley, from Grants Pass, and Dr. and Mrs. Durno from Medford, went along.

That trip was written up in a Hollywood Screen magazine, with pictures showing Ginger Rogers and Glen. She was holding up the big steelhead she caught. It weighed six and three-quarters pounds. It was the biggest steelhead caught on the Rogue that season, but the Hollywood people made it even bigger, saying it was a

Ginger Rogers (with Glen) shows the six and three-quarters pound steelhead she caught on a drift trip with Glen.   Glen Wooldridge collection

63-pounder. The party caught 125 steelhead, which they salted down and took back to Hollywood for their friends to enjoy.

But even before that, in 1940, Jean Muir, a writer for the *Saturday Evening Post,* made a trip downriver and wrote about the movie starlets and hermits along the Rogue. She included some of the Hathaway Jones stories that Glen and others along the river told her.

A local writer, Louise Stokes, went along on one trip. She was talking to old Tom Billings and asked him, "Why don't you have a cow?"

She was pretty embarrassed when he answered, "It's 70 miles to a bull."

The people we really liked to take on the trips were women. They were pretty good sports. You might think of them as being sissies, but they were better sports than men, in most cases. The average woman didn't expect to catch a fish, so when she caught one or two she was very happy about it. A man would expect to catch all the fish in the river, and then they wouldn't be satisfied.

The women were the best guests. They would do what you advised them to do, use the equipment and bait that experience had taught us was the best. But

Ginger Rogers, waiting in the drift boat.   Glen Wooldridge collection

the men, most of them anyway, had ideas of their own. They would have to try all their own ideas that wouldn't work before they would try it our way. I'd get tired of that.

If there was anything that would spoil a trip it would be liquor. I think that's no good anyplace. The only time I had a dude fall out of a boat was one who was drunk.

I guess he was drinking because he thought it would keep him dry, as on that trip we started out in a pouring rain. He had on lots of clothes and rain gear, of course, and we were going along, really hadn't much more than started good, when for some reason he stood up and fell out of the boat. We had to pull him in and go to shore to let him change clothes. That sobered him up in a hurry.

One time we were going along, just this side of Hog Creek, making a drift trip. We had just passed two guys who were wading and fishing. We went on down and I was holding the boat along, letting the dudes fish, when I looked over the side of the boat and saw the top of a man's head pop up beside me. I really just could see his hair, so I grabbed that and we pulled him to shore and dragged him up on a gravel bar.

We rolled him around, pumping the water out of him. He was heaving up this water — took on too much, I guess. He was pretty sick, but still alive, and after a while he came around okay. His partner finally got there, from upstream. They were the guys we had passed. We went on downriver, after we saw that he was okay. I never did learn who he was.

If we hadn't been right there he would have drowned. He was already gone as far as he was concerned. It was just by a big accident we were still there.

That old river has got a lot of people. I can count up twenty or thirty that I remember just right off.

Back when we were taking the fishing trips, there was a lot of army people coming in to go with us. One was an infantry colonel. He was a little guy with a little sharp mustache that he spent quite a bit of time grooming.

When you looked him square in the face he looked like a woodrat. If you've ever looked at a woodrat real close, well, that is exactly what he looked like.

He came up here year after year, for a long time, making the trips with us. Cranky, mean little wart. I never did like him, but I liked his money all right, so I'd take him along. He was a good fisherman, a really good fly fisherman, but the worst kind of a crank.

If you have never had an encounter with a fly fisherman crank you don't quite understand what I mean. But they can get so radical about this fishing with a fly that if you caught a fish with anything else they would hardly speak to you. They would think it was an insult.

On one of his trips he brought a cavalry officer with him. His name was Wallace, and the first time he spoke to me I liked him. It was just sticking out all over him that he was a real good sport.

Before we started fishing we went into Joe Wharton's to get some equipment. We had been catching a lot of fish on big Royal Coachman flies — big ones, about one and a half inches long. They did look all out of proportion, but the fish seemed to like them.

When we went in, Wallace said to me, "Now anything you can show me will be appreciated."

So I told him, "If I were you I would get some of these big flies. That's what they've been biting."

He bought a few of them, then turned around to the Colonel and said, "Colonel, do you want some of these big flies?"

The Colonel said, "Kee--riss! No! I don't gaff my fish." And he said it just as nasty as he knew how to be. So that was all that was said about it at the moment.

We went on down to the river and I could see right away that Wallace didn't have much experience casting a fly. He either hooked it in his clothes or wrapped it around his neck or somewhere else when he'd cast.

So I told him, "If you will just sit down there and let out some line, I will maneuver the fly around with the boat."

He said, "Okay," so that was what we were doing.

That is really the most effective way to catch a fish, and there will be certain spots where you can catch them. After fishing the same stretch of water over and over I could go right to the spots where they would be, if there were any.

I was giving Wallace all the breaks possible, of course, and every once in a while he would catch a fish. Nice, big steelheads. We went along and he caught four or five and the Colonel hadn't caught a one.

Finally the Colonel turned to Wallace and said, "Loan me one of your flies."

Wallace said, "No. You don't gaff your fish." And he wouldn't give him any. The Colonel never caught a fish all that day.

Well, a day or two later I went into Wharton's and in came the Colonel.

Joe asked him, "What kind of luck did you fellows have the other day, when you went out with Glen?"

The Colonel told him, "You know the s.o.b. I took along with me? He was catching fish on those big flies and he wouldn't even loan me one of them. But you can't expect anything from the cavalry, anyway, but horse manure." But he didn't put it quite that delicately.

I don't know whatever happened to the Colonel, but I imagine somebody shot him.

Boy, some of those guys who fly fished were really radicals. They just couldn't stand to see a fish caught on anything but a fly. Some of them would take a little set of scales along and a notebook. Every time they would catch a fish they would weigh it, measure it, then put it all down in the book. The date, the weather, the time of day they caught it, what they caught it on, all that would go in their little books. Then, apt as not, they'd turn the fish loose.

When the boys got big enough to go along with me, I started taking them on the river. They got to be pretty good boatmen, especially Bruce. He got to be a really good boatman, probably the best one on the river today.

I bought the lot on Oak Street, which isn't too far from my house, after the boat-building business got to going so good I couldn't build them in the garage anymore. I needed more storage space. We built the boat shop and had plenty of room to store the cedar and everything we needed to build the boats there.

And along about that time, Glenn Ballou came along. I had known him for a long time, even before he came to make a trip down the river with me. He used to work at the Three C's Lumber Company. He worked there for a long time. Then he was with the National Guards for a few years. He was in both world wars and was on the National Rifle team, in 1924.

When he retired, he came down to help me build boats. What he had done was to quit work, just retired, thinking he could do nothing, but that wouldn't work. He had to have something to do.

I used to have him make boat parts for me, when he worked at the Three C's. He was the boss of the shop down there. He was a nice man, easy to get along with, very agreeable, just an all-round good person to be with. Everything was usually all right with Glenn. You don't find very many people like that.

But he could get riled up every once in a while. I remember once I was down at the Three C's shop and they had hired a new man to work there. This new guy got mad and grabbed some tool and threw it on the floor.

Glenn just grabbed him by the collar, took him to the door and gave him a shove. That was the end of that fellow.

Glenn Ballou worked at the Oregon Caves while they were building the Caves Chateau. He was in charge of lining and waterproofing the creek that runs through the Chateau dining room. He did quite a bit of other work on the buildings such as helping with the redwood bark siding.

When Glenn came down here, after he quit working for Three C's, he asked me, "Do you mind if I just sort of help you around here?"

I told him, "I would be tickled to death to have you." So he started coming and just kept on. We had a lot of nice times together, and went many places. He must have worked with me here for twenty-five years. He was a good carpenter, really handy with woodworking tools, machines and things. He understood woodworking a lot better than I did.

He was really a wonderful person. I sure do miss ole Glenn.

On one trip down the river there was a man along who owned a plywood business in Portland. I can't remember his name, but on the trip we were using these boats made out of lumber, and he asked me why we didn't make them out of plywood.

I told him I didn't know anything about plywood, and he said, "If you will tell me how much you need I will send you enough to make a boat." So I figured it out for him and he sent it to me. After that we made them out of plywood for many years.

The plywood boats are much lighter to handle. Weight is a big factor in a boat.

Finished boat, ready for a river run, Glen's Boat Shop, 1950s.

Grants Pass Bulletin photo

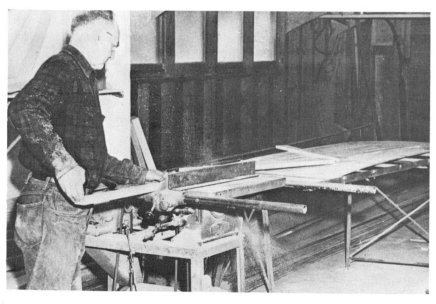

Glen, starting a new boat, 1950s.

Grants Pass Bulletin photo

Glen and Glenn Ballou team up to craft a boat, 1950s.

Grants Pass Bulletin photo

The dudes take a wild ride through Wildcat Rapids.   Bruce Wooldridge collection

Glen and lady passenger run Lower Black Bar Falls.   Glen Wooldridge collection

Bruce Wooldridge guides a party of lady dudes.
Bruce Wooldridge collection

Getting the fishing rods in action was of first importance at the camp site.
Bruce Wooldridge collection

Glen tells a tall tale to his helper while cooking flap jacks.   Bruce Wooldridge collection

Chapter Fifteen

Bears Along the River

After Glen and Sadie had the guiding business going on a pretty full schedule, they decided to buy a place downriver to spend some time relaxing during their time off from the strenuous summers and falls. The place they found, Clay Hill, above Illahe, was accessible only by boat or the trail.

The Thomases used to own Clay Hill, but they were all gone but one, George Thomas, when I decided to buy the place.

It had about thirty-three acres. The original house burned, but there was one up on the edge of the field where Sadie and I would go and stay after we bought it. We really enjoyed that. You never would see anybody, it was so isolated. We would go down and hunt and fish, just spend our vacations.

Sometimes I wonder how we managed to get up there, as I don't think I even had a motor lift, back then. And the motors were pretty under-powered, but we made it. There might have been a little more water in the river, back then, maybe a few inches, but not very much.

There were lots of rattlers at Clay Hill. We would see some big ones every once in a while. Tom Staley said he killed over twenty there one year, after he bought the place from me. It would vary a lot, sometimes there would be snakes and again not very many. I don't know why.

Every once in a while I'd see one swimming the river. They swim with their tails out of the water. Don't want to get their rattles wet, I suppose. We found one swimming across a river in Idaho, too.

A deer will swim the river, too. If a dog chases a deer, sometimes it will jump in and swim out aways. They do that in the ocean, too. Dogs can't keep up with them, swimming.

We caught a deer, a buck, one time, swimming the river. Glenn Ballou was with me in the boat. We caught up with him and Glenn caught him by the antlers, bent his head back against the side of the boat. He had his weight against him and he couldn't get loose. He was just kicking and thrashing in the water. I went back there and cut his throat, then we dragged him over to the bank.

Another time I had an odd experience with a buck. I was trapping down in Almeda country and wanted to get a deer to eat. We lived on the south side, really the west side there, and I went across the river and took a little fox terrier dog I had with me. I was hunting on one of those ridges that run to the river, and had climbed up to the top when I saw a buck down at the river side, coming uphill. He was walking right toward me.

I shot at him and he whirled and ran out of sight. Then away went the little dog, right after him. The dog barked for a while then he quit.

I ran down the ridge the way I came, so I could see them, and there they were, swimming down the river, first the buck, then the dog following him.

The dog could catch up to the deer, since the deer was wounded. He would swim up to him and the deer would turn on him, then he would swim away. Pretty soon the dog gave up and came to shore.

I watched the deer swim on down the river to just below the Almeda mine. He came to shore on the same side I was on and went along the bank. I went down there to see where he came out. He was leaving blood on the track. The dog went after him again, and ran him up into a little flat just above the river. The dog bayed him, and I sneaked up to where the dog was entertaining him.

I had shot him with the rifle at first, but I didn't want to make any more noise. He was right close, so I shot him with my 22 pistol, got him in the neck, and knocked him down. I went on up there and set my rifle down and laid the pistol down, too.

The deer was laying there with his eyes rolling around. I could see that he wasn't dead, I stepped on his horns to hold him down while I got my jacknife out to cut his throat.

But I didn't get it out. He jerked his head out from under my boot and here he was, standing right in front of me. All I could do was grab him by the antlers. I couldn't run because I couldn't get away from him. So here we went, around and around, over this little flat. He would dive at me and I would push his head aside and we would get all set and do it again. We were there for quite a while, and he was a big deer, too.

The creek had cut down through the flat and made a bank on the east side of it, about five or six feet high. As we were going around and around and I was trying to keep him off of me, it came around in such a way that his hind feet were close to the bank. I gave him a shove and his feet dropped over the bank and I had him.

He slid down the bank and just stood looking at me. I guess he wanted to rassle some more, but I sure didn't. I'd had enough of that. I got my gun and shot him.

That was sort of like having a bear by the tail. You didn't dare let go.

I saw a timber wolf down in that lower Rogue country one day. Or at least I think it was a timber wolf. And I killed an animal down there that I am not too sure about. It might have been the same animal; I don't know. It was when we were building the Payton cabin. I was living up at Clay Hill and would come down in my boat, always early in the morning, when I was working on the house. I was coasting along, down through the canyon, keeping my eye on the hillside, when I saw an animal standing up there. I kept watching it as I got closer to it; part of the time it would be behind the trees. Finally it came out and lay down. All I could see was its ears sticking up. I shot and killed it. When I went up to get it and drag it down hill to the boat, I didn't know what it was, and to this day I still don't know what it was.

I skinned it out and brought the hide to Grants Pass and showed it to the government hunter, Harry Stokes.

He examined it and said, "Well it isn't a wolf, and it isn't a coyote, either. I don't know what it is."

Harry Stokes should have known, if anyone would. He was the government hunter here for many years, and he told me he had killed thirteen timber wolves in the Evans Creek area.

It must have been a crossbreed of some mixture. I wish I had kept the hide. I could have preserved it and hung it in the boatshed for a number of years before the moths ate it up.

The last of the grizzlies in here was killed before my time, but I can remember hearing about it. My Granddad Cook said someone killed it up by Ashland. That was the last grizzly bear they knew of in this country.

I remember when I was a little boy, sitting on Granddad Cook's knee. He would tell me stories about his experiences and about the mountains and mining and all those things.

One time I asked him, "Granddad, would you run, if a bear got after you?"

He thought about it for a little while, then he told me, "No, son, I wouldn't. I couldn't outrun him, and if I had to fight him, I wouldn't want to be tired out."

Sadie had an experience with a bear, when we were staying down at Clay Hill. We had been bothered by a bear coming up around the house, so I set a trap a little ways out. I got up and was gone real early one morning and Sadie came looking for me for something. She heard this rattling and banging around the side of a little knoll, so she went around it, calling, "Glen! Glen!" and she came face to face with a bear, caught in the trap. He had pulled it up and was dragging it along, making the noise. Boy, she got out of there fast.

Those are just regular black bears, down on the lower Rogue, but they are not all black. They vary from coal black to almost yellow. A few are tan-colored and cinnamon, but they are all the same breed of bear. Once in a while you will see an old sow bear with a black cub and a brown one. Occasionally, one will have three cubs. A doe will sometimes have three fawns at a time, too, but that doesn't happen too often.

Bears feed nearly all day, but not much in the middle of winter. If you kill one in the winter or the early spring, there will be nothing in its stomach. It's stomach will be a little bitty thing about as big as my fist, all puckered up, with nothing in it.

They are full of fat, and they don't lose all of it during hibernation. They are just about as fat when they come out as when they go in.

You don't find them along the river in the wintertime. They go up in the

Old cabin at Clay Hill. Back Row, left to right, Charley Foster; Harvey Foster; Bruce Wooldridge; Tom Staley, Jr.; Glen Wooldridge; Tom Staley, Sr. Front Row, left to right, an army captain; his wife; Mrs. Staley and Don Staley.

Bruce Wooldridge collection

From left; Sadie, Glen and Bruce Wooldridge at Black Bar, 1941.

Bruce Wooldridge collection

high country where the food is. They come to the river in the springtime, when the eels are spawning, and eat them. They live for a time on those rotten eels. That kind of makes their breath smell bad a little, too.

The eels migrate from the ocean in the spring, about the same time and the spring salmon do, in April or May. They come in and spawn. You can see them if you look real close, building their spawning beds. They have a sucker mouth, and they will get ahold of a rock and work it loose and carry it out, then get another one and do the same. That's the way they build their beds. They build a little cavity in the gravel and spawn there, then they die, like salmon do.

Salmon have a different method of building their spawning beds, though. A female salmon digs her bed out with her body.

You can see the eels going upriver, if you watch, there at the fish ladder at Savage Rapids Dam. They hold on to the cement sides, let go and sort of lunge forward, through all that rushing water, then grab another hold, working their way to above the dam.

After the eels are gone, there is a period when there is very little for the bears to eat, so they live on grass and clover. They eat grass like a pig. At that time their stomachs will be just full of grass.

Clay Hill Riffle

Glen Wooldridge collection

153

They don't travel far in the early spring, maybe because their feet are tender from laying around doing nothing during the winter. If you find where one has been working, he won't be far away. I suppose that is the reason. A little later on they do a lot of traveling.

I have seen small cubs about the size of full-grown coons. When a bear is born it isn't any bigger than a rat, just a little bitty thing. If you see a cub about the size of a coon, you know the old sow bear is pretty close by. She will go a little ways, but not very far away from it.

They don't hibernate along the river, or at least I've never known them to. They go back in the mountains someplace.

Jim Payton was the champion bear killer. The first I ever knew of him, I got a letter from him in the early part of the winter ordering a boat to be built.

He told me where to deliver it when I finished with it. He had some property in Rogue River, and when he showed up — a long, tall Texan from Amarillo — I had already delivered his boat to the specified place.

I must have been the first person he got acquainted with here, as he hung around the boatshop quite a bit. I told him, "Next spring, when I get ready to start taking trips down the river, I'll take you along." He was pretty happy about that.

We went down in April, to Clay Hill, and I had quite a bit of work to do around the place. He was always telling me about his hunting experiences. He had done a lot of bird hunting, but hadn't much experience with big game.

I told him he probably could kill a bear, if he wanted to, so that really steamed him up.

Up the river, a couple of miles or more from Clay Hill, you can see some rimrock country back from the river, where the bears accumulate in the springtime. It's an open patch that faces the south, and that's where the grass starts growing first. The wild clover grows there and that attracts them.

I took Payton down the river in the boat and showed him where to get on the trail and explained to him just how to get up to that clover patch, then I went on back to working around the place.

Along in the evening he came in, really excited. "I saw twenty-one deer and three bear," he said, "I got to shooting at the bears, but I didn't hit any."

"Gee," he said, "I'd sure like to have some property in this country."

Well, it just so happened that Charley Billings, who lived down below there, owned some property on the river. He asked me to try to sell it for him.

I took Payton down and showed him the property and he got all excited about it. He gave me $1000 and told me to go down and make the deal. I went down and arranged the deal between him and Billings for the property. Then the next thing to do was to get a cabin built on it. I took a couple of carpenters down there and hauled all the material up the river to the place. We built the house and they moved in.

Well, still Payton hadn't killed his bear. This was in the springtime, and one day when I was coming upriver in the motor boat, I saw Payton over on a flat bar. He saw me, too, but he ducked out of sight in the willow bushes along there.

I didn't stop, but when I went on up by their house I saw Mrs. Payton down at the river's edge. She waved me in.

"Jim shot the mail carrier's mule for a bear," she told me.

The next time I saw Jim, I started razzing him about shooting that old jackass. He explained, "I went down to the riverbank, here in front of the cabin, and I could see something across there in the brush. I could just see the top of its back. It had its head down, feeding, so I couldn't see it. But it was black and I thought it was a bear. I shot and knocked him dead with the first shot. Then I went down to look at him. He had rolled over in a hole with his feet sticking up in the air.

"I said to myself, 'I never have seen a bear with shoes on before.' Then I knew there must be something wrong."

Jim had to go down to Charley Billings' to settle for the mule he killed. Charley told me about it. He said Payton came down and visited with him a while, then finally got around to asking him, "What will you take for that black mule that runs up there on the bar?"

Charley said he suspicioned right away that Payton had killed his mule. He told Payton, "Oh, I wouldn't sell that mule at all. He's the best mule I've got."

He kept Payton at bay there for quite a while, but finally they made a deal for the mule. I think it was $60 that Payton had to pay for the old mule, then he gave Charley $10 to help him bury it.

There wasn't any place to bury it, really. It fell in a rock pile. I ran over there in a day or so and took a look just to see what happened. They didn't have any dirt to bury him with, so they just piled brush on him and tried to set him afire. But that hadn't done much more than singe the hair on him. He was still there, and they couldn't get rid of him. I guess the buzzards finally finished him off.

So that was Payton's bear, but he finally did get to kill one, after that.

Another person I got a kick out of was Stanley Anderson who came up here and bought the ranch at Marial from George Billings. The BLM has charge of that ranch now. They call it the Rogue River Ranch, and they've made a museum out of it.

The Andersons were rich people from Los Angeles, and they just used that as a place to play for a while each summer. Stanley Anderson was a good friend of Will Rogers.

I built him a boat, and at that time motors were available, so he bought a 14 horse Johnson for it. He had me take him and his two boys down to the place in this new boat. The water was pretty low, and I didn't like to run the motor too much since it was a brand new outfit. I had taken the motor off and it was in the bottom of the boat.

Anderson said to me a time or two, "Why don't you run the motor?"

I told him, "Oh, you guys can run it when you get it down there."

But when we came to the head of Horseshoe Bend he said, "Put the motor on and let Jack run it." Jack was just a big kid, about fourteen, at that time.

So I said, "Sure. All right," and put the motor on.

Now, the head of Horseshoe Bend is three channels with bedrock sticking up between them. I told Jack, before we got there, "Now, Jack, go through the middle channel. Go through the middle one." It wasn't very wide, about twelve feet, I guess. So here we went, with Jack standing up behind me in the boat, running the motor.

When the old man saw this narrow place he shouted, "Shut it off, Jack!"

So Jack did just what he told him to. He shut it off. But that was the wrong thing to do. She turned sideways and hit the reef a hell of a blow. It knocked a big hole in the boat and Jack went overboard.

He went out of that boat just like a big frog jumping off a bank. He took the handle of the motor with him, and it poked into the river bottom. The old man almost fell out, too, and I was in hopes he would.

Anyway, Jack swam over to the reef, and we got the boat out. Now it had a hole in the side. So we had to tear the floor board out and patch the hole. I never heard anymore of "Let Jack run it." That was the end of that.

We got the boat down there, and later the old man wanted to hire me to go and show him how to run it. He said he wanted to go down to the mouth of the canyon to fish, and he wanted to use the boat to run down there. I ran it down there and back a few times, knowing damn well he couldn't do it. When we came back up to the mouth of Mule Creek he said, "Let me run it."

I said, "Okay." So we started up the river instead of down, and just at the foot of China Bar Riffle, he headed right for a boulder — just kept going in a bee-line. We ran right up on this boulder and slid off, almost tipping her over. Then we headed back for the bluff.

I shouted, "Better shut her off."

He said, "You shut it off." Well, I was sitting away up in the bow, but I got back there as quick as I could and had just reached for the motor when we hit the bank. We hit this bluff and both went end over end.

He said, "That's enough. Take it home. I'm all through."

So that was his first attempt and his last. I was glad he was quitting before he sank the boat. If he had got it down at the head of Mule Creek, he would have drowned for sure.

When you see somebody operating a boat who has been doing it all his life, you sometimes think, "All you have to do is get in there and turn the motor on. That's all there is to it." But it doesn't work that way.

Boy, that lower Rogue area was dandy country. Talk about some real good fishing and hunting, you couldn't beat that.

Bill Young, Charley Holland and I went down there bear hunting, one time. By the time we came to Horseshoe Bend it was raining like the dickens. The river came up and it rained for a week. We didn't get out of the cabin except just far enough to grab a fir limb and drag it in for wood.

When it cleared up we didn't have any meat, so we decided to go kill a deer. We took off, each one going in a different direction. I killed a couple of little deer and went back and after a while Charley came in and told me, "I killed one, but he's so big I can't pack him in."

Then Bill came in and said, "I killed two."

156

Now what in the hell are we going to do with all that meat?

I happened to know a fellow that lived up the river a little ways, so I went up to see him. I didn't know him very well, but we got around to talking about hunting and he said, "I have been trying to kill a deer, but I can't find any."

Hell, there were deer everyplace, but I got him to go back to the cabin with me and I got one of the deer on his back and I followed him home with another one.

We got rid of a few that way. We lived on venison and beans and spuds. That was about the size of our diet for the next two weeks, but I still think that's the best there is.

And fish! By golly, the river was literally alive with steelheads. We fished in a little eddie not any bigger than this room. We had an apple box full of steelheads we caught and salted down. The mule packer, MacNeill, came along, and we asked him if he wanted some fish.

We had met him on the trail, so we told him to go by and get him a mess out of that apple box. When we came home, the box and all was gone! He took the whole works. We were glad of it, though; we got rid of them. We killed a couple of bears on that trip, too.

I should have hung onto that Clay Hill place. I don't know why I ever sold it. Staley gave me $1400 for it, and I had just paid about $800 when I bought it. If I had been smart, I could have owned a lot of that property in there along the river. But we always think of these things in after years.

Glen packs out a big buck.
Bruce Wooldridge collection

Bob Wooldridge with large salmon.
Bruce Wooldridge collection

Glen and Glenn Ballou with bear skins and coyote skin. "Now I wish we hadn't killed them."   Glen Wooldridge collection

Glen with bear skins from a Clay Hill hunt, 1945.   Glen Wooldridge collection

Glen with prime Chinooks.   Bruce Wooldridge collection

Chapter Sixteen

Blasting the Channel Down the Rogue

Things seemed to be coming together for Glen. The guiding business had a full schedule for many years. And the boat building business was enough to keep him and Glenn Ballou busy in the winter months. But one problem kept nagging at him; the boulders in the Rogue. If he could have a clear channel, it would save lining and portaging the boats. That was a lot of work.

The blasting along the river was done over a wide number of years. Blossom Bar was the big job, of course. We sure burned a lot of powder there before we learned how to shoot the rocks out. But we blasted many other places to clear a safer channel all the way down to Agness.

The farthest up the river we blasted was Dunn Riffle. That was in later years, and there's a pretty good story goes along with that, but I will save that for a little later.

We shot rocks out of Innis Riffle and Carpenter's Island Riffle before you get to Galice. We shot Galice Riffle and Rocky Riffle, then down at Almeda, where the old mine used to be, we cleared that out. There was a bridge across the river, there that we had to lift the boats over, in early years. We didn't shoot the bridge out, but it is a wonder we didn't.

Then right below Galice is Argo Falls, but there isn't a falls there anymore, then comes Wooldridge Riffle, we shot both of them out. That riffle was named after me.

When we made the map that I used to promote my guiding and boatbuilding, I took Chris Cross, a writer who lived at Finley Bend, down the river with me and pointed out the different spots: riffles, rapids and falls, and told him their names. He made the map from just the one trip down the river. I tried to tell him all the names and the reasons they were named that way. One didn't have a name, that I could recall, so he named it Wooldridge Riffle.

After that, on down river, comes Grave Creek Riffle. We blasted that one out, then at Grave Creek Falls we shot some rocks out of it, too. You pass the Sanderson place, then go on down to Rainie Falls.

That used to be called Whiskey Creek Falls, then comes Booze Creek and Rum Creek. You can pretty well guess that the early day miners named them. They must have been pretty thirsty when they hiked down there. I don't think any of them ever went down any other way. When they would come back out of that canyon, they would have some big stories to tell about the terrible river and all that. That added to my urge to go down and look it over, that first time. But it wasn't nearly as bad as they thought it was.

But we made it lots easier to get through those places, otherwise you had to let the boat down with a rope, or drag it over the boulders. We opened it up so we could run right through it, even with a motor boat, later on. But, you understand, we didn't just go down the line blasting them as we came to them. We might blast some upriver, then next time do our blasting away on down-river.

I don't remember if old Ramey was around when we blasted Rainie Falls. We did quite a bit of shooting right at the falls, blasting out the lining chute, where you put the boats through. That was a toughy to do anything with. It was bedrock and pretty hard to shoot and get anything out. We blasted it half a dozen times over the years, until we could get a boat through okay.

The fishways there are natural; not many changes made to them. Except one time, in the early years, the fish commissioners went down and cleared out some stuff that washed in. Claud Bardon took them down and helped them, back before my blasting time. I remember while they were down there Claud Bardon got rattlesnake bit.

After Rainie Falls comes Tyee. That means "chief" to the Indians. I guess they thought it was pretty big or pretty bad. Then Wildcat Rapids, Russian Bar and Howard Creek. We shot rocks out of all them.

There was a big rapids at Upper Black Bar, then Black Bar Falls. It wasn't really a falls, but a steep jumpoff. Then Lower Black Bar. We worked on all of them.

Just below Black Bar is Jenny Creek. We cleaned that one out pretty good so that Witherwox, who ran the lodge at Black Bar, could get his boat up over it. He had to go down to Marial to pick up supplies.

Horseshoe Bend comes next, then Dulog. We did some blasting in them; then comes Kelsey Canyon. At Kelsey Falls we did a lot of work, changed the channel completely. We moved it from where we had been running it to the other side of the river.

We shot one rock out of the new channel, and it just went looping over some big boulders out in the middle and landed right in the old channel. We couldn't have done that in a million years if we had been trying to do it. We straightened out the channel there.

Battle Bar, next down the river, was kind of a difficult spot, too. We had to do a lot of work; because there was lots of rocks and broken channels. Battle Bar was where the early day settlers and the army battled Chief John's warriors, in the late 1850s.

The next place downriver we blasted was just at the foot of Winkle Bar, where Zane Grey had his cabin. We had to shoot some at John's Riffle, then

China Bar. There is another rapids just above Mule Creek Canyon; I don't remember that it had a name. We worked that one over, too. There were some boulders in the way right at the head of the canyon we boosted out, but we didn't blast any through the canyon. The walls are just straight up, there.

Then comes Blossom Bar. That was named by the early pioneers because of the many azaleas that grow on the north side of the river. A house was right on the trail, with the trail going right under the porch, almost. It was built during the mining days, maybe by the people who named the place.

They did quite a bit of mining at Blossom Bar, and they had to haul in all the machinery and supplies. Ruell Hawkins hauled some of it upriver, maybe from Agness, and Aubery hauled some stuff downriver, from Grants Pass. It is still there, most of it, just abandoned when they quit the mines.

Blossom Bar was the hardest place to shoot. It took a lot of bombing in there. For about one hundred fifty feet we couldn't get in the water, when we were running the river. We had to take the boats over the tops of the boulders from one to another.

We will go on down the river first, then come back and talk some more about Blossom Bar. Next we come to Devil's Stairs, just below Stair Creek Falls. We didn't do much to that; I really don't remember shooting any there, but we did shoot some at Tacoma. Then we blasted quite a bit at Clay Hill, farther on downriver. Then comes Two-Mile Riffle and Shasta Costa, between Illahe and Agness. We cleared the channel through them. Shasta Costa was an ornery one — bedrock clear across the river — wide and thin — made the water pretty shallow. We did a lot of blasting in there.

That was the farthest down we did any, just above Agness a ways. Below that there was nothing that needed shooting.

Bob Pritchett helped me some, and one of the Pyle boys was with me one time. Charley Foster helped me quite a few times. Then different people came along to help at different times. My next door neighbor, Nick Curnow, was with me one time, too.

There are a number of methods of blasting, depending on the conditions you find. For the most part, we used dynamite. It was very effective under water, much more so than on land, because you can keep the air away from it.

You take the sticks of dynamite, whatever amount you figure it will take to do the job and make it into a bundle. We always used two fuses, because we didn't want to get a misfire. We always used at least two and a half feet of fuse. That gave us two and a half minutes, from the time we lit the fuses until it would blow, to get away.

We used two giant caps to each load — two caps and two fuses — as a guarantee against a misfire. If one didn't go, the other one surely would. We would crimp the caps, with a crimper, and grease them, so water couldn't get into the primer. If that happened it would kill the cap. We'd use some kind of heavy grease, like automobile grease, anything that would shed water. You had to be careful about making them waterproof, by crimping and greasing them, because if you had a misfire and went back to see what happened, you might get bombed.

Lining boat through middle chute of Rainie Falls. The lining chute used today is to the left of this one. Glen Wooldridge collection

Now suppose that this is a big boulder. It's in your way and you want it taken out. The water is swift and flowing right down to it, then splits to one side or the other, or maybe to both sides. You can move it out all right.

We'd tie a rock to our bundle of dynamite so it would have some weight. Then we'd come up from below, especially after we got motors for our boats, and run right up to the rock to be blown.

While the fellow in the bow of the boat would be lighting his fuses, we would get in as close as possible. Run our boat right up to the rock. Then he would drop the bundle of dynamite right above the rock, where there'd be no current. There would be current on either side, but none right above the rock. Now the bundle is up against the boulder and underwater. Then we'd get the hell out of there fast.

Beforehand, of course, you have figured out just what big boulder you're going to hide behind, and where you are going to stick your head when the blast goes off. We would try to get someplace where we couldn't get hit. It would blow the rocks out in big chunks, usually. We could hear the big chunks hitting here and there, all around us, but we wouldn't get hit, unless one ricocheted off another boulder or something.

Of course you can't get your boat covered up, like you can your head. One time we got a rock thrown right through the boat, when we were blasting Clay Hill. It left a big hole in the boat.

There are some places you can't get to in the boat, when you are blasting. So the next best thing is to use a piece of pipe. You rustle up some old half-inch water pipe that has been thrown away, in sections long enough to reach from the riverbanks to the rock you are going to take out. You tie your bundle of powder to the pipe, wrap it around there good, then run your fuse up the pipe and tie that. You lay it right in there where you want it. You've got your pipe that will reach over to the shore, and you pile rocks on that. You measure and find out where it's going to come to, first, then have your rocks piled up, ready to stack on it so it will stay there. You put a rope on it, light the fuse and get out of the way.

The best powder to use is 40 percent stumping. That's not a very high percentage, but for some reason that works best. You can take a boulder that is ten feet through, put a bundle of ten or twelve sticks of dynamite under it, get it located just right, and it will take it right out slicker than a bean.

You shoot them hard! Load it heavy enough so it doesn't just break it up, or else you still have it in your way. Put in enough powder that you think will do the job, then add some more. If you can get it under the rock, so much the better, but up against it will usually roll her out.

I remember one time at Blossom Bar we shot a fifty pound box of powder at one shot. That kind of shook things up a bit. There were three big boulders leaning together with a big hole in the middle. We just put in fifty pounds of powder and eliminated all three of them.

Andy Huggins, who lived at the top of Devil's Stair and on the other side of the river, about a quarter of a mile away, came down and complained that we had shot a boulder into his yard.

Sometimes there is a large boulder that you can see buried in the gravel. You put a light charge there, try to roll it out of its hole. Get it up on top, then shoot it again.

Of course, we could have used a detonator, but we never did.

We just kept experimenting, and we made lots of mistakes. For instance, at first we thought we could get the load of powder on top of the boulder, but we found if we did that it would just break to the water line. That's as far as it would go. It won't break underneath, because the water halts it. So you put the charge under the water, against the rock; that's very effective.

At places like Blossom Bar we shot the bottom boulders out first. That is, the ones at the lower end of the channel. Then we got up above and shot the ones up there and let the water in. It made it a lot better.

When we first built a channel down through Blossom Bar, in the late 1930s, it was just a big pile of boulders all the way. Big rocks. Some of them half as big as this room. We opened up the south side, but that wouldn't do it. The bank goes up, right steep, and there were piles of heavy stuff. The blasting shook it all up so that every winter, during high water, large boulders would roll back into the channel. We'd have to go in there, every spring, and bomb it out again. It would stay open only until the next high water.

That went on for several years, then we went in there and blew a hole out through the middle and that stayed open.

We did lots of shooting, burned up lots of powder, but powder wasn't much of a problem, because the Forest Service was furnishing it. I remember they delivered a thousand pounds to me at one time, at Blossom Bar.

I wish the BLM would give me permission and the powder, I would go down and shoot Blossom Bar out again, and stop so many people from getting drowned. There have been three or four people drowned there every year for the last two or three years.

It is still the worst place on the river. You could get into trouble there quicker than anyplace. If anyone isn't familiar with the river and goes down the wrong side, they will run right into a trap, that's all. You just can't run that left side. That's been tried several times. I don't know of anybody that's been through that way.

One time some guys ran up there with a motor boat. They got above Blossom Bar and their motor went bad. They came down to our cabin with Bruce and told me their boat was up there. I told them I would run it through for them, if they wanted me to, but they wouldn't agree to that. So they went up and tried to line it down and lost the whole sheboodle. The water was high, but they could have got it through by staying on the right side of the channel. I could have towed it right down through the middle, but they wouldn't have that.

People don't realize the danger. They just don't see the danger until it is too late.

The last time I ran the river, about 1978, I followed a group of eight boats, and by the time they got to the foot of Devil's Stairs, seven of them had tipped over. Only one guy got through right side up.

I usually made a trip down, early in the summer, before I started my scheduled runs, to see if anything had washed in anywhere along the river. One year, on my first trip, I found a log right across Mule Creek Canyon. I had to go over it, that first trip down, but the next time the river had dropped, and when I got down to it, I took an axe and chopped a niche in it, loaded it with powder, put a boulder on top of that to break it down, and kicked it right out of there.

Now, about the Dunn Riffle blasting story. That was about 1949, sort of late in the blasting years. I had started a tour boat run from the city park to Hellgate and back. It was a 50 mile run, and we'd stop for lunch at Galice. That's the same run Gary Woolsey makes now, with his big Hellgate Excursion jet boats.

I meant to put two boats on the run, and the businessmen in town thought it was a great idea. They were backing me on it, the Chamber of Commerce and everybody, thinking it would be good for business. I built one boat here, in Grants Pass, a twenty-six footer that would carry six passengers. I was charging $5.50 a person. I meant to get Ruell Hawkins to put an inboard in the other one for me — a thirty-two footer — that would carry twenty passengers, if everything worked out all right, but I was holding back on that, to see how it would go.

There was a big rock that I wanted to take out, in Dunn Riffle, just below Hellgate, about fifteen miles downriver from Grants Pass. I thought it would be a little safer for the passengers, and too, I could go over it easier with my motor boat, using a prop.

I had been blasting rocks out of the river for a long time, by then, and the Forest Service had been furnishing the powder. But I kind of got ashamed of myself for bumming them so much. I went to the circuit court judge, Orville Millard, who was a pretty good friend of mine. Back then the judge acted also as one of the county commissioners. So I asked him, "Could you negotiate a deal with the county for me and get me some powder to blow out some rocks?"

He told me he would give it a try. So, through the county road department, he got me a couple of boxes of powder. I took it down and was blasting the rocks out of Dunn Riffle, and had just about finished the job, when the state police came down and stopped me.

It was Phil Bureau and Bill Allen, state policemen, who came down and arrested me. They said Orville Robertson had issued a complaint. I was supposed to have a permit, they told me.

Well I knew that, and I had gone to the fish biologist here at that time and he had issued a verbal permit. But the state fish commission was the only body able to issue a legal permit to shoot out the rocks.

While the case was pending, I don't know just when it was to come up in court, I was going down Sixth Street when I bumped into an attorney named Miller. He had been Judge Millard's law partner before Millard got to be judge.

"How are you getting along with your rock-shooting case?" he asked me.

I told him it looked like we were going to have to go to court.

"Would you like to have some help on that?" he asked.

"Sure looks like I'm going to need it," I told him. So he and his partner prepared the case. It went to justice court; Millard didn't sit on the case. But we won and I asked for my bill from Miller.

"That's all been taken care of," he told me.

Quite a long while after that, I met the judge on the street and he said, "I had to shut that up. I was right in the middle of it." He got Miller to defend me so he would be left out of it.

The fish biologist admitted he gave me a verbal permit, but he wasn't authorized to do so.

Judge Millard used to mention that to me every once in a while. "You almost got me in jail," he would say.

Bruce running Kelsey Falls before the channel was changed by blasting.
Glen Wooldridge collection

Glen and helpers blasted big rock on right (arrow) and it looped up and over large boulder in center, landing in channel at left.   Bruce Wooldridge collection

Glen tries out the new channel.   Glen Wooldridge collection

Glen's Hellgate Tours, 1949, loading out for downriver trip.   Glen Wooldridge collection

Hellgate tour boat making return trip, 1949.   Glen Wooldridge collection

Hellgate Excursions photo

Woolsey's Hellgate Excursions, 1980, in Hellgate canyon.

Blasting Clay Hill Riffle.　　　　　　　　　　　　　　Glenn Ballou, photographer

Bruce and Glen at Tyee.　　　　　　　　　　　　　Bruce Wooldridge collection

Stair Creek Falls.

Glen Wooldridge collection

Glen at Devil's Stair.   Bruce Wooldridge collection

Glen Wooldridge collection

Blossom Bar before Glen blasted the channel.

174

Lifting boats over boulders at Blossom Bar. Bruce Wooldridge collection

Bruce running Blossom Bar during high water.

Glen Wooldridge collection

Chapter Seventeen

Up the Rogue in a Boat

During those first twenty to twenty-five years of downriver guiding, Glen kept thinking how it would be to make an upriver run. As early as 1941 he was convinced that such a trip could be made. He started testing and experimenting with boats and equipment to make the trip.

He knew it was going to take a powerful motor to pull the 800-foot drop in the thirty-four mile stretch of wild river between Foster Bar and Grave Creek. The drift boats they were using at that time weren't built right for such a run, but he was sure he could build one, adapted especially for a motor, that would make the trip.

About the time he began to seriously consider the attempt, the United States became involved in World War II. Supplies needed for the trip were reserved for the war effort, and all the outboard motors produced at that time were going into military use.

When the war was over, Glen bought some of the surplus motors built for war use. They were 22 HP Evinrudes, not very well built, nor as powerful as he would have liked, but he spent time making trial runs and gauging their strength against the falls and rapids of the Rogue.

That was quite an experiment; the motors didn't amount to much, back then. I had to wait several years, until they came up with a motor I thought would do the job. In 1947, they came out with a good 22 horse Evinrude, but the propeller on it wasn't much good. We had to get them to work it over to our specifications.

If a prop isn't made right it has a tendency to slip, to cavitate, where there is a lot of air in the water. The two-blade propeller wasn't worth a hoot for upriver running. The first good one we got to work was an aluminum prop from Evinrude. It was a three-blade flat propeller.

The diameter and pitch of the prop are very important. We did a lot of experimenting to find out what would be the best job on a certain motor.

A motor has to turn up about its recommended speed or you don't get

much power out of it. So we had to change the pitch of the propeller to get it down so we could get the right rpm of the motor.

A lot of trial and error went into that stuff, but running up the Rogue was a big thing. It had never been done. That was a real good advertising stunt, good for my guiding business.

The boat Glen built for the trip was twenty feet, two inches long, with a seven foot, four inch beam. It had plenty of rake and flare. He painted it bright red so it would show up in the water.

It was a pretty sturdy boat. We made it out of five-sixteenths-inch marine plywood on the sides and half-inch marine plywood for the bottom. It had ribs made of Port Orford cedar. We were trying to build a boat that would stay on top of the water, ride the water, not plow through it.

It had two sets of oarlocks so two men could be on the oars at the same time. I asked Charley Foster and Bob Pritchett to go along with me to man the oars. They had been working with me long enough, by then, that they pretty well knew the river. We still didn't know, though, if that motor would make it up some of the worst places, so it was very important to have good men at the oars.

We took along some extra equipment, three extra props, I think, and an extra magneto assembly, and extra drive shaft pins, just in case.

Some of the places we were expecting to have trouble were Blossom Bar, of course; Tyee; Upper Black Bar and Black Bar Falls; then Rainie Falls and Grave Creek Falls. We didn't really believe we could run the falls.

We had a fairly dry winter, that year, and the river was about two foot lower than I was hoping for, but we decided to start anyway.

Tidewater Associated Oil Company furnished the gasoline, through a local dealer, and we had Fred Hale all set up to fly an extra supply down to Black Bar for us.

Several newspapers and magazines and newsreel companies had showed interest in covering the trip. When the *Oregon Journal* newspaper heard about it, they sent word they would have a helicopter fly over us to take pictures. But they couldn't get off the day we planned, on account of making repairs on their helicopter. We postponed the trip for a couple of days so they could cover it.

We put the boat in at the old ferry landing on Indian Creek, just a ways up-river from Gold Beach, on May 7, 1947, at about 7:00 in the morning. We made the run down to the mouth of the river, just to say we went from there to Grants Pass, then we took off upriver.

We didn't have any troubles until we got to Blossom Bar, but of course, we had to line the boat upriver there. At that time we hadn't blasted the channel out through the center, but we couldn't have made it anyway, with that 22 horse motor. We were grossly underpowered. Lining the boat meant we had to take the motor off the boat, carry it and all the supplies around and over the boulders and line the boat upriver like we had been lining it down on the guiding trips.

We got all that done, then we were doing all right, as well as we could expect, anyway, until we got to Marial. The state police stopped us there.

They told us Jack Mahoney, the hermit that lived down near Battle Bar, had killed his neighbor, Bob Fox, and had left a sign on a tree that he was going to shoot me. They held us over at Marial, while they were out looking for him.

Mahoney had lived, for something like forty years, in a little cabin on the hill on the south side of the river, but overlooking the river at Hewett Bar. We would see him sometimes as we went by.

Bob Fox came from Iron Mountain, Michigan, and moved onto Battle Bar, a mile or so above Mahoney's and on the same side of the river. He did some building at Battle Bar, intending to run a lodge to take care of fishing parties. Fox was Mahoney's only neighbor, really, for any reasonable distance.

A few weeks before we made the run Bob Pritchett was working for me, hauling dudes downriver, and he saw Mahoney following along down through the willows on the bank as he was drifting along, letting the dudes fish.

He could see that Mahoney had his rifle, so Bob got out of there fast. He suspicioned that this guy was going to shoot him.

Bob Fox wasn't the regular sort of Rogue River hermit. He was only about forty years old and the son of wealthy lumber people from Michigan. He had been spending quite a lot of time and money fixing up his lodge and had been living there.

He often brought in provisions and supplies on his trips from Grants Pass and gave them to his neighbors, Jack Mahoney and Jimmy Coe. Fresh bread was a luxury to the hermits, and anyone who made a trip out usually brought a fresh loaf back for each of them.

Bill Brockman lived at the Miller cabin, across the river from Battle Bar. It was the access road to his place, via the Bald Ridge road, that Bob Fox used. He would park his Ford roadster there and take his boat and cross the river to Battle Bar.

Fox's signal to Coe and Mahoney was a shot fired into the air. They would usually appear from the woods to get whatever he brought them.

Things seemed to be going peacefully for a time, with some of the men gathering at one place or another to play racehorse pinochle. Hard feelings might have developed over an imagined cheating at one of these games, but the people along the river thought Mahoney had been acting strangely for some time.

Mahoney and Jimmy Coe had words, on Mahoney's finding Jimmy at his cabin. Rumors held that Mahoney had a jar of gold nuggets stashed at his cabin, and he suspected Jimmy of coming up there to search for them.

Jimmy Coe told me about one time when Mahoney came up to his house and gave him a good going over, talking, that is, not beating. Jimmy said he let Mahoney start back down the mountain, then got his rifle and cut across a short cut and came out on the trail in front of Mahoney.

When Mahoney came around the bend Jimmy was standing there, waiting for him with his rifle leveled at Mahoney.

"Mr. Mahoney wasn't bad, atall, after that." Jimmy told me.

Bob Fox had paid Mahoney a visit, and, on finding that he wasn't home, had sat on his porch for a while before going home. Mahoney came and caught him there and told him to "git going or git shot."

Cole Rivers, the fish biologist on the Rogue, who was studying that area at that time, told of being at Fox's cabin one morning and seeing Mahoney standing behind an apple tree with his rifle pointed toward Fox's lodge.

He said Bob Fox shot three times over the top of the apple tree, "Just to let the s.o.b. know he knew he was there."

All that had happened four or five months before Glen started his trip upriver, but the rancor must have remained.

Mahoney decided to kill all of the people around that country. He called them 'honyocks,' and said he was going to kill them off.

When we got to Marial (we had been a day late in starting so the helicopter could get there) we found out that Mahoney had been there the day before. That was the day we were really supposed to be there. He had his gun with him and told the people that he was looking for me.

He had already killed Fox and left a note on a tree, at Winkle Bar, telling what his plans were and stating that he had killed Fox and had been up on the hill, to shoot Brockman. He said Brockman had company and he didn't want to disturb the company, so he didn't kill him. I thought that was a kind thought.

The murder and other happenings connected with it were reconstructed this way: when Bob Fox got up in the morning, Mahoney was waiting for him, as he had done the night Cole Rivers spent at Fox's lodge. Mahoney waited until Fox went into his woodshed to get wood for his morning fire, then shoved his 30-30 rifle barrel through a knothole, and shot Bob Fox from the back. The shot entered Fox's left shoulder, went through his body, and came out the lower right abdomen.

Fox made it back into his lodge and to his bed, where he kept a 38 caliber special, with extra shells, on a nearby window. He fired thirty-one shots, signaling for help, before he died.

Bill Brockman, at his own house, heard the shots, but was afraid Fox and Mahoney were having a shoot-out, so instead of approaching the place he went to Marial for help. They contacted the state police from Marial, and Joe Madarus, the trooper usually assigned to the area, went to investigate. It was almost night when he reached Brockman's and there was no boat available to cross the river to Fox's place. Madarus had to swim the river. He found Fox's body and a note Fox managed to write before he died, saying he suspected it was Mahoney who shot him.

A good-sized crew of lawmen and volunteers was sent to search for Mahoney. While the investigation was going on, a rock was thrown into the window of the Marial post office, with a note tied to it, reading:

> To Whom it may concern.
> It is a terrible thing to kill, but I did it.
> I would have killed that Miller Bohunk but that
> woman and kids were there. I didn't want to scare
> them, of course. They had been robbing my cabin.

The FBI and Treasury Department will get Bruckman.

Coe is in on it, too.

John Mahoney

DED BOHUNK ON BATTLE BAR.

The "Miller Bohunk" referred to in the note, was thought to mean Brockman, who was caretaker at the Miller Place. Brockman refused to be taken out of the area for his own safety. He said he would carry his gun, too, and if he met Mahoney they would shoot it out. The police put out spotters in strategic places to wait for sign of Mahoney. They knew that he could live a long time without needing outside help and that they would be in grave danger hunting through the woods for him.

But Mahoney wasn't hiding out in the woods. He had gone down to Andy Huggins place, on Half Moon Bar, and spent the night, having supper and breakfast with the frightened Huggins. Early the next day, armed with his rifle, he went to the lower end of the bar, probably intending to wait for Glen and shoot him as he came upriver.

As Glen made his way upriver, the *Oregon Journal* helicopter was flying overhead. It is supposed that Mahoney thought it was the state police, looking for him, and became frightened. Huggins reported that he heard a shot, then found Mahoney in the field at the lower end of the bar, shot through the head.

Huggins ran the three miles to Marial to report the suicide. Later a sign was found, nailed to a tree at Winkle Bar. It read:

Dead Bohunk on Battle Bar.
Take my boat to get him and put it
back where you got it. This will slow
up the skunk for some time. If I only
can get Wooldridge. I just missed the chance.

Mahoney

While most of this was going on, Glen didn't know about it. The trip upriver ran into difficulty at Black Bar Falls. They had to make four attempts before clearing this five-foot steep climb, and it took Glen at the motor and all four hands at the oars to do it.

The boat had to be lined up Rainie Falls and Grave Creek Falls, but the rest of the run was made with the motor.

Anywhere people could get to the riverbanks, they waited to see the boat come by. When Glen and his crew arrived at Riverside Park, in Grants Pass, at six o'clock in the evening on May 9, there was a big crowd waiting to greet them.

It had taken fourteen hours and fifteen minutes running time to make that first trip up the Rogue.

The story of the trip was written for several newspapers, including the *Oregon Journal* and the Grants Pass *Courier*. *Field and Stream* magazine and *Let's Get Associated* also published stories of the run.

Jack Mahoney's body was buried where it was found, on Winkle Bar.

Glen and Charley Foster running Dunn Riffle, 1947. This was a shakedown cruise before the big run.

Glen Wooldridge collection

Helicopter photo of first run up Rogue River, 1947, showing Glen's boat in Mule Creek Canyon.

Oregon Journal photo

A stopover at Black Bar Lodge; left to right; Hal Witherwox, Red Keller, Bea Witherwox, unidentified man and Glen.

Bruce Wooldridge collection

Fred Hale flew in with extra gasoline to Black Bar Lodge Bruce Wooldridge collection

End of first run up the Rogue, 1947 left to right, Bob Pritchett, Glen, and Charley Foster.
Glen Wooldridge collection

Chapter Eighteen

Up the River of No Return

Glen's run up the Rogue, in 1947, just whetted his appetite for whitewater running. He had been hearing a lot about the Salmon River, over in Idaho. People had been making drift trips down it for years, and they called it "The River of No Return," saying that it was impossible for anyone to go up it.

Glen read all he could find about the Salmon, from books and magazines, but there wasn't too much to go on. He found a Forest Service map, outdated, but showing the course of the river. He decided he would try running upriver the next year, without ever having drifted it. He knew he would have to depend on his ability to read the water to pick a running channel and locate the obstacles from what the water revealed to him.

It was 180 miles to run and the river drops 2500 feet in that distance. I never had seen the river, but I knew there had to be some pretty big rapids somewhere with that much fall to the river. It falls much faster than the Rogue.

Evinrude Motors had come out with a 33-horse outboard, at that time, and they shipped one to Glen for the trip. He built a new boat with a semi-V type keel and a high bow with a sheer forward that lifted the forefoot cleanly out of the water. At testing he found it drew about eight inches of water at rest.

I built it a little longer than the one I ran the Rogue in the year before. I made this one 22 feet long. I decided the longer boat would keep the propeller in the water longer when the boat was going up the rougher places. That cuts down on that cavitation a little.

Glen planned to make the run from Riggins to Salmon City and to take about four days for the trip. After finding as much as he could about the seasonal rise and fall of the water, he decided the proper time to make the trip would be early in July, after the initial runoff, but before the water got too low.

This time he asked Ruell Hawkins, a boatman on the lower Rogue, to go along and handle the oars.

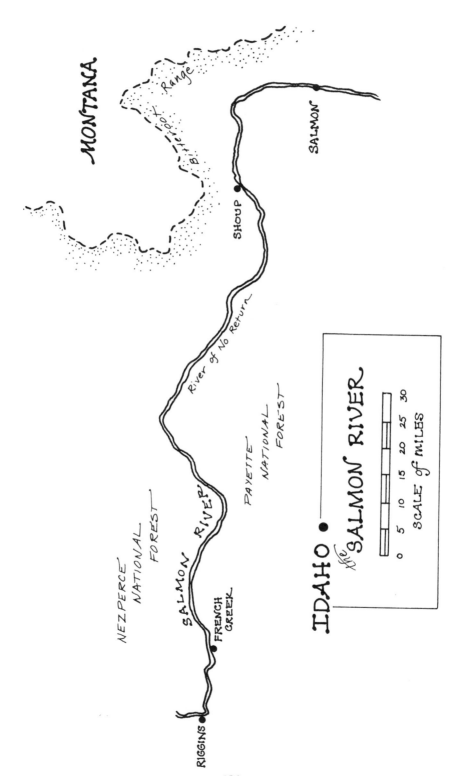

MONTANA

Bitterroot Range

SALMON

SHOUP

River of No Return

NEZ PERCE NATIONAL FOREST

SALMON RIVER

PAYETTE NATIONAL FOREST

FRENCH CREEK

RIGGINS

IDAHO ●

the SALMON RIVER

0   5   10   15   20   25   30

SCALE of MILES

Ruell was one of the Billings tribe down at Agness. He was a quiet sort of fellow, didn't have too much to say, but he was a good boatman, probably the best one on the river at that time. Tom Staley went along with us to take pictures.

They trailered the boat from Grants Pass to Riggins, then drove along the dirt road that went up the river a few miles, looking the rapids over.

Where we put the boat in, Riggins, was just a little town at the foot of the canyon. We didn't have a ramp or any special place to put a boat in the river, because there wasn't anybody boating in that country at that time. We just had to find a place where it wasn't too much trouble to put the boat in.

A crowd gathered to see what they were doing, putting a boat like that in the river. When Glen told them he was going to run upstream as far as Salmon they laughed at him, and told him that it would be a suicide trip.

One old fellow told us, "My place is upriver, just above Lake Creek Rapids. It's only about four or five miles. You can drive up that far and take a look at the river, then you'll see you can't make it."

I told him we had already been up that far and we didn't see anything we couldn't run. I offered to bet anyone of them a hundred dollars we could make it, but I didn't get any takers. But this one fellow got pretty abusive about it, telling us in rather harsh language that we would never make it over Lake Creek Rapids.

We took along a 22 hp motor for a spare and were loaded heavy, as we had to take all our gasoline and oil. We had about 400 pounds of gasoline along. We took off, and a few miles up from Riggins we came across a guy who was tending the water gauge. He told us he'd been around there fifty years and that no boat had ever made it through.

Lake Creek Rapids were pretty rough, all right, but we made it through okay.

When we got past, there was that old fellow who had told us we never would make it. He was standing there sort of slack-jawed that we had made it that far, but he still wasn't too happy about it.

He told us, "You might have lucked your way up that one, but you won't make it up Ruby Rapids, and I will be waiting down here to pick up the pieces."

Ruby Rapids did slow them down a bit. They tried to run it with the full load, but with the water so high, it was a short, steep falls. When they got to the top there was just too much grade for them to get over the hump. They had to back down and try it again, this time in the middle, with a lightened load. The boat would make it almost to the top, then just hang. The motor would be pulling, but without enough power to buck over the hump.

Finally it was necessary to back down and line the boat through the edge of the rapids and over the falls. An old miner sat on a rock on the riverbank and watched all the goings-on. Later he told that he had helped them take the boat overland.

Glen handled the boat by standing erect and using a long-handled tiller with the throttle attached. That way he could see what was ahead, at least some of the time. There are some tremendous rapids on this stretch of the river.

They camped the first night on one named the Growler, reputed to be very dangerous. Then came Mackay Bar, at the mouth of South Fork. Mackay was the first known to lose his life trying to go down by boat. Another rough one was Big Mallard Rapids, with a reputation for the loss of many boats that tried to run down it.

When the people living in the cabins along some stretches of the river would hear the sound of the boat motor, they would come running out, looking up at the sky. They told the boatmen they thought it was a plane about to crash in the canyon. They couldn't imagine its being a motor boat on that isolated stretch of the canyon.

Invariably they would tell Glen, "You can't get any farther up the river. You are going the wrong way."

His standard answer was, "Yes, we are going upriver to Salmon City. Where are we now?"

His outdated Forest Service map didn't tell him enough about the river so that he could identify the falls and rapids they were going over.

We'd been going along, looking for the Hot Springs, when we saw a fellow on the riverbank. We pulled in and asked him how far it was to the Hot Springs.

"They are about six miles up the river," he said.

We traveled on the rest of that afternoon, camped for the night, then, next morning, we ran along for quite some time before we saw another old miner. We asked him how far the Hot Springs were.

"About six miles on up the river," he told us.

Well that was just too much for Hawkins. He was a typical Indian; getting a word out of him was like pulling out a tooth. But this time he came out with, "Huh, guess we ain't losing nothing, are we?"

At the mouth of Crooked River a small creek comes in, and an old man by the name of Kleinkenheimer lived there. We knew we were getting somewhere below the fork of South Salmon River, but we didn't know just how close. We asked Kleinkenheimer about how far it was.

He said, "I don't know for sure, but I think it must be about ten miles."

"How long have you lived here?" I asked him.

He told me, "I came here in 1910." He had lived there that long, thirty-eight years, and hadn't been ten miles upriver.

We found out that Polly Creek, near there, was named after a Chinese woman, Polly Bemis, who was brought to San Francisco as a slave during the gold mining days. A miner named Bemis won her in a poker game and married her. He took her to his mining claim in the canyon and they lived there the rest of their lives. Her cabin was still standing.

At one long steep rapids they tried to run, they found they couldn't make it. Glen retreated downriver to lighten the load. They decided the easiest way would be for Staley and Hawkins to walk while Glen maneuvered the boat up the rapids. Glen made it okay, but the hikers found their way blocked by a cliff jutting out into the water. Others barricaded their path by land. Their only way of going on was to wade the river in waist deep water while clinging to the face of the cliff. Staley said their toes made it strictly by feel.

The thing we always had to watch out for was to keep from washing back into a boulder, or getting ourselves in a trap above a bunch of boulders. If the prop let go, or we sheared a pin, or the motor conked out, we would have gone backwards, slamming into the boulders. That was the greatest danger.

When we had to back down, when the boat just wouldn't make it over the top, we just slacked back on the power. Ruell was there to use the oars. He would grab them and try to get us to shore, and keep the boat from turning crossways if he could. He was our emergency power, in case something went wrong with the motor.

We had a lot of trouble with the propeller just letting go of the water. It was a poorly-shaped prop to begin with, and then with the big, bulky lower unit, it would go into a fit of cavitation, and wouldn't pull anything until we got it to grab hold again.

If a propeller isn't made right, it has a tendency to slip, to cavitate. Where there is a lot of air in the water, it just lets go. Then we'd have to go back and try it again.

But that was partly our fault. We didn't have the motor set properly in the water. The tilt was wrong. But back then we were just trying to find out something. That was pretty early in the motor boating. I found out if you tilt the prop under a little closer to the boat, you get away from a lot of cavitation. That keeps the prop in the water longer going up a steep place.

When they came to Sheep Creek Rapids, they began to think the old timers had been right about this being the river of no return. They twisted their way up and around dozens of big boulders in a steep hundred yard climb, reached the top of a steep slick and hung there. Glen could hold the boat in that position, but couldn't make it kick on over.

The bow of the boat was pointed into the air. When finally the bow did go down and they thought they had it made, the stern came out of the water and the propeller sucked air. They lost their power, and the swift water sent them spinning downstream. Hawkins grabbed the oars and kept them away from the boulders until Glen got the boat under control again.

Glen decided he would have to back the boat downriver to a landing spot and lighten the load. Throttling back on the motor, he let the current carry them, but with the power of the motor pulling against it, they weren't entirely at the mercy of the river. With the lightened load they managed to make it over the top.

Glen ran the boat only about five hours each day because of the fierce strain of handling the boat against the rough, forceful river. They camped on the sandbars at night and cooked over campfires. Wild game was plentiful in the isolated canyon and the only way into the middle section was by pack horse. They saw mountain goats, mountain sheep, lots of deer and elk, and even one baby moose.

We had been on the lookout for Salmon Falls because we had heard it was such a rough place, but we made it over it okay. In fact, we didn't even know that was what we had just run until we pulled up at Big Squaw Creek and here came two men, rushing down to the boat. One of them jumped into the boat, grabbed my hand and started shaking it. He said, "Now I have seen everything."

By the time we got to Panther Creek, not too far above the mouth of Middle Fork, we were about out of gas. We decided to take out at Shoup, the end of the road from Salmon downstream.

We felt, by that time, that we had proved our point: that the Salmon could be run. But the editor of the newspaper at Salmon City, Ronald Burke, told us he wanted to publish a story about our run.

There was another famous rapids below Salmon City, a ways, called Pine Creek Rapids. It had a bridge over it, and people had gathered on that bridge, waiting for us to come upriver. When we didn't come on up, they decided we either didn't make it that far or had been afraid to try. Burke wanted us to run on up to Salmon City so that the people could stand on that bridge and watch us go up the Pine Creek Rapids, which had a reputation for being pretty bad.

We agreed to do it and I got in touch with Carl Brower, who ran a service station in Salmon City and had him bring me a supply of gasoline. I told Burke I would lay over a day so he could get his paper out to the people. That would give them a chance to watch, if they wanted to.

When we made the run, there was a lot of people on the bridge and the riverbanks, but there wasn't much to running the rapids. It didn't amount to anything compared to all we had run below there.

When we ran on into Salmon there were several hundred people waiting to see the finish of the trip. They were all really excited. Carl Brower and another fellow, Joe Herndon, bought the boat, intending to keep it on display there at Salmon.

We didn't have to use the spare motor. And we had a couple of spare props, but the one we had on the motor was the best one we had, so we couldn't change. It took us about twenty-two hours running time to make the 180 miles. We hired a plane to fly us back to Riggins, then drove back home in the car.

The run received wide-spread newspaper coverage. Tom Staley wrote the story of the run for *Pacific Motor Boat* magazine for February, 1949 and for *Outdoor Life*, April, 1957. It was also published in *Oregon Outdoors*, 1970.

Glen and Ruell Hawkins, first trip up the Salmon River in Idaho, The River of No Return,
1948. Tom Staley photo

Glen and Ruell at first riffle above Riggins, 1948.   Tom Staley photo

Glen and Ruell on Salmon River, 1948.   Tom Staley photo

End of first run up the Salmon, "River of No Return". Glen with Carl Brower who bought the boat at Salmon City. Note people on the bridge. Tom Staley photo

Rogue River, May 7, 1948. Preparing for an upriver run.   Glen Wooldridge collection

Chapter Nineteen

Glen Stars in a Movie with a New York Premiere

The following May, 1949, found Glen on the Rogue making another upriver run. He had safety men, Foster and Pritchett, with him, and this time Elzie Abel, a Grants Pass cameraman, went along. Elzie had a new Bolex camera, loaded with Technicolor movie film. They were going to record the upriver run on film.

Glen had built a 22-foot boat and was using the four-cylinder, 33½ hp motor sent to him by the Evinrude Company. General Petroleum was furnishing the gas and oil.

We didn't have any trouble, at least not any more than expected. We had a little trouble, of course, with the cavitation, but we had learned to expect that. On most of the worst places I had to run them twice. I'd take Elzie up and get him set on the bank where he could get a good shot, then go back and run it again so he could take his pictures.

That motor took a terrific beating coming upriver, and even with a 33½ — horse this time we were underpowered, bumping up the steep falls and rapids shakes a boat all to hell.

That motor was designed to turn up about 4000 rpm. I had my eye on one over in Hubbard Wray's window (Medford). It was a 50-horse that would turn up to about 5000 rpm. I had in mind to get Evinrude to send me one like that to run the Salmon with later on in the year.

They made the trip in good time, and Elzie got about 1200 feet of professional quality pictures of the trip.

We found out on those trips that the Rogue was just as tough to run as the Salmon: only thing, there were about five times as many miles of rough water on the Salmon as the Rogue. The Salmon is a much bigger river. It doesn't have the narrow chutes like Mule Creek Canyon. We had some pretty exciting times on both of them, though.

Later that year Glen went to the Salmon again, taking along Ruell Hawkins and Bruce, Glen's son, to man the oars. Elzie Abel went to take pictures and another photographer, Merle Tobias, from California, accompanied them. They put the new Rogue #3, a 23½-footer, in at Riggins on July 11.

This time the water was about three feet above summer stage. In some places that made better running, but in others worse than the year before.

Evinrude sent me the 50-horse motor. It was quite a bit better than the 33½-horse, but we still had a little trouble. When we would back down out of a place, we would always drown the motor.

We had built a little extra transom up behind the motor, to try to overcome that, but it didn't do much good. The water still came over it, and the motor and carburetor were wide open. It would suck water into the carburetor, kill the motor, and then it'd be a job getting it going again.

We'd have to take the plugs out, spin it to get the water out of the cylinder, then put them back and get them all hitting again.

When we got to Lake Creek Rapids, we saw a fellow standing on the riverbank. When we went by he hollered out at us, "Where can I get a boat like that?"

We pulled over and I told him, "When we get to Salmon City, you can buy this one for $90."

Well, he kept in touch by Forest Service communications to make sure his boat got all the way up the river. He was Paul Keep, a college professor, over in that country. I sold him the boat and shipped him a motor. Later on I got a letter from him; all it said was, "I damned near killed myself."

A year or so later we stopped by their place and his wife said, "He made me ride on the front of the boat, watching for rocks. That isn't the way it's supposed to be done, is it?" I guess he had stopped too soon and threw her off into the water.

This time, with the lower water, we couldn't make it over Salmon Falls without lining the boat. The other time, with the higher water, we ran it.

Wasn't too much difference, except for the extra power of the motor. We had to run many of the places twice so that Elzie could get pictures. We made it okay. Guess Elzie got about 1800 feet of good film. That's the picture we show around at boat shows and fishermen's meetings when they ask us to.

Glen had another reason for remembering 1949. That was the year the state police arrested him for shooting the rocks from Dunn Riffle.

He had started his Hellgate Boat Tours, taking passengers from Grants Pass through Hellgate and back, but was having trouble making it over rougher places during the low-water season. There was danger of damaging his propeller on the rocks, but even worse danger of capsizing with the passengers aboard.

When he found he wouldn't be able to run the course with the motor riding the way it did, he started experimenting with building a motor-lift.

It took several years before it was free of problems, but he finally came up with a good, workable lift that raises the entire motor straight up out of the water to let it leapfrog over rocks and gravel in the course, even while underway.

I figured to get the prop back, away from the boat, and in the bulge of water that comes out from under the boat. That's what we were shooting for, really, with the lift. Then we could raise it and run in that hump of water instead of being down there in the rocks.

You have to remember that whatever your boat draft is, your prop is a foot deeper, without the lift. It is down there sticking out like a sore thumb, just ready to catch on anything that comes along.

With the lift, you let it down to start the motor, then raise it. That saves having to tip your motor. When you tip the motor, you get gasoline spills in the boat. The lift has a long handle to use in raising and lowering it.

You don't have to take your prop all the way out of the water, just enough to miss the obstructions; rocks or whatever it is that's in your way. We found it's really the thing for running whitewater with a prop.

It wasn't long until we were getting orders from all over the country, from U.S. Fish and Wildlife, the state fisheries, the army, guides up on the Yukon, sheriff's offices, fishermen, and surveyors. They used it over on the Snake River's Hell Canyon when they were making the survey. We got orders from Saskatchewan. We shipped them to Alaska, Florida, and even one to Venezuela. We still sell quite a few of them.

We call it the Jackass Lifter-Upper.

By then we had learned that the three-blade prop, like Evinrude made, was the best one to run the rivers with, but it still didn't have quite the right pitch. The diameter and pitch are very important. Later on, I got a fellow I knew, Whitchurch, who was a pattern maker, to help me design a prop I liked. We worked on it a while, made a model out of wood, and kept trimming it and casting it in aluminum until we got it just right.

We did the lifts the same way, made a model and cast it in aluminum. The first ones were made of steel and were very heavy.

One day, quite a while after the lifts had been on the market, I was down on the Rogue, for once without my boat, just dinking around. I saw a fellow with one of my lifts on his boat.

"What's that funny looking thing you have on your boat?" I asked him.

"Oh," he said, "that is just the thing. You can't run the Rogue without one of those." Then he went on to explain how it operated.

I asked him a few more questions about it, then I left without telling him I was the one who built it. I didn't dare tell him after pretending to be so ignorant about it.

It was April, 1951, before Glen ran up the Rogue again. That year, Kiekhaefer Corporation, manufacturers of Mercury outboard motors, sent Jack Camp, a writer, to make the upriver trip with him, and narrate a film. Dick Matt was the photographer.

Glen used a 25-horse Mercury Thunderbolt on a twenty foot, four inch, semi-V bottomed plywood boat. For ease in handling the boat, he had built a standup dashboard steering outfit. Bob Pritchett went along to handle the oars.

It was funny, because we hadn't really got started good — hadn't even got to Agness, before we sheared a pin. Then, of course, we had to line up Blossom

197

Bar, because, at that time, we hadn't blasted out the clear channel. There was a terrific drop-off there that the 25-horse just didn't have the power to pull over.

We had to run back and forth some of the rougher spots so the men could get the pictures, and we were doing pretty good until we got to Upper Black Bar. We broke a motor right in two, trying to run Upper Black Bar. Fred Hale was to bring us gasoline down there — fly it in, so we got in touch with him and told him to bring us another motor. But, of course, we didn't tell that around.

Another thing we didn't make too well-known was that we were using the Evinrude three-blade prop on the Mercury motor. All they had was a two-blade, and it just wouldn't do the job.

When we got to Rainie Falls, we had to drag the boat up the fishways. Then I didn't know whether I would be able to run Grave Creek Falls. Until that time we hadn't run it, but I gave it a try and made it okay. From there on it was easy running.

Actually we had to make another run. We went all the way back to Gold Beach and made another run for them, so they would be sure to have the pictures they wanted.

Jack Camp wrote the story for *Argosy* magazine, the August, 1951, issue. The story was titled, *Taming the Rogue,* and the cover picture was of Glen and Pritchett running Mule Creek Canyon.

Advertisements for Mercury outboards, showing Glen running the Rogue, appeared in *Argosy, Boating Industry,* and *Lakeland Yachting* that year.

Dick Matt's photos and story of the trip were in *Hunting and Fishing,* July, 1952.

The movie was called *The River Beyond.* Kiekhaefer Corporation arranged for Glen and Sadie to go to New York City to appear at the movie's premiere, shown on nationwide television. Glen made an appearance at the New York Boat Show and the entire column, *Hooks and Bullets,* in the New York *World-Telegram and Sun,* by Ray Thillinger, was about Glen.

When we went to New York, that was a big build-up. You see, after we made the picture, the following year they asked Sadie and me to come to New York as their guests. They put us up in a big hotel, the Roosevelt, I think it was, and told us we could stay as long as we wanted to. They gave us a guide to take us around the city. So we saw the city all right — went down in those gopher holes.

Then we went to the mouth of the Hudson, where the Statue of Liberty is sitting out in the river.

While Glen and Sadie were in New York, after their appearance at the movie's premiere, Glen was a contestant on THE STRIKE IT RICH SHOW. He was asked to appear for an invalid boy from Mississippi who wanted $255 to buy a gas heater for his home.

I did all right until it came to music. I don't know anything about music. But I won about $300 for him, I guess. I don't really know how we managed to get in on all that. I don't know who was pulling the strings. I think the things that impressed me most were the subways and the Statue of Liberty. We were there about a week, then we had all of New York City we needed, so we flew home.

Back home, Glen was caught up in his schedule of river trips. Some pretty important dudes signed on: former commanding general of the Army Air Force Carl Spaatz; Lt. Gen. Ira C. Eakers, U.S.A.D. retired; Noah Dietrich, Executive Vice-president of Hughes Tool Company; Dr. H. Herzikoff, Los Angeles surgeon; Dietrich's brother; and a friend, Mr. Elliot.

That trip led to other trips by the Generals, bringing General Twining, and others with them.

I remember when they came, there was whole schmeer of generals. Six of them. Ruell Hawkins and me, and someone else, Bob Pritchett, I guess, took them downriver.

They bought some property from me, and decided to build a cabin. It was Generals Spaatz and Eakers that bought it. By that time they were retired, and Spaatz was working for Newsweek magazine, and Eakers for Hughes Aircraft, but all the generals used it. It was twenty acres just across the river from Brushy Bar.

I built them a boat, and Ruell Hawkins was running it for them, bringing in the materials to build their cabin. Then, after they got the cabin built, he kept running it for them, because they just couldn't manage it.

I sure got tickled at that Indian, Hawkins, one day down there. He was coming upriver in his motor boat, and here were the generals. They had got over a little riffle in their boat and couldn't get back up.

It wasn't much of a place to get over, but they didn't know that. Hawkins had to help them back up over the riffle.

He was talking to me about it, later on, and he said, "And these are the guys that are protecting us."

He was running the river in that boat of theirs when he lost his life. There had just been a rise of high water, and it had undermined the river banks, and trees had tumbled in.

That was about five miles above Gold Beach. He had taken the boat down to Gold Beach, and he and another man were coming upriver; when he got to those trees he ran the boat in between them and stopped. When he came out and turned up river the motor died. He washed back into the tops of the trees and capsized.

The other man jumped into the tops of the trees when the boat turned over, but Ruell was on the side away from them, and he couldn't reach them. He washed on downriver and was drowned.

That was too bad that we lost him. He was really a good man. A good boatman, a good fellow, nice to get along with. A good companion; pretty sharp, too.

In April, 1952, Ted Trueblood, a writer for outdoor magazines, and photographer Harold Rhodenbaugh came to run the Rogue with Glen and Bob Pritchett. The river was high from recent rains and snowmelt when they began their trip from Gold Beach, adding to the challenge of the twenty-foot boat and thirty-three-horse Evinrude motor.

Trueblood, writing the story for *True* magazine's *Fishing Yearbook*, 1952, describes Glen's running one spot on the river this way:

"At Clay Hill Rapids, a few miles farther on, I deliberately turned away from the stream to watch him as we moved into the whitewater. He was standing spreadlegged, his muscular body perfectly balanced. His left hand held the steering arm; his right gripped the post behind the seat. His coat was flying open in the wind of our own making and his misshapen felt hat was pulled down tight.

The steady good humor still was in his face, but it was masked over now by a gleaming mixture of rapture and determination. This was it. This was one of the great times. This was what he loved, and as his sharp eyes scanned the rapids for hidden rocks they were as unaware of my scrutiny as those of a soaring eagle. It was the river and the man, alone, and the boat and motor were part of him, of course.

We edged along the side of the fastest water, nosed up and across a slick, hung a moment on the brink and then shot on away across a pool. I didn't grip the life preserver quite so tightly after that." (used by permission of author).

When they got to Blossom Bar, they found it was a regular waterfall about five feet high. Pritchett climbed a cliff and tied a rope to a madrone tree, and they pulled the boat upriver to near the falls. By using a set of blocks fastened to the bow ring and the rope from the cliff, they maneuvered the boat along the rocks, some thirty to forty feet, until they got it above the falls, then carried all the equipment and the motor up and mounted the motor again to make the trip on upriver.

This time, too, they had to line the boat up the fishways at Rainie Falls, but ran Grave Creek Falls.

The next year Glen decided to sell his schedule, boats, and equipment to Bob Pritchett and concentrate on building boats in semi-retirement. He, like Glenn Ballou, found it was easier to plan retirement than to carry it out.

Glen and Bob Pritchett during filming of Mercury Motors movie, title, The River Beyond.   Dick Matt, photogragher

Running Upper Black Bar Falls during the 1951 filming.   Dick Matt, photographer

This was the largest wooden boat Glen built. It was shipped to be used on the Snake River.
Bruce Wooldridge collection

Glen, showing one of the first Jackass motor lifts.   Glen Wooldridge collection

Los Angeles Boat Show, about 1952, Glen, center holding up the magazine. Glenn Ballou is third from right behind boat.
Glen Wooldridge collection

Chapter Twenty

Christmas Rescue on the Roaring Rogue

By 1955, Glen had been running rivers for forty years, in just about every stage of water except high flood. He had always given way to flood waters, with the twisting, rolling, up-rooted trees and debris they carried. That is why the Christmas flood of 1955 was to prove the true test of his courage and skill of boatmanship.

The storm started on the weekend of December 16, with snow and freezing rains falling over the Pacific Northwest. Trees toppled under the weight of the ice, and powerlines went down. Mud slides stopped traffic on some highways. Many airports were closed. Heavy winds and up to two inches of rain were general over the entire area. Grants Pass was deluged with 3.07 inches, but the Rogue crested at only 7.8 feet about noon on Sunday, the 18th.

By Monday, warm air was coming into the state and causing a general thaw. The heavy downpour continued, however, and by Wednesday there was flooding over all the Pacific Northwest. Nearly all the creeks and rivers were over their banks in Western Oregon. The Rogue was at 9.98 feet, and rising about eight inches an hour.

On Thursday it was evident that a crisis situation was at hand. Civil Defense Director Lloyd Haynes, took charge of Josephine County, and put an embargo on all non-essential travel and phone calls not connected with the emergency.

Eight Greyhound buses, with over 300 people on board, were stranded when the Rogue, now at high flood stage, buried the Pacific Highway under ten feet of water at Savage Rapids Dam. In Northern California whole communities were being evacuated. All roads leading into the Rogue Valley were closed. The C and OC railroad bridge over the Rogue, just outside Grants Pass, fell to the river's rush.

The Rogue rose to 30.1 feet, the highest since the turn of the century. It had done extensive damage to the Grants Pass area. Downriver, in the Lower River Road section, rescuers were using boats to remove families stranded by the flood. The governor called the National Guardsmen to duty in the Grants Pass area.

The Rogue crested at 31.16 feet on Thursday and started dropping a little, but the small village of Galice, downriver from Grants Pass, was isolated because of a slide at Hog Creek. There was a bottle-neck blockage at Hellgate Canyon, causing the washout.

Fred Hale, local pilot and owner of the Grants Pass Air Service, reported that, on the lower Rogue, a home and the Brownell cabin at Marial had been washed away, and also a cabin at Paradise Bar. Black Bar Lodge's airstrip was gone, too.

By Saturday, Christmas Eve, thousands of persons had been evacuated from their homes in Southern Oregon and Northern California. The receding waters and lessening rain gave people hopes of clearing their mudfilled houses and getting on with the mopping-up process, but reports came from the weather bureau that another storm was on its way into the area.

Fred Hale was our local flyer, and he was the manager of the airport here. He also did the flying into the Rogue River Canyon. He supplied Black Bar Lodge with anything they might want. He would fly in there, maybe once or twice a week, with food, or whatever their requirements were. They had a kind of landing strip there, anyway they called it a landing strip.

When this big storm came, the day before Christmas, the sheriff, Lloyd Lewis, came down here and told me Fred Hale had flown into the canyon and was due back at 11:00 that morning and he hadn't returned. They were somewhat concerned about it, and he asked me if I would go in there in a boat and look for him.

At that time that was one of the biggest floods we had ever had on the Rogue. It got up to something like 32 feet here. It was too late to go down the river that night. It would be dark before we could get to Almeda to put the boat in, so we decided we would wait until the next morning. That would give him a chance to get out of there, if he was going to get out.

The next morning we had a report that a flyer had flown over that part of the river and it had cleared enough so that he could see a light. Someone had a fire burning at the mouth of Howard Creek, which is about four miles upriver from Black Bar Lodge.

Planes had been sent downriver Saturday afternoon to make a search. Ed Scholtz, a Forest Service pilot, accompanied by Orval Looper, a smokejumper, checked as far down as Agness without spotting anything. Deke Miller, who had a place a few miles farther downriver than Black Bar, made another fruitless flight. George Milligan, from Medford Mercy Flights, took Harold Conners along as spotter, and they made an after dark search. They were the ones who reported the fire on the south rim of the canyon at Howard Creek.

There was no way of getting into the canyon by plane, and the area was either fogged in or the rain would be falling so heavily they couldn't tell exactly what it was they were seeing on the canyon's rim.

The next morning, Christmas Day, Bruce and I took my boat, a twenty-one foot plywood one, with a 20-horse Mercury motor, and went down to Almeda and put it in there. It must have been about 11:00 when we put the boat in.

We started out, in all that water, and it was a completely new river to me.

The high flood stage had covered all the guide marks. Rocks that had protruded from the water were now completely submerged. Others that had stood twenty-five feet or more out of the water were now the dangerous ones, just barely sticking out of the water.

The only way we could tell where we were was by the contour of the mountains. At Rainie Falls there wasn't even a ripple to tell us where the falls should be. It was just smoothed out with the rest of the river.

There was stuff washing down the river, trees and parts of houses and things, but we didn't hit any of it, fortunately. But that part of the river wasn't the really bad part.

When we got down to Howard Creek, or in that vicinity, we went as slow as we could, to see if we could spot anything. But there was nothing until we got to Black Bar. The river had risen until it was right at the edge of the cabin at Black Bar Lodge, and there was a sheet pegged to the lawn, so we knew that this was it. That was a signal; if anyone flew over they could spot the sheet spread there.

So we pulled in and tied up. When we went into the house, there was Fred, on a cot, burned until he was not recognizable. He was a big man, weighing about 230 pounds, and his ears were partly burned off, and of course his hair was all burned. He looked like a roasted turkey. His face was swollen so that his eyes were shut and couldn't see.

When we went in and Fred heard me talking, he said, "Hello, Glen. I knew you'd come."

Well, that kind of got me. Imagine, a guy having that much confidence in another one.

There were two men staying at the Lodge, Bill Brockman and Red Keller. They had found him when his plane crashed and brought him down to the lodge, but they had no way of getting him out of there. It would have been impossible to land a plane on the airstrip. It was completely underwater.

We had to take one of the seats out of the boat to make room for the cot. Then the four of us carried him down and put him in the boat and we started on down to Marial.

Before we started out from Grants Pass, Virgil Hull made arrangements to meet us at Marial, with an ambulance, in case we found Hale and he needed to be brought out that way.

Glen wasn't aware of it at the time, but the whole countryside around Grants Pass was on the alert in the rescue efforts. Virgil Hull and Norman Webb had started out with a power wagon ambulance, but they knew they wouldn't be able to make it through the mud and snow slides on the Robert Dollar logging road, in from Glendale, which they planned to take.

Bill and Lloyd Ford, owners of Ford Brothers Logging Company in Josephine County, volunteered to open the way for them. They took their crew, including Dick Hayes, Mel Johnson and Pete Ingalls, and attacked the road, making it in seventeen miles before they decided to turn off and go over Mt. Reuben. They bulldozed their way to the top of Mt. Reuben in a blinding snowstorm with two feet of snow on the ground.

The power wagon ambulance followed, as did Tom Winneford in a Jeep with radio equipment, to keep contact with the airport and Forest Service crews.

Another crew; Debbs Potts, Dewayne Dahl, Howard Lewis and Darrel Woolsey, was forcing a road through from Galice road to Grave Creek Bridge. They made it to the bridge by nightfall, then returned to Rand Forest Station for the night.

Two ground crews were also on the river. A Forest Service crew; Ray Marchant, Bruce Lathrop, Steve Martin and Bob Pruitt, went down the north rim of the canyon. The other crew; Cole Rivers, the fish biologist; Al Zenor, Shorty Melville; and Al Chapman; started down the south side.

Many others were involved, including George Douglas from the Oregon Aeronautics Board in Salem, and George Felt, Aeronautics Search and Rescue from Roseburg, who brought in Unicom radios to assist the Forest Service; logging radio networks; and ham radio operators who were relaying messages between searchers and the airport.

Standing by the airport were Ben Spaulding, Hale's assistant air rescue director; Frank Wagoner, a friend of Hale's who had come for a visit the day before Hale made the flight; and many others who remained at the airport for the duration of the search.

Horseshoe Bend, just below Black Bar, I knew had to be awfully bad, with the water that high. My first thought was to walk down and look it over, before we started down, but there wasn't any use to look at it, we had to run it anyway.

So we took off with Hale, Bruce and I, and it was raining a terrible storm! It hadn't stopped yet.

Horseshoe Bend is about two miles below Black Bar. You go right around a hair-pin curve there. It almost meets itself. A mountain comes off and ends right there and the water whips on around this point. It creates a terrific turbulence.

I had never seen it with the water this high before, but even in normal high water it is a very rough place. So we started down and here was a big boulder, as big as this house, and the water was just parting around it.

The right side looked like the best way to go, and I had to make a quick decision; I didn't have much time; we were going full blast. So we went to the right.

Then we discovered, when we got around that boulder, we were heading for a series of sharp bedrocks. We had to make a quick turn off to the left and that headed us directly into those big breakers. There wasn't any other place to go.

We hit the first breaker and went over it pretty good, but we went under the next one and it loaded the boat full of water. We hit with such force it broke the cot and Hale went down into the water in the boat. The water was about level with the seat, which means that the boat was about three-quarters full of water.

Well, that water killed the motor and there we were, helpless; but, fortunately, there were no more big breakers below us or it would have really swamped us. We would never have made it out of there.

We had put in two buckets, because we knew we would have to bail. They were about six-quart size. So we both grabbed a bucket, and we did a menace-able job of pumping that water out of there. Boy! It looked awfully bad, and of course, all this time, we were going like the dickens down that canyon.

By the time we had traveled a couple of miles we had her down pretty good. Bruce was supposed to handle the oars and keep us out of trouble, but we were pretty helpless, anyway.

We got the water down pretty good, and I got to monkeying with the motor and, by golly, it started! Then, of course, the water ran to the back of the boat. Bruce got back there and bailed it out — threw it all out — and every-thing was lovely. We were on our way again.

Then our next real bad spot was Long Gulch. We had to go down on the left side, and it was terrifically rough, down through the middle and left side of the river.

Water shot across and onto a mountain, boiling up about twenty feet high, and we had to cross the river before we got there.

There was a series of big rollers — they weren't breaking much, but they were about eight to ten feet high. It looked pretty woolly out there, but we had to cross it, that's all.

We just had to, so away we went, and we ran the motor wide open as much as we could. You have better control — it rides better — everything is better if you have the power on it.

Well, we ran that out and got on down to Marial. We landed in the orchard; the water was that high. Bruce ran up to the house to see if he could get some help. When we got there, fortunately, Rick Venner and Akesson were there. Venner had a station wagon, so he brought it down and we stuffed Hale into it and took him down to Marial's place.

Marial was out for the winter, and we just moved in and took possession of her lodge. We stripped Hale's clothes off him and put him to bed. He was freezing from getting soaked with the cold rain and being burned, too. We got a fire going, heated water and filled fruit jars and stuck them around him in bed. We got him kind of thawed out, then someone thought to go up on the hill to Mrs. Gordon's house to get her.

She was a registered nurse. She was down there in a few minutes and took charge of Hale. There wasn't really much she could do, as she didn't have much to do with. She did have some morphine and she gave him that, off and on, to kind of ease his pain.

So there we were, stuck, no way to get out, no communication.

I wanted to take him on, after we got him to Marial and couldn't get him out of there any other way. I suggested we just put him in the boat and take him on to Gold Beach, but Mrs. Gordon objected.

"You get him cold and wet again," she said, "and he's liable to take pneumonia."

It would have been quite a little ride on to Gold Beach. We would have had Mule Creek Canyon, Devil's Stair and Blossom Bar ahead of us, but it wouldn't have been any worse than we had already been through.

Hale told us the way it all came about. He had flown in at that particular time, to take a man in who lived down there. His house had washed away and his wife was down there — Mrs. Overton, at Marial — and they somehow got word out that the house was gone.

He asked Hale to fly him in there at the first opportunity.

It was on Christmas Eve that Fred flew him in, and on his way down he dropped off a parcel of fresh meat and other things at Black Bar Lodge. Brockman and Keller, at Black Bar, didn't see the package, so when Hale came back he could see that they hadn't found it. He circled around to try to point it out to them. A wind current caught his plane and flipped him right into the side of the mountain.

He knew he was going to crash, so he headed his plane between two trees. They sheared the wings off the plane, but Hale managed to open the door and roll free. It was just a miracle he did, though, because later I saw the plane and right where it was sitting an oak tree was just far enough back that he could manage to open the door. If he'd stopped a foot sooner he'd never have got out of there. He'd have burned up.

It broke the gas tank, when he crashed, and splattered him with gasoline. That caught fire, and he rolled down hill, right at the back of the lodge. I don't know how those guys got the fire out, but they did. His body wasn't burned so badly, but there was a big spot on his leg that was burned.

The Ford brothers' road building crew was making its way through four and a half feet of snow with the cats and dozers, building a road for the power-wagon ambulance and radio-equipped jeep. They had forty-two miles of logging roads to conquer and much of it was washed out. They repaired these washouts by falling trees and pushing fill into the chasms. One washout they had to bridge was forty-five feet wide, and the creeks and streams were all in high flood stage.

Trees, storm-fallen across the road, some three feet thick, had to be cut-up and winched aside. On the north side of Dutch Henry peak, it took them two hours to make a mile of progress. The cat never stopped; the crews took turns keeping it in operation.

On Monday, along in the afternoon, there was a break in the weather, and a plane came down the canyon. They couldn't fly into it before because of the rain and fog.

It was Deke Miller, sailing in to make a landing at his place about four miles below Marial. Venner ran down the trail and met Deke coming up. He had seen my boat and figured out what happened. Miller came on up to Marial's with Venner and we told him how badly Hale was burned. He flew out, then, to Grants Pass and got Hale's doctor. Dr. Mikkelson.

When they came back they had to land at Miller's and walk up the trail, which they said was almost completely gone, with all the trees down and mud-slides.

At Black Bar, when Brockman and Keller saw Fred's hands burned so badly, they wrapped them in towels and poured Wesson oil on them. I don't know what good that did, but anyway, that was the best treatment they could think of.

When the Doctor came, he unwrapped them and took a pair of forceps and just peeled that skin off, just like taking a glove off, fingernails and all. Boy, that was quite a job! Then he treated them and the rest of Fred's burns.

Miller got word out to the Coast Guard at Coos Bay, and they were to fly a helicopter in and pick Fred up, but when they brought it down from Portland they were grounded at Roseburg on account of the weather.

On Wednesday, the Ford brothers got the road punched through with the dozers and the ambulance came in. It had taken them about 28 hours to get through. Not more than thirty minutes after they came in, the army helicopter landed up in Anderson's field. They put Fred in the ambulance and took him up and loaded him in the helicopter. They flew him to the hospital, where the doctors did a lot of skin grafting and got him back in good shape. He lives down close to Sacramento, now. He flew some, after that; then he went down and took charge of the airport where he lives.

Bruce flew out from Marial, on Tuesday, with Deke Miller, but I stayed until after they picked up Hale. I flew out with Ed Scholz and Jack Hollis. The biggest problem we had, aside from Hale's being hurt so bad, was a food shortage. There were ten or twelve people there and not much food, since Marial had intended to be out for the winter. But the few people who were living around Marial pooled their food and shared with us.

Bruce and I were on the river about three and half hours, and it was about fifty miles from Almeda to Marial. Boy! That was the biggest and roughest boatride I ever had. That was just too much of a good thing. When someone asked Bruce about it he said, "That's where I learned how to pray." It was really dangerous.

Nobody wanted to do it, I guess, but we had to. Fred Hale was a good friend of mine and when a man is in trouble you've got to do something about it.

I knew we were taking a big chance, and, luckily, we won.

Black Bar Lodge. In 1955 flood the water was to the edge of the cabin. A sheet was pegged to the lawn as a signal to pilots who would be hunting for the downed plane.
Bruce Wooldridge collection

Glen, running the river just below Black Bar Lodge when the water was at normal level. During the flood of 1955, the water was over all the boulders in the picture. In fact, it was much higher. Bruce Wooldridge collection

Glen, at Lower Black Bar Falls. This cliff was under water during the 1955 flood. Bruce Wooldridge collection

Flood, 1955, showing Grants Pass area. Looking downstream with the old railroad bridge in foreground, Caveman Bridge in distance.

Josephine County Historical Society

The Big Flood on the Rogue, 1964, Caveman Bridge, Grants Pass.

Josephine County Historical Society

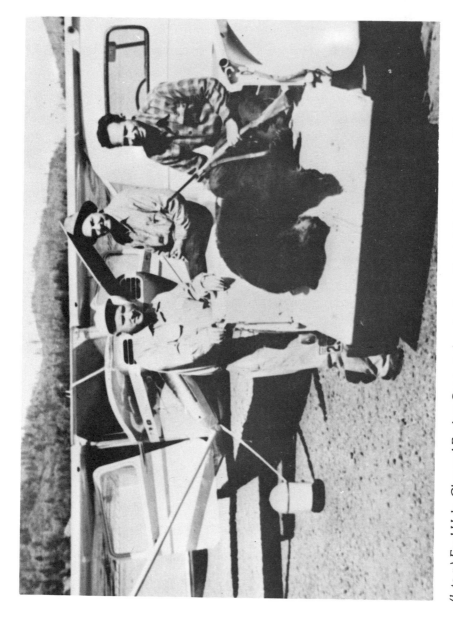

(l. to r.) Fred Hale, Glen and Reuben Garcia, in happier times. Garcia killed the bear and Hale flew in to haul it back to Grants Pass.
Glen Wooldridge collection

Chapter Twenty-One

Good Companions: Good Times on the Rivers

Retirement living didn't suit Glen Wooldridge any better than it had Glenn Ballou. They had no trouble finding things to keep them busy. Building boats could have taken all their time, as they had a ready market for all they could build, but a little time had to be given to river running, just for the fun of it.

Glen and Sadie bought land at Long Gulch, in an isolated spot on the lower Rogue, and made plans to build a retirement cabin on the ridge overlooking the river. Glen and Glenn Ballou hauled the building materials for the cabin by motor boat from Marial, and Glenn Ballou did most of the carpenter work. When it was finished, it was a good place to stay when they weren't on the river. They named it *Dungydon.*

Glenn Ballou never tried to operate the boat; he never did learn anything about it. He just wanted to go along for the ride. He was a good friend, a really good one.

The cabin wasn't the answer to the Wooldridges' retirement plans, however. Sadie's health wasn't very good. She had been having respiratory problems, and didn't like to spend the winters on the river. Glen always had other rivers to run, and he didn't want to spend the summers there, so they finally gave it up.

Glen Ballou and I had some good times together. We took some nice trips. One time we went to Bella Coola, British Columbia. First we drove up to Williams Lake, then went west of there about 200 to 300 miles, out across that plateau country, over a bumpy road.

We took along a boat, and were pulling it with a Volkswagen van. There was one hill about ten miles long that was really a toughy. I didn't know if we would ever get back out of there with the boat. But we didn't have to worry about it, we sold the boat.

While we were there we built a boat for Elsee, the fellow who owned the resort where we were staying. He said he would like to have a boat like mine, so we told him to get the material and we would build him one. We built it right

The cabin Glen and Glenn Ballou built at Long Gulch.
Bruce Wooldridge collection

Glen and Glenn Ballou, hauling freight to the cabin site at Long Gulch.
Glen Wooldridge collection

there at the resort. We stayed there for about three weeks; then when we started to leave, we asked him how much we owed him for staying there.

"Nothing," he told us. "You built the boat for me: that's payment enough."

I'd like to go back to that Bella Coola country. It impressed me as being a really wonderful place to live. It's isolated, but the surroundings are beautiful: big, high mountains; a real nice river, actually right on the beach on an arm of the inland passage.

But what impressed me most was the people. We never met anyone who didn't speak to us, and half of them would start a conversation. I really liked that. They hadn't been subjected to the cutthroats and thieves like a lot of city folks have. Most of them were descended from the Indian tribes of that area.

The supply boat made a trip in there once a week, and when it came, everyone dropped whatever they were doing and went running. It was a small place, but I don't know what the roads are like now. They weren't very good then, but that's been a lot of years ago.

It really would be a nice place to live. There must have been some kind of air service, in case of an emergency. There was only one little store, maybe two. I went over to get a newspaper and they told me, "We don't get a newspaper. The news is stale before it gets to us, anyway, so we just don't bother getting it."

Glenn and I were down at Clay Hill, on the lower Rogue, one time, and it was storming pretty bad. We got word that a woman staying at Half Moon Bar was sick and thought she had to get out of there. The river was high, pretty mean, with lots of drifts running. It looked pretty wild, but we thought it was an emergency. We went up in the boat and got her and took her down to Gold Beach, in all that flood. We took her to the hospital, but by the time we got there with her, she was feeling lots better.

I remember going up through Huggins Canyon. There were logs and drifts and lots of crap running, but we thought it was an emergency and we had to go through.

There were lots of bear in that lower Rogue country, so Glenn and I decided to advertise in the archery magazines that we would take people on trips into that country to hunt them with bows. We had several men come up to go along.

We had quite a bit of bear meat to do something with, and we would stop over at the Long Gulch cabin, where we had a cooker. So we just canned up the bear meat and put it on the shelf. When the dudes came down, sometimes we would feed them bear meat. They got to liking it pretty well, but I never could eat it.

Howard Bearss and his brother went bear hunting with us one time. We went down to Horseshoe Bend and were out hunting when we saw this bear coming around the mountainside. He was coming down the trail right toward us, but we were on the opposite side of the river. He walked down until he got right opposite us, then just turned around and walked back up the hill the way he came. They shot at him a few times, but didn't kill him. Then, when we got

The sign for the new cabin tells the world Glen's retirement plans. He's dun gydon.

Glen Wooldridge collection

A couple of nice half-pounders for dinner at the new cabin. Glen Wooldridge collection

Glenn Ballou draws kitchen duty at Dungydon.   Glen Wooldridge collection

back into the boat and were going downriver, Howard saw a bear on the bank. He threw his gun up and took a shot, killed that bear while the boat was bouncing over the riffle.

Carroll Cornell and I went downriver, one time, fishing and hunting. I was rowing the boat along while Cornell fished. He caught a nice steelhead, weighing about two pounds, and we planned to have him for dinner. We pulled the boat up at Horseshoe Bend and went up the mountainside hunting, but we didn't see anything. When we got back to the boat there were bear tracks all around the boat, and in it, but no fish. The bear had made off with Cornell's steelhead while we were out looking for him.

I took another guy from Grants Pass bow-hunting down in that country; I won't tell you his name. He saw several deer standing on the side of the hill, not very far away. He shot arrows all around them, so many it looked like an Indian attack. They would just raise their heads and look at the arrows landing, then go back to grazing.

There were always other things popping up that brought the Rogue and Glen to the public's attention. In 1955, Glen invited President Eisenhower to come to the Rogue, in October of the next year, to spend a week fishing with him and General Nathan Twining, Air Force Chief of Staff, at Glen's lodge. General Twining was an old hand on the Rogue, along with the generals, Ira Eakers, Curtis LeMay and Carl Spaatz.

The story received nationwide coverage. It was accompanied by telephotos of Glen's first trip up the Rogue. Everyone waited for Ike's reply. That date would be in the heat of the election the next year. They thought if Ike accepted, it would give an inkling as to whether he would be running again, but he didn't accept.

In 1958, Glen and Bruce took TV personality Truman Bradley and his party down the Rogue. They were photographed running some of the fiercest rapids, and spent two days shooting film for the TV show, *Target*. The trip was also made into an Olympia beer commercial, shown on the west coast.

Another unusual boating adventure Glen had on the river was treasure hunting. It wasn't ancient treasure, but the loot from a robbery at the Pay 'n Save grocery store in Grants Pass in 1961. When some of the stolen goods were located in the river, just below the Hellgate Bridge, Glen took his boat and assisted skin-divers Chuck and Don Jaynes in recovering it. He held the boat in the current, above the spot where the safe was thrown in, while the divers went down into the icy water, clinging to a loop at the end of a rope slung from the boat, to retrieve a sack of checks and papers from the safe.

There was always a crowd of young river runners hanging around Glen's boatshop when they had time off. They urged him to plan a trip to show them how to run the Rogue upstream.

Glen agreed, and the last week in April, 1962, was chosen as the likeliest time to make the run. Glen built three boats for the trip. He would operate one, asking Bonnie Riggs, a Roseburg writer, and Elzie Abel, his Grants Pass photographer friend, to be his passengers. His boat was powered with twin Mercury 25 hp motors. Bruce Wooldridge ran another of the boats, and Dr. W.H. Roberts, a Medford dentist, and his son, Bill, the other one. Both of these boats were powered by single Mercury 45s.

Six of the boatmen built three other boats, under Glen's supervision and by his plans. They were Chuck and Dick Shorbe, Bruce and Gary Coome, Bob Curry and Tom McEuen.

These boats, built of three-eighths-inch plywood, were around eighteen feet long, with six and one half foot beams. They had flat bottoms, strengthened with fiber-glass coating, and wide, upswept bows.

One boatman, Gordon Hatch, was using an earlier design Wooldridge boat with a 30-horse Mercury motor. He hesitated to start the trip, knowing he might be underpowered.

Other passengers were Harry Howard, Darrel Woolsey and Bill O'Malley.

They put the boats in at Agness, on April 28, and ran up the rapids as far as Devil's Stairs without any difficulty. At Devil's Stairs, below Blossom Bar, Glen had them pull over and walk up on the rocks to check it out before making the run. He pointed out the best route through the rapids.

About fifty people drove over from Grants Pass and hiked into the area to watch the run through Blossom Bar. The show wasn't as exciting as it might have been. The boatmen didn't have any difficulty there, except that some of the boats took on a lot of water.

The biggest difficulty came at Washboard. It was so steep and rough the boats hung on the wave crests, lugging enough energy to go over. Chuck Shorbe's boat hit a wave so hard it was carried backward, taking on a load of water. He had to pull to shore, bail out, then let his passengers walk up while he made the run.

He had another close one at Kelsey, when his motor went dead right in the middle of the drop off. Luckily a quick pull on the starter rope got it going again.

All the boats suffered damages to equipment from the pounding of the rough water. Glen said he knew one man who named his boat *Old Hernia* because of the shaking.

The motor mounts weren't rigid enough, and the weight of the motors buckled them, making it necessary to strengthen them with steel when it was available. Some of the men attached their motors directly to the boats transoms when their mounts gave way.

Bruce Coome had trouble at Battle Bar. His motor wouldn't start and they suspected a wet coil from so much wear and tear on it. They wrapped Scotch Tape around it, but still didn't get any fire. Finally the others had to go on, leaving him and Gary to make their way back downriver to a place where they could take their boat out of the water. Before the party reached Wildcat Riffle, however, the Coomes caught up with them. They had wrapped the entire coil with Scotch Tape to keep the water out.

Bailing wire came in handy, too, for making repairs to throttle controls which were jarred loose. Little could be done for props which were damaged from hitting the rocks.

All the boatmen made it through to Rainie Falls, however, where they took about two hours to line the boats up the fishways. Grave Creek Falls was navigated without too many problems, but the Coomes' boat had trouble again at Innis Riffle. A hidden boulder took the whole lower unit of their motor, causing them to drop out of the run. The rest of the boats made it all the way.

Bonnie Riggs wrote the story for *Sports Afield,* and it was published in their Spring, 1963 issue.

That same year a new invention revolutionized outboard motor boating on whitewater rivers. It enabled Glen to streamline his boat design into the sleek Wooldridge Sled on the market today.

This invention was Dick Stallman's Outboard Jet Unit, a snail-shaped housing replacing the lower unit of propeller housing on the outboard motor. Its intake siphons in water and whirls it around the spiral housing, then shoots it out in a thousand-gallon-per minute stream. Mounted with the forward edge of the intake scoop flush with the bottom of the boat, and its trailing edge only one and a half inches lower, the jet unit allows the boat to run in only three inches of water over gravelly riverbottoms or rocks.

Stallman, the 34-year-old inventor from San Carlos, California, had been working on the jet unit on the Rogue, in the Agness area. He believed that testing the equipment on the Rogue was probably the toughest test he could give it.

Dick got in touch with me through Larry Lucas, who ran the Lucas Lodge, at Agness. Larry told him he should see me for ideas about the testing, then Larry called me and told me, "There's a fellow here who has something I think you ought to have a look at." So that was the beginning of my being involved.

Stallman and his father manufactured bearings. Dick was a machinist, and he thought up the idea of the jet unit. He got some books from England, where they had done some research, and studied up on the idea. He started tinkering with it, and he is a pretty shrewd fellow. He was wise enough to put these ideas together and get it to work.

He told me he wanted to give it a test, to run it from Gold Beach to Grants Pass, so I furnished the boats for the run. I had a 35-horse Evinrude and he had two Johnson motors. He made a jet for my motor and had his Johnsons mounted with jets. We went over to Gold Beach and made the run upriver.

When Glen and Stallman made the proving run, they were in the boats Glen built. Glen's was a sixteen-footer, and he was using the single 35-horse Evinrude. Stallman was using an eighteen-foot boat with the Johnson 25s. Both boats were six-and-one-half feet on deck with a five-foot beam at waterline. The steering controls were conventional, allowing 180 degree maneuverability in the jet units.

Making the trip with Glen, in his boat, was John Inkrote, from Grants Pass. Stallman had his father, Ralph Stallman, from Oakland, California, and a writer-photographer, Bert Goldrath, with him.

The party took four days to make the 120-mile trip, breaking it up into easy 30-mile-per-day runs. They averaged about 22 miles per hour actual running time on the entire trip. The water was low for the season, but with the jet units enabling them to navigate water as low as three inches, they encountered no problems and had no mechanical difficulties. They lined the boats at Rainie Falls and Grave Creek, but ran the rest of the river by power.

Popular Mechanics, Sports Illustrated, Popular Boating, and *Boating* all ran the story of the trip in 1963 issues.

We were grossly underpowered on that trip. We had quite a tussle to get up the river. The jet wasn't perfected, and the motor wasn't suitable for the job. After I ran the jet a while I decided the Mercury was the answer, because it has high rpm and will wind that thing up.

I talked to Dick about that, and he told me, "It's against the principal of a pump to run it at high revolutions."

"Well," I told him, "these old feeble things aren't doing anything."

I kept hounding him; finally he said, "Well, if you will get me a motor, we'll try it." That's where the jet for the Mercury was born.

I ordered him a new Mercury. I didn't even see it, just had the company ship it to him. Then in a month or two I got a letter from him and he said, "This thing is really doing a good job."

There were lots of improvements to be made, and anytime I could suggest anything, which I did on several occasions, I'd tell him and he'd go ahead and try it. Of course I was in a much better position to test it than he was.

The last time he was here he had a 200-horse Mercury — a V-6, I think it was — with a jet. We took it down to Galice country and ran it back and forth. Just that motor alone would cost more than $4000. It worked out all right too.

The advent of the jet unit gave whitewater runners much more leeway in running rivers. Glen had fun playing with the jet unit and adapting his river boat to use it. It enabled him to run in water that even his Jackass motor lift had denied him before.

He and Taylor Cain, who designed and built the original Caveman Campers in Grants Pass, made a couple of exciting trips in 1963. With Bill Pruitt of Grants Pass, they made a trip on the far reaches of the upper river. They put the boat in at Shady Cove and ran to the mouth of the South Fork of the Rogue, ending about two miles below the Pacific Power and Light powerhouse at Prospect. Until the jet unit was developed, this hadn't been motor boating waters.

The other notable trip Glen and Taylor made that year was down the Rogue and back in a two-day weekend. They started from Grants Pass on Saturday morning and ran down as far as Illahe. Next day they went on to Agness, turned around, and made the upriver run, passing under the Caveman Bridge, Grants Pass, about 3:30 p.m. on Sunday. On this trip was the last barrier of running the Rogue fell to Glen's boat. He bounced up through the fishways at Rainie Falls, just like going up a giant staircase.

Stallman's Outboard Jets became popular across western boating waters almost immediately. On Alaskan rivers it was used on work boats and by commercial fishermen. Game wardens found its maneuverability in shallow waters suited to their purposes. Water skiiers could use it with safety because it had no propeller blades to endanger them in the water.

The next "unrunnable" river to fall to Glen's onslaught was the Klamath, in California. He and Casey Wineski, from Illahe, jet-boated up the Klamath from Happy Camp to the Highway 99 Bridge, in July, 1964, without making portage.

The Klamath is a pretty wild river, all right, just about as wild as any I've seen. In fact, there are several falls that we weren't too sure we could run. The big falls, below Happy Camp, we knew we couldn't run. It is just straight up, so we put in above that.

At one place I could see three falls on the river at one time — all whitewater — very pretty. We ran them all. Hamburg Falls was one of the toughest, but we made it okay. That is, I made it; Casey had to get out and hike around. But I believe now that we could run it with several people aboard. Put on a couple of motors and we'd be sure of making it easily.

We were using a sled, about 16 feet long, with a 50-hp Mercury, with an Outboard Jet. It's quite a ways through there — close to 90 miles. We spent the night at the lodge at the Big Foot Ranch, which burned down not too long after we made the run.

We couldn't have done it with a propeller, but we made it okay with the jet. I think I could run it again, not later than the first of June, when we have

some water. I wouldn't want to run it again when we didn't have any water. That kicking up dust here and there, that's getting too shallow. When it gets down that low it doesn't make a good trip.

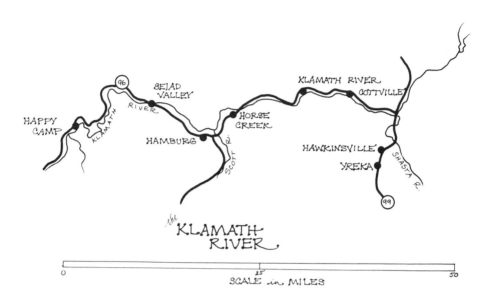

Glen with Truman Bradley, from the TV show "Target", on the Rogue during the making of Olympia Beer commercial.
Glen Wooldridge collection

Herb Whitchurch, Glen and Glenn Ballou relax on the porch of Dungydon cabin.
Glen Wooldridge collection

Glen at the 1959 celebration at Agness.
Glen Wooldridge collection

The Moosegooser. Two men brought this boat from Alaska to make a run up the Rogue. It tipped over in Washboard and one man was drowned. The boat washed up at Horseshoe Bend.
Bruce Wooldridge collection

Chapter Twenty-Two

Yukon Fever

In the mid-sixties, Glen tried making his boat hulls of molded fiber-glass, but didn't like the way they turned out. On a trip to Seattle, he came across some aluminum boats at a marina, and bought a load of them to sell at his boatshop in Grants Pass. They were made by the Monarch Boat Company in Arkansas.

Later he and a friend, Carl Locke, made a trip to Arkansas, to the Jett Boat Company, and arranged to have aluminum boats made to his specification.

That was the first time I had heard of welded aluminum boats. They were making them at a little bit of a place, Friendship, Arkansas. I went back and bought some boats, a truck load or two.

I asked them why they called the boat company "Jett," and they told me that was the owner's name. I guess I was thinking about the Jet Outboard Units.

We crossed the Mississippi while we were back there seeing about having the boats made. We crossed between Greensville, Mississippi, and the Arkansas line. We had breakfast there and ordered something on the menu; I don't know what it was. When it came, it looked like little eels or angle worms. I didn't eat it.

The Mississippi River was running so slow you had to watch it awfully close to tell if it was moving at all. It doesn't seem to be moving much, probably about a half-mile an hour. It was wide, flat and dirty, not much like our rivers up in this country.

Carl Locke had just moved up here from down south. He was a retired welder, and had had an aluminum shop for twenty years or so. He was over here quite a bit of the time, and one day he said to me, "I understand this aluminum welding, and if you will get some material, I will build you a boat."

Well, that sounded good to me, so I arranged to have the material for him. He had his own equipment, and he built the first aluminum boats we made in my shop. They were really good, and I could see that they had a lot of merit.

Glen stand beside the boat used in the 1948 trip up the Salmon. This picture was taken about 20 years later. Arman collection

Glen cooks huge steaks on Salmon River boat trip with Red Boyer helping out at the campfire, about 1969. Arman collection

Glen built a wooden boat to use as a model or pattern for the aluminum sled. The boats proved very serviceable. In time, they were making them "to last a life-time," of .0110 marine aluminum, and it was almost impossible to knock a hole in one of them.

The proven quality of the sled boats led to the making of the drift boats of aluminum also. These were made of .080 marine aluminum, about fifteen feet long and with a forty-eight inch bottom, flaring to a seventy-eight inch top beam. They were advertised as the "tuffest drift boats ever built."

Glen equipped the boatshop with welding equipment to build both the drift boats and sleds. He was marketing the Jackass Lifts, and had the dealerships for both Outboard Jet Units and Mercury Outboard Motors. He had designed and was selling an adapter bracket to convert a standard fifteen inch transom to accommodate the Outboard Jets. It was adaptable for a long shaft motor.

Glen designed and marketed steering controls for stand-up boating, with an optional seat, built like a cycle seat, that allowed the operator to sit or stand astride. The boatman faced forward, and the height of the seat, or the standing position, allowed him to look at the water ahead for fast decision-making.

When it became hard to obtain ash and fir oars, Glen developed aluminum oars to market. Anything he didn't consider safe for his own use he wouldn't market. He wouldn't get out on the river in his sled boat without a pair of oars along.

He had blueprints drawn for a do-it-yourself wooden sled boat and advertised them in boating magazines. The plans started with building the jig and took the builder through each step until the boat was ready for its first coat of paint. A sketch-type plan for the drift boat was sold, also.

Glen didn't let all that business interfere with his running rivers, however. He would load the latest and best Wooldridge sled from the shop on his trailer and head for some whitewater river that hadn't been run, or maybe just rerun one of the more exciting ones. There were always sportsmen eager to go along.

Jet boat trips on the Salmon, the Snake and the Rogue were yearly outings, as were drift trips down the Rogue. These were eagerly awaited by doctors and businessmen from Portland to Los Angeles.

In 1968, Glen; his sons Bruce and Bob; stepson Robert Black, from Southern California; Dr. David James from Portland; and Dr. William Roberts from Medford made a hundred-mile trip up the Snake, boating the Hells Canyon section.

The next year a group of Grants Pass men, including Don and Red Boyer, Bob Griffith, Bob Arman, Carl Locke, and Dr. James, accompanied Glen for another run on the Snake and Samon, taking three boats.

Sometimes the boat trips would be combined with a boat delivery so that Glen could explain the operation to the new owner. Orders came in from just about everywhere in the Pacific Northwest and points beyond. One order came through a Portland marina for two of Glen's boats to be shipped to New Zealand.

Alaska, too, was a prime marketplace for the boats and lifts. It was through an enthusiastic customer, Don McNaughton, at Anchorage, that Glen arranged his longest and most time-consuming boat trip. In 1970, he took a party of eighteen

The 1962 trip up the Rogue when Glen led six boats. This picture was taken between Dulog and Horseshoe Bend.

Bruce Wooldridge collection

Rest stop, 1962 trip up the Rogue. Bonnie Riggs, left, takes notes for her story for Sports Afield magazine.

Bruce Wooldridge collection

people on a 700 to 800 mile cruise on the Yukon-Tanana-Chena rivers, with side trips up tributary streams.

I made a plane flight the year before, looking the area over, and decided it would be a worthwhile trip. NcNaughton and Marc Stella, a bush pilot up in that country, were my contacts. They made all the arrangements and made sure there were enough barrels of gasoline scattered along at the Indian villages for us to have plenty for the run.

Don and Red Boyer, who'd made several runs with me on the Salmon and Snake rivers, decided to go along. Taylor Cain and his wife, Teresa, kept talking of going. One day Teresa told me, "If Taylor doesn't hurry up and make up his mind to go, I'm just going to take our boat and go anyway."

Taylor and Bob Pruitt were pretty busy, along then, doing whitewater guiding on the Rogue, the Owyhee, and some of the Idaho rivers, but the Yukon Fever got the best of them, too. Bob said he'd do the cooking for us.

The Armans, Bob and Florence, offered to drive my pickup up the highway, hauling the boats. We stacked them high, three of the sled boats and Robert Black's inflatable Zodiak. We put them all on one trailer. The motors were carried in the bottom of the pickup and we made a sort of shelf in there for the Armans to sleep on.

Then we put in the camping and cooking gear, just anywhere we could find room. Some of it in the pickup and some in the boats, where we thought it would ride without hurting the boats. It was pretty heavily loaded, so we started them off about eight days before we were to make the trip.

Taylor and Teresa Cain; Bob Pruitt; Robert Black; Bonnie Riggs; a writer from Roseburg; and I went by plane.

Two young lieutenants with the Army Engineers went along. They were Steve Abel, Elzie Abel's son, and his friend, John Best. Steve had learned how to run the Rogue with me.

Al Lent and Mabry Ogle, a couple of Grants Pass businessmen, and the Boyers drove up the highway. Lent towed his own boat.

Our guide on the river was to be Richard Ketzler, an Indian Chief from the village of Nenana. Another Alaskan, Bob Carroll, who had something to do with the Bureau of Indian Affairs in that area, went along. The four Alaskans were in McNaughton's boat. Marc Stella was a bush pilot to the Indian villages on the Yukon and Tanana. He flew emergency services for them, carrying them out to the hospital when they would get sick or hurt, or bringing in food supplies. He flew the plane for the women when they would go to the hospital to have their babies, so about half the children were named after him. He never had been on the Yukon in a boat, though.

I guess the thing that impressed me most, about the whole trip, was the people along the Yukon River. There were three Indian women at Circle who hadn't ever gone much of anywhere except maybe to Fairbanks. They lived their whole lives right there in one house. They took us up and showed us their house, raised a board up in the floor and showed us their refrigerator, a hole down into the permafrost.

While we were there at Circle City, where we put the boats in the Yukon, a fellow came down where we were getting the boats loaded and noticed the lift on my boat. We got to talking about it, and he told me he had been using one and really liked it. He was glad to meet me when he found out I was the one who had made it.

On this trip Glen declared his intention of being a dude. He would sit back and let someone else run his boat; but, of course, it didn't work out that way. Before the party made it to Fort Yukon they really had a laugh on Glen. He had been running all those terrible whitewater rivers in Oregon and Idaho, and here he was running along the big, flat Yukon and got his boat stuck in a sand bar.

Yeah, I really stuck her in tight. You couldn't read the water on the Yukon. There wasn't anything happening on top to tell you what the bottom looked like. And the water was so loaded with silt, we couldn't really tell where the bottom was.

Everyone had to pull their boots off and get out and rock the boat to break the suction loose. They were laughing so hard we couldn't hardly break it loose. They said I must have high-centered on the Arctic Circle. I think Teresa got some slide pictures of that.

The big fishwheels that the Indians had set out in the river were really something. They turned with the current, picking up the salmon and letting them slide down into the holding boxes. That way of catching fish is lots easier than when I was doing gillnetting, back in my younger days. The Indians who owned the fishwheels told us they sometimes took as many as 200 salmon a day from one wheel.

At Fort Yukon we met Suzy Peters, who worked in the post office. She and her husband, Johnny, and a friend of theirs, Willie, took us to a real nice camping spot. It was just off the mouth of the Porcupine River.

They told us about their families on the Yukon in early days. Johnny was an Athapaskan, and his family was from the upper Porcupine area, but Suzy told us she had seven different nationalities, including Indian and Eskimo, in her background. Her father was an early-day trader on the Yukon.

One of the most impressive things on the whole trip was when four of us took a side trip up the Porcupine River. Taylor, Bonnie, Florence and I. We caught our first northern pike and saw some bald eagles and golden eagles.

When we were about twenty miles up the river, we saw two wolves run down the riverbank and into the water and start swimming across. We were downriver quite a ways from them, but I speeded up the boat and caught them in midstream, circling them a few times.

I guess the current was so strong that it was taking all of their effort just to swim across. They didn't pay any attention to us in the boat, anyway. Taylor took a couple of pictures of them, there in the water. When they reached the bank they just hightailed it to the willows, never looking back.

We camped next on Birch Creek, at an old line camp for fur trappers. A couple of old cabins they had used were still standing and in good shape. They were made of squared logs, with sod roofs. The permafrost had melted under the cabins through the years of use and the cabins had sunk into the ground until they were only about five feet high.

The Alaskans with us caught some large pike, weighing about twenty pounds or so, and the hunters shot some grouse and spruce hens so we could eat off the land.

At the little village of Beaver, Jack Van Hatten, who runs the store, came out to meet us. We had seen him in Fairbanks, where he had told us he'd have gasoline for the boats. We filled up our tanks there. I met a schoolteacher at Beaver who built a boat using the plan I sell. He made it somewhat longer than the boats we use on the Rogue. I guess it is a good thing he did. He had just killed a huge moose and brought it home in that boat. He was dressing it out when we went over to his house.

We camped on Beaver Creek and had grouse and fish cooked over the coals. Some of us slept in the boats right on the water, but most of the crew just put their tents or shelters on the riverbanks. They were pretty shook, next morning, when they found smoking grizzly spoor about one hundred feet from where they were sleeping. During the night we heard foxes barking and loons calling.

From left, Bonnie Riggs taking a picture of Glen and Taylor Cain cooking dinner. Woman in parka at right is Suzy Peters from Fort Yukon. Arman photo

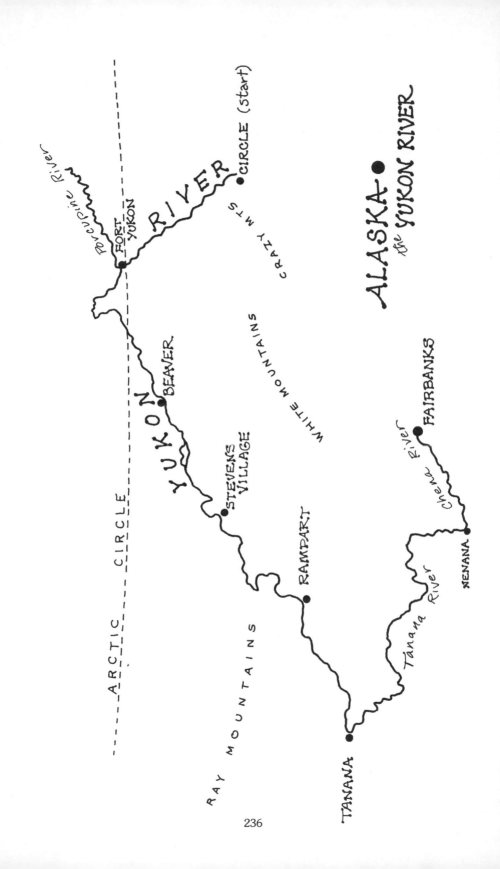

ALASKA
the YUKON RIVER

CIRCLE (start)

FORT YUKON

Porcupine River

YUKON RIVER

CRAZY MTS

BEAVER

WHITE MOUNTAINS

STEVENS VILLAGE

ARCTIC CIRCLE

RAMPART

FAIRBANKS

Chena River

NENANA

Tanana River

RAY MOUNTAINS

TANANA

Red Boyer killed a moose, and we had moose liver and blueberry muffins for breakfast. Then we went on down to Stephens Village, filled up with gasoline there and visited the natives a little while. We got a good look at some dog teams there. They told us that those dogs they had staked out on the upper bank of the river could hear a boat coming, and if it was a village boat they had one kind of howl, but if it was a strange boat they howled a different tune. They could hear a boat coming ten minutes before a person could.

After that we went to Ray River and Richard Ketzler, the Indian chief who was with us, caught the first shee fish I ever saw; big, thick bodied things weighing thirty to forty pounds.

The river was wide and comparatively smoother than any of the rivers we were all used to running. In some spots it was a mile or so wide, but you couldn't tell it, because the islands looked like the other banks. I was impressed by the eroding away of the banks. As we went along in the boat, huge chunks of the bank would just slide off into the stream. The way the trees grew showed the age of the islands. They had a regular cycle of growing, and as the sandbars would build up, certain trees would sprout, then give way to another species; that way they would rebuild the little islands in the river.

Before we got to Ramparts Village, the river narrowed to just one channel. The Indians were dressing salmon on the riverbanks at Ramparts. The men cleaned the dog salmon to dry for their sled dogs' winter food. The women were preparing silver salmon to smoke for their own use. They called it "Squaw candy."

The old man who ran the store at Ramparts took us into what he called the world's largest deepfreeze. It was a permafrost cavern where he stored his supplies. He showed us some of his Yukon gold. He had a couple of big nuggets, one weighing about six ounces.

Then, just before we got to Tanana, we stopped at a cabin where an old bachelor, Gus Nordor, lived. He had been fishing and his fish were piled up on the landing. He must have had a dozen or more big salmon. His meat cache was built high on stilts so the bears couldn't get to it. He had a pretty nice garden and a tight little cabin.

Everybody told us that Squaw Crossing, after we started up the Tanana River, was a pretty bad place if the winds were high and coming from the right direction. But it was calm and we didn't have any trouble.

When we stopped at Manley Hot Springs, everybody had to go down and have a bath in the hot springs bath house. Then we went to the lodge and had dinner and spent the night. They grow most of the fresh vegetables used in that part of the Alaska right there in big greenhouses. In and around the lodge were mastodon bones they had found in the riverbanks in that area.

Some of the party flew out from Tanana, and Bob Pruitt left us at Manley and caught a plane back to Oregon. He had some guide trips he was scheduled to take. We went on to Nenana, Ketzler's village, then up the Chena back into Fairbanks.

The excursion was interesting and the companionship great, even if it wasn't as exciting as a whitewater run. One exciting moment did come to the crew in

Glen's boat when he ran out of gasoline in midstream. When the motor went dead and the boat leveled out, water started pouring into the boat where the drain plug had been pulled to allow the water in the bottom of the boat to run out. As long as the boat was going the water didn't come into it; but when it stopped the water started flowing in through the drain hole. Steve Abel felt around in the water, located the plug and stuck it back in the hole.

Then, when Glen looked for his funnel to put gas in the tank from a barrel he was hauling, he found out it was in one of the other boats. The young lieutenants, aided by Bonnie and Florence, hoisted the barrel in the middle of the boat, in the middle of the river, and sloshed enough gasoline into the tank to allow them to reach the other boats and shore.

Glen had the last laugh on the other crews who had accused him of high-centering on the Arctic Circle. Later on during the trip four of the boats, at one time, were mired in the Yukon mud, and had to be pushed by hand to a deeper channel.

I enjoyed the trip a lot, but I think if I was to do it again, I'd spend more time in the villages getting acquainted with the people. That's the part I missed the most, but it was pretty late in the season and we felt we had to hurry.

I would like to go back up there and spend all summer. I would make a run on up the Porcupine, just as far as possible. I really would like to see that country away up that river. When we were on that little jaunt we did make, the wind started blowing and the waves on the river got pretty rough for a while.

All in all, I think we had a pretty good trip. We get together and talk about it sometimes.

The story of the Alaskan trip was published in Mercury Outboard's magazine *Outdoors*, in April, 1972, by Florence Arman, and in an Alaskan magazine by Bonnie Riggs. Other articles about Glen were in *Ford Truck Times*, summer 1971 issue; and *Outdoors*, January, 1972.

Glen prepares for bed in his boat under the midnight sun, Yukon trip, 1970.

Bonnie Riggs photo

Glen, with his boat stuck on the Arctic Circle! left to right; Bob Pruitt, Taylor Cain, Bob Arman, Florence Arman and Glen, trying to decide how to break the boat loose.
photo made from slide taken by Teresa Cain

Glen's boat on the Yukon, 1970.   Arman photo

Chapter Twenty-Three

Up the Fraser's Hell's Gate Canyon

At Age 79

In 1972, Ted Trueblood, associate editor of *Field and Stream* magazine, came back to the Rogue. This time he and Glen and Glenn Ballou made an easy, extended vacation type cruise down the Rogue. Trueblood wrote a biographical article about Glen, including the account of the trip, in *Field and Stream*, June, 1972.

Shortly after that, Glen headed a party to run some of the Montana rivers. Dick Stallman took his twin boys along in his boat; Robert Black took his boat; and Glenn Ballou rode with Glen.

We were going to Three Forks, in Montana, where Lewis and Clark camped when they got to the head of the Missouri. The Madison, the Jefferson and the Gallatin all run into the Missouri in that area.

We drove from Grants Pass directly to the Snake River and put the boats in, then went up to Hell's Canyon and played around a while. We went from there, intending to run the Salmon, but when we drove up the road above Riggins and looked at the river, they voted me down. They didn't like the looks of that.

So we didn't put in the Salmon at that time. We headed out for Montana, going first to Butte. Stallman had sold an Outboard Jet to the manager of the television station there, so we went to see him.

When we told him we were going to run the rivers, he said, "I will go with you." We spent the night with him. He took a television camera along, so got pictures of running those rivers.

We went down the Missouri for several miles, then came back and went up these tributary streams, the Jefferson, the Madison and the Gallatin. We took the fellow back to the TV station and had an interview with him to be put on the air, but we didn't stay to see the broadcast.

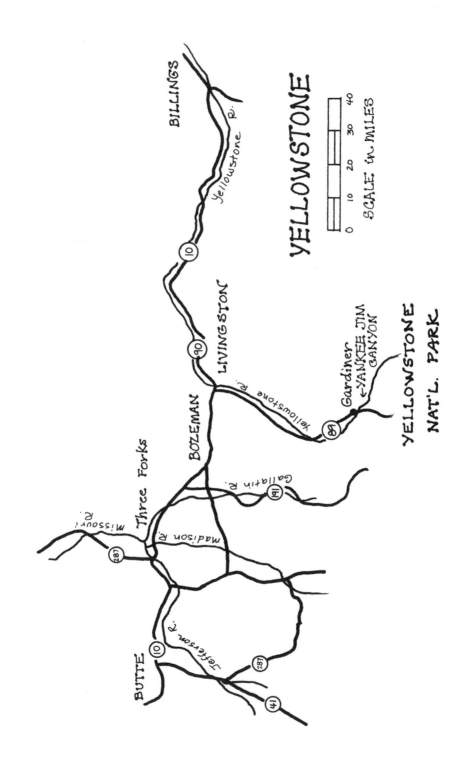

YELLOWSTONE

SCALE in MILES

0   10   20   30   40

BILLINGS

Yellowstone R.

10

LIVINGSTON

90

BOZEMAN

Yellowstone R.

89

Gardiner
←YANKEE JIM
CANYON

YELLOWSTONE
NAT'L. PARK

Three Forks

Missouri R.

287

Gallatin R.

191

Madison R.

BUTTE

10

Jefferson R.

287

41

The pictures themselves probably wouldn't be too exciting. Those rivers are just about like the Applegate here, with shallow, gravelly bottoms. I didn't see a riffle on one of them.

When we left there, we went to Livingston and put the boat in the Yellowstone and ran it for quite a number of miles, up and back. Then we went up the Yellowstone, by road, for a couple of hundred miles, to the upper part.

People had been telling me about the Yankee Jim Canyon, saying, "Nobody runs the Yankee Jim," so that was what had me interested. Ted Trueblood was the first one who told me about it, when he was here.

As we drove along the canyon, we saw signs along the road saying, Yankee Jim Canyon. We went down and had a look at it, then drove on up to Gardiner, a few miles up from there, not far from the Wyoming line, just almost to the edge of the Yellowstone National Park.

We saw a boat in a guy's yard, so we went over and talked to him. I asked him if he ever boated the canyon. He told me, "I drifted down it once, but no more. I don't want any more of that."

We went to the forestry department to see if they knew the best place to put a boat in, and they told us to go back down by the canyon, to the second bridge, cross it and go about six miles. We did that and found a place where we could get to the river. They didn't have any landings, just a place where we could squeeze the boat through the brush and put it in the water.

We ran the Yankee Jim Canyon, which is only about a mile long, but has some good rapids. It's about like Mule Creek Canyon, only wider and lots of

Glen and one of the Stallman boys running the Yellowstone River.

Glen Wooldridge collection

243

boulders. It isn't smooth sailing like Mule Creek, and right at the top of it is a real whitewater dandy. We got just below that and Glenn Ballou's new camera blew up, right at the critical moment. I put him out on the bank and told him to monkey with it while I went on up the canyon.

I ran up it and back down and that was the end of that. It was really tough, all right, really steep with a lot of whitewater — lots of fun, but I had a good motor, so there wasn't any problem.

It would have made a dandy picture if we could have got it. Stallman came up that far, below the steep place and got some pictures from the shore, but not while my boat was in the water. I had to run it on the left, as I couldn't get up the right side, and the camera would have to be on the opposite side. It would have been shooting too far across the river. He'd have needed to get close in to get a good picture of me running the canyon, there.

I guess we went about a hundred miles on the Yellowstone, both ways. It is a beautiful river for people to play on. Golly! You'd think there would be people playing on that river, but we didn't see another boat on the whole trip, and not a dozen fishermen all together.

I wanted to run the Yellowstone, through the National Park, in the boat, but they informed me that it was unlawful to run the boat through the park.

While I was in Gardiner, I picked up a little booklet telling about Yankee Jim. He built a toll-road through the canyon, in the early days. He charged $2.50 for a wagon and team to use his road. Cattle and sheep were 5¢ a head. Then the railroad came along and went right through his yard and spoiled his business.

When we came back, Stallman wanted to come by North Fork, by Boise, but I told him, "You go ahead, I am going back by the Salmon River and have fun. So he decided to come with me. We camped on the Salmon and spent some time running up and down it.

Glen made another trip on the Salmon, The River of No Return, a year or so later. It was different from any he had ever made. He and Glenn Ballou; the Stallman family; Bonnie Riggs; and Dr. and Mrs. James from Portland, made a raft trip downriver with Bob Smith, who makes scheduled runs on the river.

Bonnie called the 36-foot pontoon raft the "Salmon-Hilton," because of its modern conveniences; propane stove and refrigerator, kitchenette, folding chairs and waterproof roof.

Glen said it was all right, but he had been up that river a couple of times before. This time, though, he did get to be a dude and see the scenery.

During the next few years Glen found many excuses for boating the Rogue. He was called on to do search and rescue work, and pick-up duty at the Memorial Day boat races. Testing new boats and equipment took some time, too.

When the "FBI Story" and "Gunsmoke" TV shows filmed movies on the Rogue, he was called on for technical advice and to run his boat in many of the more dangerous places while the movies were being filmed.

He was amused when Efrem Zimbalist, Jr. told him, "I have been wanting to meet you. I have heard so much about you."

Glen's son, Bruce, and grandsons, Mike and Mark, took over the ownership and management of the Wooldridge Boatshop in Grants Pass in the early 1970s. Bob, Glen's other son, opened a Wooldridge boat shop in Seattle, Washington, leaving Glen with more free time.

For several years he had been hearing about the Hell's Gate Gorge on British Columbia's Fraser River. It was reputed to be impossible to run.

This 120-foot wide crack in the Coast Range funnels the drainage from the upper Canadian Rockies, some 200 million gallons per minute, on its way to the sea.

Simon Fraser, the first white man to look into the gorge's fury, called it "A place where no human being should venture." On his exploration trip in 1808, he and 23 companions had to abandon their canoes and make their way downstream on an Indian-made spider's web of ropes and tree trunks secured to the crags above the chasm. Fraser gave the river the name, "Waters of Hell."

In modern times fishways had been built to allow the sockeye salmon to go up the chasm. The current was so swift it would sometimes throw them twenty feet out of the water to their deaths against the rock walls, when they would try to buck the waters of the stream.

The only time a boat had ever made it up through Hell's Gate Gorge was in 1880, when the Canadian Pacific Railroad was being built. Two Columbia river-boat pilots, the Smith brothers, took the steamboat *Skuzzy*, through. In addition to the *Skuzzy's* engine, they used a steam winch and 160 Chinese laborers on the banks, with ropes, to get the steamboat through.

In 1968, a raft load of people tried to run the gorge, but one person lost his life and 12 others narrowly escaped when their raft was engulfed in one of the dangerous whirlpools.

Glen looked the canyon over from the bridge which now crosses the gorge, and decided he would give it a try. The water depth in the gorge would have been best in August, but he wasn't able to make the trip until September 20, 1975.

He had Bruce, Mark, and Mike design and build a 21-foot-long aluminum sled, and he powered it with two 85-horse Mercury motors, equipped with Out-board Jets.

It became a family outing when Bruce decided to back Glen with his boat, a 17-foot aluminum sled built at his shop. He used a jet-equipped 150-horse Mercury motor. Mike and Mark went along.

Others making the trip were Glen's other son, Bob, his wife, Ann, and daughter, Stacy; Bob's son, Glen, and his wife; Robert Black; and Jim Berning, from Grants Pass.

They put the boats in at Hope, about 36 miles downstream from the gorge, and camped for the night. There was a little excitement next morning early, when Bruce awoke and found his boat missing. He didn't stop to dress, but grabbed Glen's boat and took off, catching the drifting boat several miles downstream. It was a breezy trip, but Bruce came back towing the boat.

When the news spread that Glen was going to make the run at 11:00 a.m., many spectators and newsmen thronged the fishways trying for a good view and camera angle.

It looked wild from the bottom of the gorge. If I hadn't already been up

above and looked at it, I'd have been skeptical about running it, but I was pretty sure I could make it.

Glen's red boat was in front, with Bruce's silver one about ten boat lengths behind, when they entered the rapids below the gorge. The bows of the boats rode high from the force of the water and the power of the motors. It looked as if they were going to hit it head on, to tackle the mass of water that was boiling down at almost twenty miles an hour.

I thought at first I could go straight ahead, at the left shore, but at the top it's pouring off too steep, a drop of about five feet or so. If it is too steep, too abrupt, and you happen to hook your bow in that, you go to the bottom. You have to look out for that. We had to go up the left side, then cut across one or two big breakers to get to the slick, into the middle.

It was awfully swift, really rolling, especially when we were on top of it. We certainly had to use all the power we had.

When they pulled up at the rockpile, in the calmer waters above the gate, Robert Black and Bob Wooldridge, who had made the first trip upriver with Glen, gave their places to Bob's wife and daughter and young Glen's wife for the return trip.

Three women, and they thought it was exciting. Going down you have to keep up pretty good speed. The boat is thrown sometimes three or four feet out of the water. When the jet is out of the water it sucks air, cavitates, but it catches hold again when the boat hits water.

After all their own party had made the run, Glen invited riders from among the spectators. Two women from the TV station in Vancouver made the trip, then the TV cameramen rode through. A Chinese delegation was there, studying the fisheries, and Glen asked them if they would like a ride, but they declined.

After eight trips through, we ran out of passengers. I was kind of glad. When we left the gorge, we went about 25 miles up the Fraser to the mouth of the Thompson, where it comes out of the Black Canyon.

You can look down the canyon, oh, 300 feet or more. It looks kind of spooky. Next morning we took off up that river. It was a beautiful ride. We never stopped until we got to Spence Bridge. I really believe the Thompson was the hardest to run.

There are ten miles of whitewater, several big rapids, but the nicest part of it you can't see from the highway. Beautiful!

To Glen, the nicest water is the hazardous rapids. Beautiful means dangerous, full of whirlpools and narrow rocky channels.

One place I had to get right over against the bank, in a really tough spot. Here was an Indian who had crawled in there fishing. I had to run within six feet of him. He couldn't hear the motor for the roar of the river, so the first he knew we were there, we were right in his face. Talk about a guy being bug-eyed; he was really astonished!

I think that trip was the most fun I ever had.

Glen, in a Wooldridge aluminum drift boat, 1972.   Ted Trueblood photo

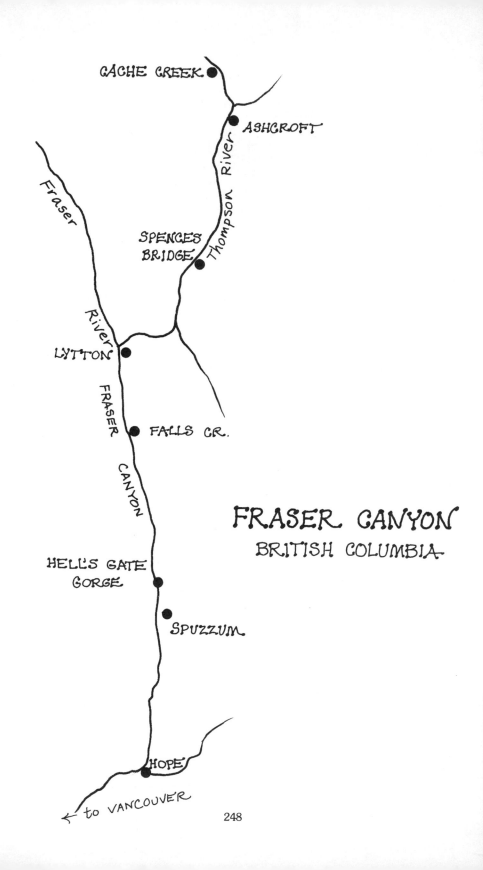

CACHE CREEK

ASHCROFT

Fraser

Thompson River

SPENCES
BRIDGE

River

LYTTON

FRASER

FALLS CR.

CANYON

FRASER CANYON
BRITISH COLUMBIA

HELL'S GATE
GORGE

SPUZZUM

HOPE

← to VANCOUVER

248

Ted Trueblood and Glen check out an Outboard Jet on Glen's sled boat, 1972.   Glenn Ballou photo

Glen tests out his rig at Caveman Bridge, Grants Pass, before taking it to the Fraser River, B. C. for the Hell's Gate Gorge run in 1975.   Arman photo

Glen making the first trip through Hell's Gate Gorge, Fraser River, British Columbia, 1975.

Robert Black photo

An upriver run at Grave Creek Falls, early 1970s.   Arman photo

Glen making a downriver run at Grave Creek Falls, in the early 1970's.   Arman photo

Old-time gillnetter Al Schmidt showing Glen a steelhead he caught, early 1970s.
Arman photo

From left; Glen, Howard Bearss and Al Schmidt, all old-time gillnetters, checking over an old gillnet, early 1970s.
Arman photo

Young Glen Wooldridge, Glen's grandson, runs the Thompson River, British Columbia, in a welded aluminum inboard built in the Wooldridge Seattle boatshop.
Glen Wooldridge collection

Glen at the 1965 celebration of his 50th year on the Rogue River.
Kerbyville Museum photo

Chapter Twenty-Four

Settling Down in the Eighties

Until his 79th year, Glen always had excellent health, except for a bout with arthritis in one of his feet. But even before the Fraser River run, he started suffering from a circulatory problem. While he was planning the Fraser run, Bruce tried to talk him out of making it. He told him, "Dad, you can't make that run. You can't even walk between your house and the boatshop without zigging and zagging along."

Glen told him, "Well, Son, that river won't be straight. It makes a few zigs and zags, too."

Surgery helped Glen get back in good condition before he made the boat run, but both he and Sadie had recurring illnesses in the following years. Sadie had been in poor health for some years. She still suffered from, and was frequently hospitalized with, chronic respiratory problems. Glen had several heart attacks, thought to be minor, at that time.

They were further saddened by the death of their friend Glenn Ballou, in 1976. He had been a big part of their lives for many years. Old friends Larry Lucas, Howard Bearss, Al Schmitz, and others followed him in death.

Sadie died in 1977, and Glen suffered a severe heart attack. He was hospitalized the day of her funeral. He improved under the doctor's care, with his family and friends rallying around. When he was able, he spent time visiting Bob Wooldridge and his family in Seattle.

At 81 he married Mary Miller, who had lived next door to the Wooldridges for many years. His health improved, and he reorganized his workshop in his garage and started building wooden boats again. When he built one to his liking, a regular old timer with two sets of oarlocks, he and Dr. Roberts planned a drift trip on the Salmon. They talked Bruce into going along.

We drove over and put the boat in at Corn Creek below Salmon City, then had to hire a young woman to drive the car to about 25 miles above Riggins.

Glen and Mary Wooldridge, 1978.   Mary Wooldridge photo

Glen, to keep busy, builds a wooden boat in his garage, 1978.   Arman photo

She charged $120 plus the cost of gasoline. It was 320 miles to drive around by Riggins. She figured the gas at a possible $35. She was to leave the pickup at a little park there above the river and give the key to Paul Filer, who lives just across the street.

We had to wait all day, from early in the morning until late in the afternoon to get to the landing, there were so many people and boats. We finally put the boat in there and went across the river and stayed the night, then took off the next morning.

There were a lot of boats on the river, but we seemed to travel a little bit faster than the rest of them. About the second night out we camped on a sand bar on the south side of the river and it began to get cloudy, started raining, thundering and making a hell of a racket. We got under a tree, the best we could. It was pretty dark, except for occasional lightning flashes. Along in the night, I felt water running in my bed. It was running in at one end of my sleeping bag and out the other. I thought, "That's enough of this." So I got up and built a fire out of a pile of driftwood someone had gathered, and stayed there the rest of the night. Along about ten or eleven o'clock it stopped raining, but my bed was soaked, by then. I had a big fire going, so I got things dried out.

Next morning, when we got started, we went about two or three miles and came to where there had been a cloudburst up in the hills above the river. About a thousand tons of debris had washed down the mountainside and into the water. The river was just full of trash from then on. It is hard to describe, but the eddies were just simply full of it, wherever there was a still place. It was all over the river. Boy! I'm glad we didn't camp in that place or we would really have got soaked up. A lot of water had to come down that mountainside to wash that much debris into the river.

One spot we almost got into trouble. We were going to run a place, and a great big boulder, nearly as big as this room, was sticking up there. We had to drop down, then cross to one side to get by it. In the process of crossing, Bruce sprung one of his oarlocks. It flipped out and he lost his oar. We were right above this big boulder, so right up on it we went! It washed us off to one side. If we had gone the other way it would have swamped us, but it gave us a good thrill, anyway.

That was the closest we came to having any trouble, but that could have been a dandy. We were in really swift, heavy water.

The river was extremely low, with lots of boulders and lots of whitewater — really difficult. I wouldn't want to do it that way again.

That was a beautiful drive going in from Sun Valley over the Bitterroot Range and Sawtooth Range, then driving in to the head of the Salmon. It makes wonderful trip.

We saw one old guy with a covered wagon and two mules. He was walking along, leading his mules, with his dog tied behind the wagon. That would have made a good picture.

In 1979, Glen had other recurring heart attacks, and this time open-heart surgery was necessary. Doctors performed two bypasses and implanted a new valve. Recovery has been slow, but steady.

257

Jerry's Jet Boats, Gold Beach, 1978. The Glen Wooldridge waits for passengers at the dock.   Arman photo

A loaded boat, named The Ruell Hawkins, returns from Agness.   Arman photo

Any day at the Wooldridges', while Glen was recuperating from the surgery, he would have three or four visitors or groups of people. Dudes who made trips in early years on the river would stop in to talk about some incident that happened on their particular trip. Nearly every one of them insisted their trip was one of the high points of their lives. River guides who learned the river under Glen's tutelage dropped by; river runners like Ron Hainline, who originated the Wild River Trips from Gold Beach to Paradise Bar; Bob Pruitt; Taylor Cain and others.

They brought pictures of people and places on the river for Glen to identify; dug out old movies made of drift trips some forty years ago, and gave him paintings made of early day trips.

Since Glen has recovered, he is asked to put in an appearance when groups of sportsmen and river runners are meeting. They show the movies of his trips up the Rogue, the Salmon and the Fraser Gorge and ask Glen to narrate them. Each appearance is always to an overflow crowd. Background talk is of where the steelheads are running, or the condition of the river at Blossom Bar, or who lost a boat and how, until the picture starts.

At a recent showing, when Glen stood and watched the film of himself in the boat, climbing rapids of the Rogue, he said, "I'm just like an old fire horse who hears the firebell, when I see that whitewater. I have a great yen to be out there, doing it all over again."

A group of talented and gifted children from Riverside grade school, Glen's old school, in Grants Pass, has taken Glen as their local history project. They have access to a film of an early day drift trip, and they plan to raise money to have it copied for use in local schools. They plan, also, to write a biography of Glen for school children.

They asked Glen to come and speak to them and they recorded his answers to their eager questions about his life on the Rogue in the early years.

Yes, Glen really started something when he pushed off for his first guide trip downriver sixty-five years ago. Interest in whitewater running is high. The first sunny day in Spring brings out the boats from the garages and sheds. Kayaks, rafts, drift boats and canoes line the Rogue River as far as Grave Creek Bridge, where the wild section begins.

Memorial Day weekend brings the racers to Grants Pass for the big river race. That is also the time permits are required for boating the wild section of the Rogue, until after the Labor Day weekend. Non-commercial permits are obtained through a lottery by application to the Siskiyou Forest Service.

According to river guide Mel Norrick, there are 175 guides on the Rogue in Josephine County alone. At a Chamber of Commerce meeting, in 1980, he outlined present recreation on the Rogue by saying that some 4,500 persons would take guided river runs on the Rogue that year. An additional 2,500 would take guided fishing trips with the thirteen outfitters operating on the Rogue. He quoted a reliable source as estimating recreation on the river would bring over $4,000,000, with a turn-over value of $16,000,000, to the Rogue recreation area.

With the high interest in river running, Glen is often asked for his own rules for running rivers safely.

My theory of whitewater river running has always been "proper equipment, properly used, and a healthy respect for the river."

Of course, you aren't going to learn to swim until you get your feet wet, and it's the same with boating. But I don't advise beginners to start with the worst water they can find.

But I'm not trying to scare anyone off, either. I have had over sixty-five years of whitewater running, and I wouldn't have missed it for the world.

Drift boating is becoming very popular on many of the rivers, nowadays. If you are thinking of drifting, I would suggest you make your first trip with a good river guide. That way you will have a chance to see the river and also how it is done.

A good sound drift boat, at least 15 feet long, with a 4½ foot bottom and a six foot beam is the best choice. You'll need three good 8½ to 9 foot oars. Be sure to carry that extra oar; you never know when you will break one or lose one overboard.

Oarlocks should be fastened in the sockets so they can't bounce out while you are rowing. That's what happened to us on the drift trip on the Salmon. The oarlock sprung and jerked the oar right out of Bruce's hand. Also, be sure the oars fit the oarlocks.

For lining a boat, and just general safety, you'll need a fifty-foot bowline, or rope. You don't want to ever use a chain for an anchor line; sometimes you need to cut it quick, if you get hung up in swift water. Put your anchor right out into the current. It holds better there and when you throw it out, be sure your weight is back away from the bow. Then when you pick up your anchor, have someone else get in the stern with an oar to hold the boat in the current. If you have a motor, you can use it, but be careful not to get the prop caught in the bowline.

Everyone in the boat should wear a life vest. A person hasn't got a chance if they are thrown out of a boat into the Rogue's rough waters without one. Their chances aren't too good, even with one. That old river has taken a lot of lives, just since I have been on it. You oughtn't to overload a boat, either. Three adults are just about all that can ride safely in a drift boat.

If you plan to run whitewater rivers with a motor boat, you shouldn't get one less than 18 feet long; longer is okay. My years on the river have taught me that the wide bow boat is best. The first three or four feet of a sharp bow craft does nothing for river boats in an upstream run through whitewater. The sharp bow tends to cut in to the breakers and throw the boat off course. We found that out in the early-day runs on the Rogue and Salmon. That can be dangerous. I used boats like that when I first started boating, but it was always my ambition to get them up on top of the water instead of plowing through it.

A 50-horse motor is the smallest that will do the job with a light load. A 70-horse Evinrude will carry a pretty hefty load.

If you have a shallow-water problem, the Jackass Lift will help a lot. Attach it to the transom of the boat, and you can raise the prop in the water while underway. Use a handle and stand up for better visibility. When lifted to drydock position, it will lock there until released, and can be spring loaded for easier lifting.

If you are using a lift and a standard shaft motor, the boat transom should be 18 inches. It will take a little time to learn to use the lift, but when you do, you wouldn't take many times its cost for it.

But you want to always carry an extra prop, just in case some unusual circumstance damages the one you are using. As I have said, a three-blade prop is best in whitewater.

The Outboard Jet is very good for whitewater running, although it does cut the power output the same motor would have with a propeller. Just use a little bigger motor and you get the extra power you need. I prefer to use the jet in whitewater, because it doesn't cavitate as much.

There really isn't any comparison in using a prop and a jet, because each has its own advantages and disadvantages. The jet will run in more shallow water. If the boat draws six inches, you can run it in about eight inches of water, if you are not too heavily loaded and run at the proper speed. The jet will allow you to load and unload in more shallow water, too.

If you want a good boat and live in some out-of-the-way place where delivery presents a problem, you might want to build your own. We saw boats, made by my plans, operating on the Yukon in 1970, and they were proving satisfactory. One man, a school teacher in Beaver, had just hauled home an awfully big moose in one of them when we were there.

Proper steering controls are a must. Most controls are poor for whitewater running because of sluggish performance. The boat must be quick in turning, because the obstacles are coming at you very fast and, if your controls don't respond, you are in trouble, especially if you are going downstream. If I am going to use the controls on a run, I check them out very closely before I start. We developed our own stand for controls using a tiller. The use of the tiller instead of a wheel gives greater maneuverability.

You have to always keep your eyes open for trouble. It takes just about all your attention to run the river safely. Reading the water comes by experience. In whitewater every motion on top of the water is caused by something on the bottom. You have to learn what each rooster-tail of whitewater means. You learn where the boulders are and just how they are situated on the bottom by what is happening on top.

One of the worst things you can do while running the river is to drink. I always hated that. It seems to me people shouldn't dim their minds with that stuff when there is so much on the river to see. It seems like it takes away the enjoyment. There's enough excitement just running rivers. That's the way I always felt about it.

This boating has turned into a big thing, hasn't it? Lots of guys working at it now. A whole industry. It's all over the country, now, scattered everywhere: California, Montana, Idaho, Washington. I don't know whether it has crossed over into British Columbia yet, but I would think it would. All the times I have been up there I have seen two rubber rafts.

Glen, just below Galice, 1940. Note this boat was built of small strips of wood nailed from the top.
Glen Wooldridge collection

This boat is believed to be the one with Glen at Galice, 1940. Glen and sons built it for Mr. Anderson who bought the Billings ranch at Marial in 1931. It was rediscovered in an old shed at Marial after the BLM bought the ranch, about 1978.

Grants Pass Courier photo

The same boat, now protected under a shelter at Rand Forest Station. Glen checks out the bottom, 1981.

Arman photo

What I would like to do, now, is to build a boat and go up and run that Thompson River. If I had enough time, that would be a beautiful trip. There is so much country, so much river to play with. There must be 500 miles of beautiful water. A lot of it I have never seen. I'd like to see that. Gee! That would be fun, to just go way back up there and take something to eat and a sleeping bag, wouldn't it? And just fiddle around. It would be like it was down here 50 years ago.

Bob Pritchett says we had the good times on the Rogue, he and Charley Foster and me, back when we had it all to ourselves. It was a lot of hard work, drifting the Rogue back then, lining the boats at Rainie and Grave Creek Falls, hauling them over boulders at Blossom Bar, then bouncing over those rough roads, hauling the boats back home. But sometimes we wouldn't see another boat from the time we left Grave Creek until we got to Agness. It was so quiet on the river bars you could hear the gravel washing along the bottom of the river.

We had some good times, all right. If I had my life to live over again, I wouldn't change it much. Not everyone gets to do just exactly what he wants to do in his life, and make a good living doing it. According to my notion, running rivers is a pretty good way to spend your life. And when it comes to whitewater rivers, the Rogue is still the best river to run.

The End

Lifetime Permit to Float the Rogue River

In recognition for his contributions to whitewater boating and guiding on the Rogue River, the United States Forest Service, Bureau of Land Management and State of Oregon, hereby jointly grant GLEN WOOLDRIDGE a lifetime permit to float the Wild Section of the Rogue Wild and Scenic River. Issued this 13th day of Nov. 1981 by:

Richard E. Worthington
Regional Forester
Pacific Northwest Region
U.S. Forest Service

William G. Leavell
Oregon State Director
U.S. Bureau of Land
Management

Victor A. Atiyeh
Governor
State of Oregon

Glen's unique lifetime permit to run the Rogue River. It was issued to him on November 13, 1981, by the five agencies governing the Wild and Scenic section of the Rogue, at a dinner sponsored by the Rogue River Guides Association. Participating in the ceremony were officials from the BLM, State Marine Board, State Scenic Waterways, Forest Service, and the board representing the counties. The permit was signed by Governor Vic Atiyeh, State BLM director Bill Leavell, and Forest Service official Dick Worthington.

BIBLIOGRAPHY AND SUGGESTED FURTHER READING

Unpublished Manuscripts

Hefferan, Peggie Gibson. Notes on the history of the Weasku Inn.

Hemphill, Corene. Notes on Glen Wooldridge; Pioneer guide on the Rogue River.

Rivers, Cole. "Memories of Characters of the Lower Rogue River Canyon." Oregon Fish and Wildlife. 1960s

Rivers, Cole. "Rogue River Fisheries." Oregon Fish and Wildlife. 1963

Newspapers

Rogue River Courier (Grants Pass)
Medford Mail
Gold Beach Gazette
The Oregonian
Grants Pass Courier
Medford Mail Tribune
Oregon Observer
Oregon Journal

Books

Atwood, Kay. *Illahe.* Kay Atwood. Ashland, Oregon. 1978

Beckham, Stephen Dow. *Requiem For A People.* University of Oklahoma Press. 1971

Beckham, Stephen Dow. *Tall Tales of the Rogue River;* The Yarns of Hathaway Jones. Indiana Un. Press 1974

Dodd, Gordon B. *The Salmon King of Oregon.* University of North Carolina Press. 1974

Grey, Zane. *Rogue River Feud.* Curtis Publishing Co. 1929

Grey, Zane. *Tales of Fresh Water Fishing.* Haper and Bros. 1928

Hill, Edna May. *Josephine Country Historical Highlights.* Vol. 1 Josephine County Library System and Josephine County Historical Society. Grants Pass, 1976

Hill, Edna May. *Josephine County Historical Highlights.* Vol. 2 Josephine County Library System. Grants Pass. 1979

Johnson, Olga Weydemeyer. *They Settled in Applegate Country.* Olga Weydemeyer Johnson. Grants Pass, 1978

Quinn, James M., Quinn, James W., King, James G., *Handbook of the Rogue River Canyon.* Quinn. Medford. 1978

Sutton, Jack. *The Mythical State of Jefferson.* Josephine Country Historical Society. Grants Pass. 1965

Sutton, Jack. *110 Years with Josephine.* Josephine County Historical Society. Grants Pass. 1966

Periodicals

Arman, Florence "Another River to Run." *Southern Oregon Sunrise Magazine.* November 1977.

Arman, Florence. "Beginning at the End." *Outdoors.* April, 1972

Arman, Florence. "The Man, the Boat, the River." *Outdoors.* January, 1973

Arman, Florence. "Wrong Way Wooldridge and the Uphill River Boat." *Ford Truck Times.* Summer, 1971

Bowman, Hank Wieand: *Encyclopedia of Outboard Motor Boating.* Barnes Publishing.

Camp, Jack. "Taming the Rogue." *Argosy.* August, 1951

Dodd, Gordon B. "The Fight to Close the Rogue." *Oregon Historical Quarterly.* December, 1959.

Grey, Zane. *Country Gentleman Magazine,* 1926
    Reprinted in the Grants Pass Courier, 1926.

Goldrath, Bert. "Conquering the Wild, White Rogue." *Popular Mechanics.* May, 1963

Goldrath, Bert. "Up the River On a Fire Hose." *Boating.* 1963

Hemphill, Corene. "The Big Three Conspiracy." *Oregon Outdoors.* June, 1979

Holm, Don. A series of three articles. *The Oregonian,* February, 1971

Matt, Dick. "Whitewater Cowboy." *Hunting and Fishing.* July, 1952

Muir, Jean. "Hermits Who Hate Hollywood." *Saturday Evening Post.* February 9, 1940

Phelps, Alva W. "Rogue River." *The Cherry Circle.* November, 1950

Purdum, William B. "Guide to the Geology and Lore of the Wild Reach of the Rogue River Oregon." *Bulletin Number 22.* Museum of Natural History. University of Oregon. May, 1977

Riggs, Bonnie. "We Ran the Rogue Uphill." *Sports Afield.* Spring, 1963

Riggs, Bonnie. "The Yukon River." *This Alaska.* April, 1971

Staley, Thomas, Sr. "Up the River of No Return." *Pacific Motor Boat.* February, 1949

Staley, Thomas, Sr. A short recap of the River of No Return article. *Outdoor Life,* 1957

Thompson, Jon. "Going the Wrong Way Up a One-way Stream." *American Boating.* March, 1975

Trueblood, Ted. "A River in His Blood." *Field and Stream.* June, 1972

Trueblood, Ted. "We Bucked the Mighty Rogue." *True Fishing Yearbook.* 1952

Wharton, Joe. "Down the Rogue to the Sea." *Oregon Outdoors.* October, 1941

Wooldridge, Glen. "Up the Roaring Rogue." *Field and Stream.* September, 1947

    . "Shooting the Rogue." *Let's Get Associated.* September, 1947

        . "Ginger Rogers Goes on a Fishing Trip." *Screen Guide.* May, 1947

Other articles appeared in *Western Outdoors,* 1963, *Northwest Archer, Sunset Magazine,* 1948, *Los Angeles Times,* 1960. And other magazines and newspapers.

INFORMATION GIVEN ORALLY BY:

Glen Wooldridge, Sadie Wooldridge, Glenn Ballou, Bruce Wooldridge, Robert Black, Taylor Cain, Al Schmidt, Squeak Briggs, Bob Pritchett, Pauline Shier, Howard Bearss, Bob Pruitt, Hattie Hogue, Bill Young, Bob Arman, Gene Gilpin, and others.

INDEX

(Please note: There is no listing for Glen Wooldridge, the Rogue River, nor Grants Pass because of the frequency of their use in the text.)

269